Design for Reliability

T0344444

IEEE Press
445 Hoes Lane
Piscataway, NJ 08854

Design for Reliability
Information and
Computer-Based Systems

Eric Bauer

IEEE PRESS

A John Wiley & Sons, Inc., Publication

Published by John Wiley & Sons, Inc., Hoboken, New Jersey.
Published simultaneously in Canada.

For general information on our other products and services or for technical support, please contact our Customer Care Department within the United States at (800) 762-2974, outside the United States at (317) 572-3993 or fax (317) 572-4002.

Wiley also publishes its books in a variety of electronic formats. Some content that appears in print may not be available in electronic formats. For more information about Wiley products, visit our web site at www.wiley.com.

Library of Congress Cataloging-in-Publication Data:

Bauer, Eric.
  Design for reliability: information and computer-based systems / Eric Bauer.
    p. cm.
  ISBN 978-0-470-60465-6 (hardback)
  1. Reliability (Engineering)   I. Title.
  TA169.B385 2010
  620′.00452–dc22

                                2010028409

Printed in Singapore.

10 9 8 7 6 5 4 3 2 1

To Sandy, Lauren and Mark

Contents

Part One   Reliability Basics

1. Reliability and Availability Concepts 3

2. System Basics 31

Part Three   Design for Reliability

Figures

Tables

Preface

As networked systems and services become more integrated into the fabric of our personal and professional lives, we expect those services to be continuously available. A popular term for this expectation is *24/7/365*, meaning service is available 24 hours a day, 7 days a week, 365 days a year. Technically this expectation is quantified as *service availability*, and *99.999%* or *five 9's* is a common requirement for *highly available* systems. This 99.999% availability means that a system has no more than 5.26 down-minutes per system per year. This book gives students, system architects, engineers, developers, testers, project and product managers, and others knowledge and techniques to develop systems to meet customers' expectations for high availability. When the system is available for service, customers expect valid service requests or transactions to be reliably executed with acceptable quality. Thus service availability and service reliability are complementary characteristics. This book assumes readers have basic familiarity with networked computer systems; advanced knowledge of software, hardware, and networking concepts is not required. This book treats reliability and availability both qualitatively and quantitatively.

Failures are inevitable in the real world. All large software products contain some residual defects that will eventually be activated; hardware will eventually fail; human maintenance and provisioning staff will make mistakes; network infrastructure will fail; and so on. Traditional quality activities strive to reduce the number of residual software, manufacturing, and documentation defects and otherwise reduce the failure rate, but the rate of failures cannot be driven to zero. Fault tolerance assures that inevitable failures are automatically detected and recovered with minimal service disruption to achieve the high service availability expectations of 24/7/365 or *five 9's* systems. Ideally, reliability and robustness mechanisms are so effective that end users are unaware that a failure has even occurred.

This book is organized into three parts: reliability basics, reliability concepts, and design for reliability.

Part One, **Reliability Basics**, contains the following chapters:

1. **Reliability and Availability Concepts** explains the fault to error to failure progression and the failure recovery process.

2. **System Basics** frames the elements of a typical system, its context in a broader networked solution, and the services that a system provides. Subsequent chapters will use this system, solution, service, and activities framework to methodically address reliability.

3. **What Can Go Wrong** defines eight broad categories of errors that can produce critical failures of systems. This error vulnerability framework is used to drive design, analysis, and robustness testing.

Part Two, **Reliability Concepts,** covers:

4. **Failure Containment and Redundancy.** Reliability is achieved by isolating failures to modules that can be rapidly detected and recovered with minimal service impact. Service impact can be further minimized via module redundancy to enable service to be rapidly shifted to an operational redundant module, rather than having service impacted until the failing module can be restarted or repaired. This chapter explains concepts and mechanisms for failure containment and recovery.

5. **Robust Design Principles.** Various architectural and design techniques can minimize a system's inherent susceptibility to errors, and thus enable many faults and errors to be mitigated without having to activate dramatic recovery actions. This chapter reviews general principles and techniques that complement failure containment and redundancy to improve system reliability.

6. **Error Detection.** Rapid accurate detection of errors—ideally before errors escalate to service-impacting failures—is crucial because this triggers automatic failure recovery mechanisms. Error detection and failure recovery mechanisms must operate fast enough to keep the duration of service impact within the system's maximum acceptable service disruption latency requirement. This chapter reviews detection techniques to address error categories and types presented in Chapter 3.

7. **Analyzing and Modeling Reliability and Robustness.** This chapter reviews reliability block diagrams, failure mode and effects analysis, and the basics of system availability modeling. In addition to software and hardware failures, human errors also contribute to system downtime. Systems are operated by staff that uses documented or undocumented procedures and policies when operating, administering, maintaining, and provisioning the system. The quality and robustness of these procedures and operational policies has a significant impact on both the observed failure rate and the time it takes to successfully complete emergency recoveries of outages. This chapter gives design basics for reliable procedures, and information to help enterprises deploy robust operational policies that will maximize the likelihood of highly available system operation.

Part Three, **Design for Reliability,** covers:

 8. **Reliability Requirements.** Clear, verifiable requirements are the first step in any design, and system reliability should be designed like any other feature. This chapter reviews how to define complete and verifiable reliability requirements.

 9. **Reliability Analysis.** Qualitative reliability analysis is the first step to assure that it is feasible for the system's architecture and design to meet the system's reliability requirements. This chapter reviews reliability analysis techniques.

10. **Reliability Budgeting and Modeling.** A system's downtime can be quantitatively budgeted and modeled to assess the feasibility and likelihood of meeting the system's service availability requirement. This chapter reviews the budgeting and modeling activity to produce detailed quantitative targets for failure rates, switchover latencies, coverage factors, switchover success probabilities, and other characteristics that should be used as detailed design specifications and to drive robustness test case definition.

11. **Robustness and Stability Testing.** The ability of a system to automatically detect, isolate, and recover from failures is called *robustness*. System robustness can be verified through formal testing by confronting the system with plausible and likely failure scenarios and verifying that the system recovers automatically with minimal service disruption. Stability testing verifies that the system is stable under an extended heavy and varying load of end-user as well as operations, administration, maintenance, and provisioning traffic. This chapter covers strategy and planning of both robustness and stability testing.

12. **Closing the Loop.** Failures and outages are inevitable when systems are broadly deployed and heavily used. This chapter details how field outage events can be analyzed to drive reliability improvements in future system releases. Initial system releases rarely achieve the system's ultimate, asymptotic service availability requirement. Best practice is to construct a *reliability roadmap* to methodically drive the system to achieve the ultimate service availability target on a schedule that balances the demands of customers with the supplier's business needs. This chapter explains how to construct a reliability roadmap.

13. **Design for Reliability Case Study.** A case study of design for reliability diligence of a networked system is given to illustrate the considerations that are appropriate for developing a high availability and high reliability system.

14. **Conclusion.** Reviews how all of the above activities fit into the overall system design lifecycle to produce robust systems that achieve customers' expectations for service reliability and service availability.

15. Appendix: Assessing Design for Reliability Diligence. Weaknesses and gaps in a project's design for reliability diligence can be identified by asking the various members of a project team focused questions. This chapter explains how to complete an actionable design for reliability assessment.

This book is organized for students and professionals to read in chapter order. Professionals with system reliability experience will find it useful to read Chapter 3, "What Can Go Wrong," before jumping to Part Three, "Design for Reliability." Professionals should also note that the "Appendix: Assessing Design for Reliability Diligence" material can be useful when assessing the reliability diligence and risks of systems that are developed internally or sourced externally.

Acknowledgments

The author acknowledges the valuable input of Doug Kimber, who provided insight on many aspects of system reliability and thoughtful suggestions on organizing the material in this book. Working closely with Randee Adams, Xuemei Zhang, Meena Sharma, Abhaya Asthana, and Richard Riley on various Alcatel-Lucent and former Lucent products and solutions offered numerous insights into the practical aspects of system design for reliability. Jim Runyon and Karl Rauscher encouraged the author to consider how the Bell Labs "8i" framework might be applied at the system level to improve service availability of individual systems. Chun Chan, Don Jackson, Hans Wellman, Werner Heissenhuber, and Herbert Ristock contributed on system reliability and robustness. Neil Witkowski and Ted Lach contributed on hardware reliability. Bill Reents shared the graphic images of hardware failures that appear in the text. Anil Macwan contributed on procedural reliability topics. Tapan Chakraborty, Brad Van Trueren, and Tom Cook contributed on hardware fault insertion. The author acknowledges Gus Derkits, John Franey, Debbie Fleming, Xu Chen, Laurent Moquet, and Yves Lebreton for the hardware images included in the book. Finally, the author acknowledges Niren Choudhury, who originally asked the author to work on system design for reliability.

Part One

Reliability Basics

Chapter 1

Reliability and Availability Concepts

This chapter reviews the basics that underpin system design for reliability:

- Definitions of reliability and availability in the context of systems and services
- How faults are activated to become errors and evolve into failures
- Failure recovery and high availability
- Quantifying downtime and service availability
- Attributing responsibility for downtime and outages
- Overviews of hardware and software reliability

1.1 RELIABILITY AND AVAILABILITY

Reliability is defined by the IEEE as *"the ability of a system or component to perform its required functions under stated conditions for a specified period of time"* [IEEE610]. For example, a failure rate, such as the frequency of software crash or failure, measures reliability; mean time to first failure is a simple reliability metric.

Availability is defined as *"the degree to which a system or component is operational and accessible when required for use"* [IEEE610]. For example, the probability that a car will start is a measure of the car's availability. A simple mathematical formula to compute service availability is:

$$Availability = \frac{Uptime}{Uptime + Downtime}$$

Design for Reliability: Information and Computer-Based Systems, by Eric Bauer
Copyright © 2010 Institute of Electrical and Electronics Engineers

Since both the numerator and denominator of the formula are in the same units (time), the units cancel out and the value of availability becomes dimensionless. Because availability is dimensionless, it is generally expressed as a percentage, such as 99.999% or "five 9's." Table 1.1 shows the relationship between number of 9's and down-minutes per system per year.

Table 1.1   Availability as a Function of Number of 9's

Number of 9's	Availability	Annualized down-minutes per system	Practical meaning
1	90%	52596.00	Down 5 weeks per year
2	99%	5259.60	Down 4 days per year
3	99.9%	525.96	Down 9 hours per year
4	99.99%	52.60	Down 1 hour per year
5	99.999%	5.26	Down 5 minutes per year
6	99.9999%	0.53	Down 30 seconds per year
7	99.99999%	0.05	Down 3 seconds per year

Note that although many people speak of "99.999% system reliability," they often actually mean *five 9's service availability*.

Service availability is essentially based on the simple model that a system is either "up" or "down," and transitions between those states are fairly well understood; this abstraction maps well to critical service failure events, such as system crashes. However, failures occur that can cause a few isolated operations to fail without bringing the system down. Readers will be familiar with these service failures, such as when their wireless calls drop or fail to complete, or when they have to use the "reload" button on their web browser to reload a page that did not display properly. Assuming the network or server did not actually go down, the service failure will not be reflected in the service availability metric. Service reliability measures the rate of successful user interactions or transactions when the system is up, such as rate of successful transactions, successful call completions, or successful web page displays. As service reliability is often very good, it is often more convenient to measure service *un*reliability as defective transactions or interactions per million attempts. For example, 15 web page loads per million might fail, or 37 database update transactions might fail per million attempts, or 27 calls per million attempts may fail to be established with acceptable voice quality. Although the servers or network probably did not go down, some individual users experienced unacceptable service. Thus, users experience unacceptable service either when the system is down (which is measured via service *unavailability*) or when the system is up but fails to complete their service request properly (which is measured via service *unreliability*). This book addresses designing systems that deliver both high service availability and high service reliability.

1.2 FAULTS, ERRORS, AND FAILURES

Failure is defined as *"the inability of a system or component to perform its required functions within specified performance requirements"* [IEEE610]. *Error* is primarily defined as *"the difference between a computed, observed, or measured value or condition and the true, specified, or theoretically correct value or condition. For example, a difference of 30 meters between a computed result and the correct result"* [IEEE610]. *Fault* is defined as *"(1) A defect in a hardware device or component; for example, a short circuit or broken wire. (2) An incorrect step, process, or data definition in a computer program"* [IEEE610]. Faults are said to be *activated* to become errors, and errors can lead to failures. For example, a software defect (**fault**) in the stopping condition of a *do/while* loop is activated when executed to become an infinite loop **error**, which prevents the system from replying to a user's request within the specified time and thus produces a service **failure**.

Faults can be residual software defects, design weaknesses, or vulnerabilities of internal components and external elements. Practical realities assure that no large and complex software product is ever completely free of residual software faults; defects are inevitable. Hardware components are vulnerable to physical phenomena like bearing wearing out on hard disk drives that eventually cause them to fail. Documented installation and planning guides, procedural instructions, user interfaces, and so on can be unclear, incorrect, misleading, or otherwise prompt humans who operate, administer, maintain, or provision the system to perform incorrect actions. Unexpected, extraordinary, and malicious inputs and conditions challenge deployed systems, and these can exceed the system's designed parameters or expose residual software defects.

Quality activities focus on reducing the number of residual defects in a system's software, hardware, and documentation through careful development and testing processes. For example, written specifications, designs, source code, test plans, and documentation are methodically reviewed and diligently tested. Best-in-class quality organizations will often analyze defect data to predict and quantitatively manage the number of residual software defects (faults) to assure that a system is of appropriate quality before deploying a software release to customers.

An error is an activation of a fault that causes incorrect behavior. Fault activation is a function of the system's profile of operation, including operating time, operational environment, workload, and other characteristics. Most errors will be minor and not cause notable impact, but some may escalate to cause some or all of a system to become incapable of functioning and thus cause a service-affecting failure. For example, consider a common programming error—not initializing a pointer or an array index variable that is used to store or write data—as a sample fault. This fault would be activated by executing the code that uses this pointer or array index variable. Depending on the previous contents of the uninitialized variable, the value of other input parameters, the system state, the application logic, and the memory map, the system will attempt to write data to some location in the process's address space. If the computed pointer or array index value is outside of this process's writeable address space or the address is misaligned, then the CPU is likely to raise a processor exception and the operating system is likely to cause abnormal termination of the process, thereby producing a system error. If the computed pointer or array index value is a properly aligned address within the process's writeable address space, then the data write is likely to complete successfully without immediately producing a system error. If the system accesses or executes memory that was compromised by the erroneous data write, then a secondary error is likely.

Some errors will escalate and catastrophically impact system operation, thus causing critical failures. If a system doesn't recover from the initial failure promptly, then a cascade of secondary failures may be triggered. These concepts are illustrated with an ordinary pneumatic tire on an automobile or truck in Figure 1.1. A nail on the road presents a hazard or fault that can be activated by driving over it, thereby puncturing the tire to create a hole that leaks air (an error). Over time, this air leak will cause a repairable tire failure, commonly called a "flat tire." If the driver doesn't stop driving on a failed tire quickly enough, then the tire will become irreparably damaged. If the driver continues driving on a flat tire even after the tire is damaged, then the wheel rim will eventually be damaged.

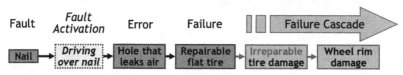

Figure 1.1 Fault Activation and Failures

Robustness is defined as "*the degree to which a system or component can function correctly in the presence of invalid inputs or stressful environmental conditions*" [IEEE610], which encompasses tolerance of hardware and software faults as well as human and external faults.

1.3 ERROR SEVERITY

Errors are generally classified by severity, with *critical* (often "severity 1"), *major* (often "severity 2"), and *minor* (often "severity 3") being commonly used. For example, consider the definitions of *critical*, *major*, and *minor* severities from the telecommunication industry's TL 9000 quality standard [TL9000]:

> *Problem report—**critical**: Conditions that severely affect the primary functionality of the product and because of the business impact to the customer requires non-stop immediate corrective action, regardless of time of day or day of the week as viewed by a customer on discussion with the* [enterprise] *such as:*

a) product inoperability (total or partial outage),

b) a reduction in the capacity capability, that is, traffic/data handling capability, such that expected loads cannot be handled,

c) any loss of emergency capability (for example, emergency 911 calls), or

d) safety hazard or risk of security breach.

*Problem report—**major**: Product is usable, but a condition exists that seriously degrades the product operation, maintenance or administration, etc., and requires attention during pre-defined standard hours to resolve the situation. The urgency is less than in critical situations because of a lesser immediate or impending effect on problem performance, customers and the customer's operation and revenue such as*

a) reduction in product's capacity (but still able to handle the expected load),

b) any loss of administrative or maintenance visibility of the product and/or diagnostic capability,

c) repeated degradation of an essential component or function, or

d) degradation of the product's ability to provide any required notification of malfunction.

*Problem report—**minor**: Other problems of a lesser severity than "critical" or "major" such as conditions that have little or no impairment on the function of the system.*

Note that some organizations formally or informally include a severity above *critical* such as *emergency* to capture extraordinary events of extreme scope or duration—for example, a failure that is large enough to be reported as a news item in trade publications or general media (e.g., *Wall Street Journal*, Cable News Network, etc.), or that will require external reporting (e.g., for regulatory or contractual compliance), or that triggers liquidated damages payments to customers for violating service-level agreements.

1.4 FAILURE RECOVERY

Failures are typically recovered or repaired by a process that follows three simple steps: failure detection, failure isolation, and failure recovery. Consider recovery illustrated in Figure 1.2 from the road hazard example of Figure 1.1. The example begins with the error of a hole in a tire that leaks air. Some cars will automatically alert the driver when the tire pressure drops below a minimum threshold, while other drivers must rely on a change to the feel of the car's handling, or increased road noise, or perhaps the honking and waving of other drivers. If the road is rough or the driver is distracted or for other reasons, then the driver may not detect the failure right away. After detecting the failure, the driver must safely stop the car. After stopping the car, the driver inspects the tires to diagnose if a tire is flat. While isolating a flat (failed) tire visually is often trivial, isolating failures to a specific repairable or replace-able unit is often nontrivial. The failure is "recovered" by manually replacing the failed tire with the spare. After installing the spare tire and stowing the

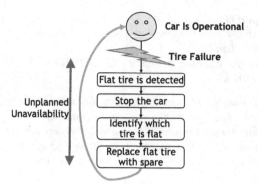

Figure 1.2   Tire Failure as Simple Robustness Example

flat tire, the car is again operational. This completes the *unplanned* downtime associated with the tire failure. Eventually, a planned activity of repairing the flat tire, reinstalling the repaired tire and returning the spare tire to its stowage compartment, must be completed. As the car is unavailable while the tire is repaired and reinstalled, and the spare is returned to its compartment, that period may be considered as planned downtime or planned unavailability.

Generalizing the failure recovery example of Figure 1.2, one can see the three basic robustness steps:

- Failure occurs.
    1. Error is **detected** by system or human being.
    2. Error is diagnosed to **isolate** failure to a repairable or recoverable unit. While it is easy for a human being to visually diagnose which tire has failed, most failures are not trivially isolated by simple visual inspection. For example, consider the challenge of diagnosing typical automobile engine failures to the specific component that must be replaced. The mechanic may follow troubleshooting procedures that rely on both on-board and off-board diagnostics to hypothesize which replaceable unit has failed and must be replaced. If the mechanic incorrectly diagnoses the failure (typically referred to as a *diagnostic failure*), then troubleshooting continues and another likely component failure is hypothesized and that component is repaired or replaced. Ineffective diagnostics can lead directly to higher repair costs and longer unavailability incidents, as any car owner with an intermittent or hard-to-diagnose failure can attest.
    3. Fault is repaired or recovered. Hardware failures are typically repaired by replacing the failed module; software failures are often repaired by restarting a process or the entire system; damaged data may be restored from backup or repaired/rebuilt using system tools, and so on.
- Service is restored.

Sometimes additional actions are required to restore the system to full operational redundancy and readiness (e.g., repairing the failed hardware and/or restocking of spare equipment), but these repair actions are usually completed on a nonemergency basis, and often are not service impacting.

1.5 HIGHLY AVAILABLE SYSTEMS

To reduce cost, typical consumer and commercial systems are permitted to experience some unavailability during failure recovery or repair. For example, tire failure, battery exhaustion of a portable electronic device, or software crash of a PC application all require recovery or repair procedures that include a period of service unavailability. In some commercial, industrial, public safety, and other applications, service unavailability is so costly that it makes business sense to invest more in system hardware, design, and development to minimize service unavailability following failure. Highly available systems are designed so that no single failure causes unacceptable service disruption. To accomplish this, systems must be designed to detect, isolate, and recover from failures very rapidly. Practically, this means that failure detection, isolation, and recovery must be both automatic and highly reliable, and hardware redundancy must be engineered into the system to rapidly recover from hardware failures. A basic robustness strategy for a highly available system is illustrated in Figure 1.3.

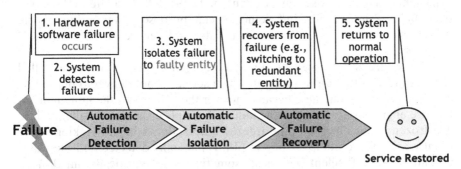

Figure 1.3   Simplified View of High Availability

Consider each step in Figure 1.3 separately:

1. **Failure.** Hardware, software, human, or other failures will inevitably occur.

2. **Automatic failure detection.** Modern systems are designed to detect failures via myriad mechanisms ranging from direct hardware mechanisms like parity checks, to direct software mechanisms like return codes or expiration of timeouts, to environmental sensors like temperature or moisture sensors, to sophisticated indirect mechanisms like

throughput monitors. Highly available systems will have several tiers of failure detection so that if one detection tier misses the event, then another tier will catch it some time later.

3. **Automatic failure isolation.** The system must correctly diagnose or isolate the failure to the appropriate recoverable module so that proper recovery action can be initiated. Fault isolation should be as fast as possible so that failure recovery action can be promptly activated to shorten service outage, but not so hasty as to incorrectly isolate the failure and activate a wrong recovery action. In addition to prolonging the outage event, activating the wrong recovery mechanism (e.g., restarting the wrong software module or rebooting the wrong processor) may unnecessarily impact end users who were not affected by the failure event itself. The situation when a failure is not isolated to the correct recoverable or repairable module is called a *diagnostic failure*.

4. **Automatic failure recovery.** After isolating the failure to the proper recoverable module, then highly available systems will automatically activate the recovery action, such as switching service to a redundant module or restarting a software module.

5. **Service restored.** The system returns to normal operation when service is restored onto the redundant module.

In high availability systems, failure detection, isolation, and recovery occur automatically, and the duration of impact to service should be minimal. Typical high availability systems will automatically detect, isolate, and recover from failures in seconds, but some special purpose systems like optical transmission equipment will detect, isolate, and recover from failures in milliseconds.

If a failure is not automatically detected by the system, then a so called "silent failure" situation will exist in which service is not delivered but recovery actions are not activated because neither the system nor the human maintenance engineers are aware of the failure. A simple example of a silent failure is a frozen water pipe: the pipe freezes, cracks, thaws, begins leaking water silently, and will continue leaking until it is manually detected and the water is manually shutoff. Silent failures are sometimes euphemistically called *sleeping* failures to indicate that the system hasn't noticed the failure because it is "asleep." For example, an underinflated or flat spare tire may be sleeping in an automobile for months or years before being detected. In contrast to sleeping failures, a system might be "dreaming" that a module is operational when it has actually failed, thus misleading surveillance and maintenance engineers. For example, a defective fuel gauge in an automobile might incorrectly report that there is fuel when the tank is actually empty. Depending on system architecture and the specific failure, these silent failures may directly impact users (e.g., a server is down, but the operations team doesn't know it) or they may not immediately impact users but put the system into a simplex or vulnerable state (e.g., spare tire is flat, but the driver doesn't know it).

If automatic failure detection, isolation, and recovery mechanisms are not themselves highly reliable, then excess downtime will be accrued while human beings manually detect, diagnose, and recover unsuccessful automatic failures, as shown in Figure 1.4. If the system does not automatically detect the initial failure, then the failure will probably escalate or cascade to produce more service impact until it is either automatically detected by the system or is manually detected by a human operator. Note that highly available systems typically have several tiers of automatic failure detection, isolation, and recovery mechanisms to increase the overall likelihood of successful automatic recovery. If the system's automatic failure isolation indicts the wrong recoverable module, then the automatic recovery action will not clear the failure, and thus will require manual failure diagnosis by a human operator. If the automatic recovery action fails, then intervention by a human operator will typically be required to clear the failed recovery and restore service. Assuming that automatic failure detection, isolation, and recovery is at least moderately effective, human operators who do detect a failure will often monitor the status of automatic robustness operations before taking any manual action to avoid disrupting automatic failure detection, isolation, and recovery actions that could be progressing (perhaps slowly). Figure 1.4 illustrates the possible interplay between automatic robustness mechanisms and manual recovery.

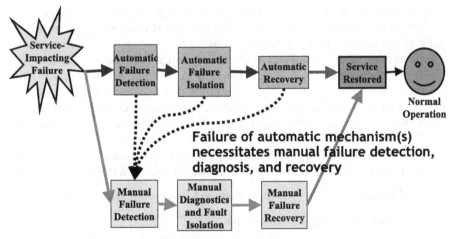

Figure 1.4 Automatic and Manual Recovery

In the real world, robust systems typically follow an elaborate automatic recovery process. There are an infinite number of possible failures that can confront a system. Beyond hardware and software failures, other systems or users can send malformed or malicious requests, human operators can make mistakes, and supporting systems or infrastructure can fail. Myriad failure detectors are integrated throughout the system, such as parity detectors in hardware and timeouts in software. When these mechanisms detect a failure, then alarm correlation software should isolate the true failure. A recovery strategy is then executed, such as switching service to a redundant element, or restarting a software module. Unfortunately, no single automatic recovery strategy is always effective, and thus a secondary—often more severe—recovery action may be required. For example, if restarting a failed process does not restore service, then it may be necessary to restart all application software on a processor or perhaps restart the processor or entire computer, or take other recovery steps. Thus, the system monitors progress of the automatic recovery, and if the system does not recover promptly, then a secondary recovery mechanism may be activated. There are usually human operators who are responsible for monitoring and maintaining systems, and if the responsible human operators deem that automatic recovery is not progressing acceptably, then they can initiate a manual recovery action. As a practical matter, not all automatic recovery actions succeed either because automatic failure detection, isolation, or recovery didn't work properly, or because the human operator didn't want to wait long enough for automatic mechanisms to complete.

1.6 QUANTIFYING AVAILABILITY

The period when service is available is called *uptime*; the period when service is unavailable is called *downtime*. While most personal and consumer electronics devices support only a single user at a time, most enterprise and commercial systems support many users simultaneously. To account for variations in failure impact to end users for multiuser systems, one can prorate service downtime by capacity lost. For example, a 10-minute outage that impacts half of a system's users or capacity is logically equivalent to a total (100%) capacity loss outage of 5 minutes. Prorating of capacity loss is a practical way to capture the impact of smaller events that affect only a portion of a system's users or subscribers.

Service downtime is the sum of outage duration prorated by capacity lost for all failures in a particular time period. Mathematically, this is:

$$Downtime = \sum_{Failures} OutageDuration * PortionOfCapacityLost$$

Consider each of the input factors separately.

- **Portion of Capacity Lost** captures the portion of system capacity that was impacted by the service outage. Some events, such as power failure, will render a system completely unavailable, and thus 100% of system capacity is unavailable. Other failures may impact only a portion of a system's capacity, such as if users are distributed across several process or hardware instances and one of those instances fails. For example, if user data is distributed across 5 hard disks, each user's data is confined to a single hard disk, and we assume that users are uniformly distributed across the five hard disks, then the failure of a single hard disk will nominally impact 20% of the system's users. Note that some systems can experience partial functionality outages in addition to partial capacity outages. For example, a voice-mail system might both record messages from callers and play back those recordings to subscribers; if one of those functions fails (perhaps the system can play back previously recorded messages but not record new messages), then that might be considered a 50% loss of functionality and 50% could be used for Portion of Capacity Lost.

- **Outage Duration** is duration of service unavailability for the failure event. Outage duration is normally measured in seconds or minutes and lasts from start of service disruption until service is restored. This duration generally includes the time to detect, isolate, and recover service from the failure.

Section 1.1 explained that availability can also be expressed as:

$$Availability = \frac{Uptime}{Uptime + Downtime}$$

Rather than explicitly calculating uptime, one can simplify the calculation to:

$$Availability = \frac{TotalSystemMinutes - DownMinutes}{TotalSystemMinutes}$$

- **TotalSystemMinutes** represents the number of in-service systems multiplied by the number of minutes in the reporting period. For example, the month of April has 30 days or 43,200 minutes (= 30 days times 24 hours per day times 60 minutes per hour). If 50 systems are in-service, then the *TotalSystemMinutes* for April is 2,160,000 (= 50 systems times 43,200 minutes per system).

- **DownMinutes** is the cumulative, prorated service downtime accrued by the in-service systems in the reporting period. For example, assume that in one 30-day month, 50 deployed systems experience three outages:
  1. 10-minute outage impacting 25% of a single system's users. For example, assume that users are uniformly distributed across four identical frontend processes on each system and one of those processes failed.
  2. 20-minute outage impacting one-third of a single system's primary functionality for all users. For example, consider a social networking site that supports two broad functions: users can their own post content, and users can search and read content posted by others and themselves. If a failure prevents users from posting new content but does not impact the ability to search and read previously posted content, then that failure could be considered a 50% functionality loss event.

3. 30-minute outage impacting all of a system's users. For example, imagine that a janitor plugs a vacuum cleaner into the same electrical circuit providing electrical power to the server hosting the service, and when the vacuum cleaner is turned on the circuit breaker trips, thus causing power outage to the server and a total service outage.

Thus,

$$Downtime = 10*25\% + 20*50\% + 30*100\% = 42.5$$

$$Availability = \frac{2,160,000 - 42.5}{2,160,000} = \frac{2159957.5}{2,160,000} = 0.99998 = 99.998\%$$

Note that some service impairments may be so brief or minor that they will not be classified as outages. For example, few people would classify a momentary disruption of residential AC power that caused lights to flicker as a power outage.

Since there are 525,960 minutes per average year (365.25 days per average year * 24 hours per day * 60 minutes per hour), annualized down-minutes are often expressed as "availability" via the following formula:

$$Availability = \frac{525,960 - AnnualizedDownMinutesPerSystem}{525,960}$$

Five 9's (99.999%) availability works out to be 5.26 prorated down-minutes per system per year. *Four 9's* (99.99%) availability is about an hour of downtime per system per year (52.6 down-minutes); *three 9's* is about nine hours of annualized downtime.

1.7 OUTAGE ATTRIBUTABILITY

Service outages generally have a single primary cause and may have additional contributory causes that prolong outage duration or increase outage extent. The various causes may be attributable to system or equipment suppliers, system integrator, the enterprise operating the system, others, or a combination. By clearly defining responsibility for actual outage causes, suppliers and enterprises operating the systems can proactively manage their respective outage responsibilities to minimize the overall risk of any outage. TL 9000 factors outage attributability into product or supplier-attributable, enterprise-attributable, and external-attributable outages, and this taxonomy is applicable to a wide range of systems.

1. **Product-attributable or supplier-attributable outage.** Some outages are primarily attributable to the design or failure of the system's software or hardware itself. The telecommunications industry defines product-attributable outages [TL9000] as follows:

An outage primarily triggered by
a) *the system design, hardware, software, components or other parts of the system,*
b) *scheduled outage necessitated by the design of the system,*
c) *support activities performed or prescribed by an organization* [system supplier] *including documentation, training, engineering, ordering, installation, maintenance, technical assistance, software or hardware change actions, etc.,*
d) *procedural error caused by the organization* [system supplier],
e) *the system failing to provide the necessary information to conduct a conclusive root cause determination, or*
f) *one or more of the above.*

2. **Enterprise-attributable outage.** Some outages are primarily attributable to actions or inactions of the enterprise operating the equipment. The telecommunications industry defines this category (called *customer-attributable outage,* in which *customer* refers to the enterprise operating the equipment) as follows [TL9000]:

An outage that is primarily attributable to the customer's [enterprise's] *equipment or support activities triggered by*
a) *customer* [enterprise] *procedural errors,*
b) *office environment, for example power, grounding, temperature, humidity, or security problems, or*
c) *one or more of the above.*

3. **External-attributable outage.** Some outages are attributable to external events beyond the control of either the enterprise operating the system or the system supplier. The telecommunications industry defines this category as follows [TL9000]:

Outages caused by natural disasters such as tornadoes or floods, and outages caused by third parties not associated with the customer or the organization such as commercial power failures, 3rd party contractors not working on behalf of the organization [system supplier] *or customer* [enterprise].

Real outages may have a primary cause and one or more contributing factors that caused the outage impact either to increase (e.g., via a failure cascade) or to prolong outage recovery, or both. For example, the primary cause of a flat tire may be an external-attributable road hazard like a nail, but the outage may be prolonged if the driver (*enterprise,* per the taxonomy above) is unable or unwilling to repair the tire himself and had not previously joined an automobile club that could quickly arrange for a repair technician to change the tire. Interestingly, outages are occasionally prolonged by enterprises for deliberate policy reasons. For example, if a small-capacity loss outage occurs on a system during a peak usage period and recovering service will require taking the entire system out of service briefly (e.g., to restart the system), then the enterprise may elect to defer the system recovery to an off-peak period to minimize service impact to other users. Conversely, if an outage occurs in an off-peak period, then under certain circumstances the enterprise may elect to defer system recovery to normal business hours to avoid the incremental cost of paying maintenance staff overtime to perform the work in off-hours. While the downtime associated with an initial product-attributable failure and unde-layed service recovery might reasonably be assigned to the supplier, additional service downtime accrued due to deliberately deferred service recovery should be assigned to the enterprise.

Obviously, system integrators and suppliers should focus on minimizing product-attributable outage causes, and enterprises should focus on both mini-mizing enterprise-attributable outages and mitigating the risk of external-attributable events. For example, enterprises can install uninterruptable power supplies to mitigate the risk of variations and disruption in external, commer-cial AC power. System integrators and equipment suppliers often provide recommendations and guidance to enterprises to minimize risk of enterprise- and external-attributable outages, such as offering training for enterprise staff to minimize risk of human error.

1.8 HARDWARE RELIABILITY

System hardware is packaged in field-replaceable units (FRUs) that can be individually replaced. Replaceable parts on home appliances, automobiles, computer systems, and other products are FRUs. Hardware reliability addresses how often each of these FRUs will fail. The following sections give a basic review of hardware reliability, service life, and return rates, and discusses typical system considerations related to hardware reliability.

1.8.1 Hardware Reliability Background

Hardware reliability is much better understood than software or system reliability for several reasons. First, hardware fails for physical reasons, and persistent (versus transient) hardware failures can be thoroughly analyzed to determine the precise failure mode and the likely root cause(s). Second, since early electronic hardware (e.g., vacuum tubes) was often prone to high failure rates, engineers have been working to understand and improve hard-ware reliability since at least World War II and the physics of hardware failure are now well understood. Third, actual hardware reliability of deployed ele-ments is generally easier to measure in the field than software reliability because hardware failures generally require physical replacement of failed FRUs and/or rework of failed connections to repair, rather than simply restart-ing, a system, or reseating an FRU that reboots some or all of a system's software.

Hardware failure rates generally follow the so-called "bathtub curve" illustrated in Figure 1.5. The X-axis shows operational time and the Y-axis shows failure intensity or rate. Some FRUs will quickly fail to operate because of weak components, solder joints, or manufacturing quality factors. FRUs that

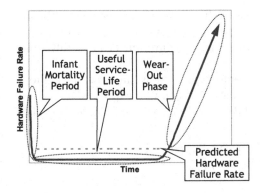

Figure 1.5   "Bathtub" Hardware Failure Rate Curve

fail to operate the first time they are powered on in the field are often called "dead on arrival" (DOA). Over the first days and weeks of operation, some poorly manufactured parts and assemblies are likely to fail; the time when weak FRUs fall out is called the "infant mortality period". The rate of early life failures declines quickly as the weak hardware fails and the failure rate stabilizes; the period of stable hardware failure rate is called the "useful service-life period." As the useful lifetime of the hardware expires, the hardware enters the wear-out phase and the rate of hardware failures increases due to wear-out factors. At some point in the wear-out phase, all hardware elements will have failed, and thus the curve ends.

1.8.2 Hardware Reliability Prediction

Hardware failure rate prediction methodologies estimate the failure rate in the useful-life period. MIL-HDBK-217F [MIL217F] and Telcordia's SR-332 [SR332] standards for hardware reliability prediction are common in the industry. Prediction methodologies consider various factors, including the parts used in the design and assumptions about operational characteristics like ambient temperature. Assumptions and prediction models tend to be conservative, so observed hardware failure rates during useful-life periods are often much lower than standard prediction methodologies calculate. As customers expect hardware failure rates to be less than predicted failure rates throughout the useful service life, hardware suppliers have historically been motivated to give conservative hardware failure rate predictions to minimize the risk of exceeding official "predicted" hardware failure rates. Since different prediction methodologies and different prediction assumptions can give significantly different failure rates, it is useful to calibrate and validate a supplier's predictions against historical data to understand how pessimistic or realistic their predictions are likely to be. Hardware failure rates are highly dependent on temperature; the higher the temperature, the higher the hardware failure rate and perhaps the shorter the useful service life. Thus, if the assumed ambient temperatures are not consistent with the actual ambient temperatures of deployed systems, then the predicted hardware failure rates can be different from actual observed values.

Hardware failure rates are commonly expressed as "failures in 1 billion hours" (FITs). Alternately, hardware failure rates may be expressed as "mean time between failures" (MTBF). MTBF and FIT rates are mathematically related as

$$MTBF_{Hours} = \frac{1,000,000,000}{FITs}$$

1.8.3 Hardware Service Life

Although MTBF and service life are often expressed in the same unit (hours or years), they are completely different concepts. Hardware service life is the period that hardware should operate before the hardware failure rate rises above the predicted hardware failure rate as wear-out failures increase. A predicted hardware failure rate estimates the rate of failure during the useful service life, rather than during the wear-our or infant mortality periods. While the hardware service life of most electronic devices is significantly longer than the expected useful life of the system those devices are in, some devices with mechanical parts may have service lives that are shorter than the expected useful life of the system. As hard disk drives have moving parts with lubricated bearings, they generally have a hardware service lifetime of less than 5 years. For example, a hard disk drive manufacturer may quote a mean time between failures (MTBF) of 1 million hours, which is mathematically equivalent to a predicted failure rate of 10^{-6} failures per hour (10^{-6} is the mathematical reciprocal of 10^6 MTBF). The designed hardware service lifetime might be 5 years (43,430 hours) and the predicted hardware failure rate during that useful lifetime might be 10^{-6} hardware failures per unit per hour. An MTBF of 1 million hours is equivalent to an MTBF of 114 years, but with a designed hardware service life of 5 years, very few units will survive to even 10 years. Experience and common sense assures us that the moving parts in a typical hard disk drive will wear out after *far less* than a century of actual service. Figure 1.6 graphically illustrates this example for a hypothetical hard disk drive.

Service life creates a reliability risk if customers expect to keep the system in service beyond the designed hardware service life of any individual FRUs because of the increasing hardware failure rate that occurs after the FRU enters its wear-out phase. Having some FRUs with a shorter lifetime in a complex system is a very common phenomenon. For example, consumers expect to replace the tires and battery on their car at least once before the car wears out, and they accept that light bulbs, appliances, carpets, roofs, and so

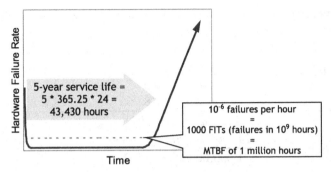

Figure 1.6   MTBF and Service Life of Sample Hard Disk Drive

on will require replacement long before their house reaches the end of its useful life. Thus, system suppliers should carefully design to assure that hardware elements that are likely to fail before the system reaches the end of its designed hardware service life can be easily replaced. Just as light bulbs, batteries, and tires can be replaced relatively easily, failed fans, hard disks, batteries, and so on should be easily replaceable in the field so that customers are not forced to endure prolonged service disruption or exceptional expense to replace worn-out hardware components. Like automobile manufacturers recommending maintenance schedules to replace filters, tires, batteries, and other components that are not designed to last the entire useful service life of the automobile, both hardware and system suppliers should clearly communicate the service-life expectation of any FRUs that are expected to wear out before the system itself reaches the end of its useful service life.

1.8.4   Hardware Return Rates

While some system hardware elements like batteries and fans are considered consumable and are discarded on failure, most hardware will be repaired following failure. For repairable hardware, the rate at which hardware elements are returned for repair is a common measure of hardware reliability, and hardware return rates are a reasonable proxy for the hardware failures that customers experience for nonconsumable hardware units. Hardware return rate measures are generally expressed as *annualized return rates*, and may be further subdivided into *time windows*, such as TL 9000's metrics:

- Early Return Index (ERI) measures hardware returns in the first 6 months after shipment.
- Yearly Return Rate (YRR) measures hardware returns 7 to 18 months after shipment.
- Long-Term Return Rate (LTR) measures hardware returns more than 18 months after shipment.

Hardware reliability predictions can be converted to equivalent annualized return rate predictions as follows:

$$\mathrm{Re}\,turn\,Rate_{Annualized} = \frac{1}{MTBF_{Annual}}$$

$$\mathrm{Re}\,turn\,Rate_{Annualized} = \frac{24*365.25}{MTBF_{Hourly}} = \frac{8,766}{MTBF_{Hourly}}$$

$$\mathrm{Re}\,turn\,Rate_{Annualized} = \frac{24*365.25*FITs}{1,000,000,000} = \frac{FITs}{114,077}$$

As explained in Section 1.8.2, "Hardware Reliability Prediction," hardware suppliers often use fairly conservative assumptions so that the best estimate of actual return rates will generally be below prediction.

The hardware return rate metric is complicated by several factors:

1. **Not all hardware returns are attributed to hardware failures.** Inevitably, some returned hardware FRUs will be tested at the repair center and found to function properly with *no trouble found* (abbreviated *NTF*; sometimes called *no fault found—NFF*). No-trouble-found hardware is generally attributed to a variety of causes including software failures misdiagnosed as hardware failures, and diagnostic failures in which functional hardware was incorrectly deemed to have failed and was thus returned. In addition, unused materials may also be returned to the supplier because too much material was ordered, or because the order was changed or canceled or for other reasons. Hardware may also be returned in response to product recall or change notices to have recommended corrective changes applied. The percentage of confirmed hardware failures as a portion of total returns often varies significantly based on the nature of the FRU. High NTF rates are a concern because although the hardware reliability does not appear to be a problem, one or more root causes are forcing customers to spend effort and cost to manually remove and return hardware that had not failed.

2. **Uncertainty in the actual number of FRUs in service to normalize returns against.** It is very easy for hardware suppliers to count how many FRUs are shipped from their factory, but it is not very easy to know how many FRUs are actually in service. There is always a delay between the time an FRU is shipped from a factory to the time that the FRU is installed in a system and powered on. Some individual FRUs will be promptly delivered to customer sites, installed and powered on; other FRUs will endure logistics or staging delays; some FRUs will be stocked as spares, and may not be installed for years; some FRUs may never even be sold. The uncertainty of actual number of FRUs in service is often highest in the early months of production

as the logistics and delivery process is being refined and spares pools are created.

3. **Uncertainty of in-service time of individual returned FRUs.** Because complex systems are generally built from many different FRUs and systems cannot go into service until all required FRUs are available on-site, installed, configured, and brought into service, variable logistic and business delays add uncertainty between the time a FRU was shipped by the hardware supplier and the time the FRU begins normal, continuous operation. In addition, some FRUs will be held as spares, and these may spend months or longer in factory packaging without ever being powered on. Thus, it may be hard to reliably determine how many hours of service a particular FRU sustained before it was returned. Just as automobiles include odometers to maintain a persistent count of the distance driven, the best practice is for each FRU to record wear-out-related parameters like power-on hours and maximum operating temperature in persistent-on-FRU storage as part of an "odometer."

4. **Not all failures are returned to the equipment manufacturer's authorized repair center.** Just as automobile owners are not required to take their cars to factory authorized service centers for repairs, system owners may send their failed FRUs to competitive repair centers, and thus hardware suppliers may have no visibility or knowledge of those failures. With inexpensive or short service life FRUs, customers may simply discard the failed unit rather than returning it for repair.

Despite these complicating factors, hardware return rates are an excellent measure of actual hardware reliability. Hardware suppliers should be able to provide return rate data for each FRU, and the confirmed hardware failure rate should be well below predicted hardware failure rate. If the overall return rate is above prediction or the no trouble found rate is substantial, then there is significant risk that system owners may experience higher apparent hardware failure rates than predicted. After all, a perceived hardware failure (even if it is later deemed to be "no trouble found" by the repair center) causes maintenance engineers to take the time to replace a FRU and the expense of returning that FRU, restocking a spare, and so on. From the system owner's perspective, a confirmed hardware failure and a no trouble found failure have similar cost, but the no trouble found pack may offer an incremental intangible cost of uncertainty surrounding the true root cause of the failure and thus elevated risk of failure recurrence.

1.8.5 Hardware Reliability Considerations

The primary considerations when selecting hardware are obviously functionality ones, such as:

- **Does the hardware deliver the required functionality with adequate performance?**
- **Does the hardware meet the physical design requirements?** (e.g., size, weight, form factor, power)
- **Does the hardware operate reliably in the target environment?** (e.g., temperature and humidity range, shock and vibration tolerance, presence of dust and corrosive gases, altitude, etc.)
- **Does the hardware meet the cost target?**

Hardware reliability is a secondary consideration for hardware options that meet the primary requirements. The fundamental business question when considering hardware reliability is

- **Will the hardware failure rate be acceptably low throughout the system's designed service life?**

Note that higher hardware failure rates may lead to higher operating expenses associated with increased hardware returns and sparing-related expenses. Acceptability of hardware failure rates is fundamentally driven by how often customers will tolerate executing hardware repairs or maintenance actions on the overall system. Just as consumers evaluate reliability of their automobile based on how often the car is in the shop rather than on the failure rate of individual subsystems or components, system owners are likely to consider how often they have to replace any board or FRU on a system rather than the failure rate of individual blades. Thus, there is likely to be some flexibility in failure rate requirements of individual FRUs so long as the overall hardware failure rate remains low enough that the customer doesn't have to repair hardware too often. Deep knowledge of customer expectations enables one to estimate the maximum acceptable system hardware repair rate, and manage individual FRU failure rates to be low enough to meet the overall system target.

End customers will expect hardware reliability to be below predicted failure rates and may include business remedies, such as contractual penalties with liquidated damages, if hardware returns exceed predicted values. System suppliers should assure that appropriate business arrangements are made with original equipment manufacturers so that risk of premature (i.e., warranty) or excessive hardware failures is covered by the hardware manufacturer who is best equipped to manage the risk.

1.9 SOFTWARE RELIABILITY

Although software doesn't physically break or fail in a persistent way that can be easily examined with an optical or electron microscope, it does fail or crash. Figure 1.7 shows an instance of the infamous *blue screen of death* software failure from Microsoft Windows®, which many readers will have personally

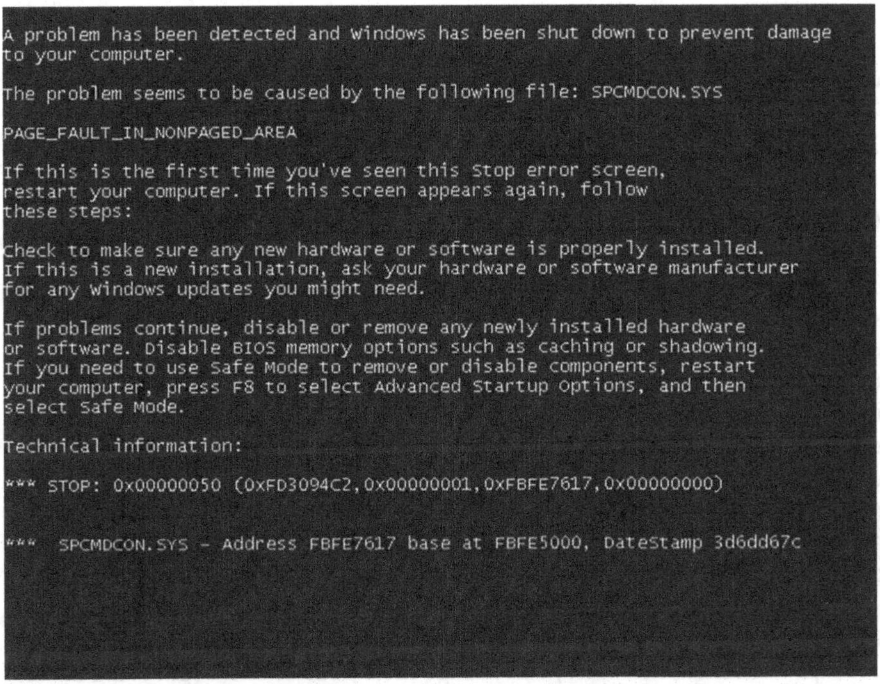

```
A problem has been detected and windows has been shut down to prevent damage
to your computer.

The problem seems to be caused by the following file: SPCMDCON.SYS

PAGE_FAULT_IN_NONPAGED_AREA

If this is the first time you've seen this stop error screen,
restart your computer. If this screen appears again, follow
these steps:

Check to make sure any new hardware or software is properly installed.
If this is a new installation, ask your hardware or software manufacturer
for any windows updates you might need.

If problems continue, disable or remove any newly installed hardware
or software. Disable BIOS memory options such as caching or shadowing.
If you need to use Safe Mode to remove or disable components, restart
your computer, press F8 to select Advanced Startup Options, and then
select Safe Mode.

Technical information:

*** STOP: 0x00000050 (0xFD3094C2,0x00000001,0xFBFE7617,0x00000000)


*** SPCMDCON.SYS - Address FBFE7617 base at FBFE5000, DateStamp 3d6dd67c
```

Figure 1.7 Blue Screen of Death

Source: Figure taken from Wikipedia, http://en.wikipedia.org/wiki/File:Windows_XP_BSOD.
png, June 15, 2010.

experienced. In addition to the dramatic "blue screen," a critical software
failure event may simply be called a *crash* or *system hang*. Practically speaking,
software reliability is measured as the rate of critical software failures (e.g.,
crashes, hangs, blue screens), as in "application X crashes once a month unless
we reboot the system."

Software reliability growth theory [Musa89] posits that there are a finite
number of defects in a piece of software that can be exposed in a particular
operational profile. While hardware wears out over time, software does not;
new defects don't spontaneously arise over time in software as cracks and
physical breakdowns arise in hardware. Thus, as residual software defects are
discovered and removed, there are fewer defects left to be exposed in a particular operational profile. Fewer critical residual software defects should be
encountered less frequently in normal operation, and thus should yield a lower
software failure rate. This is generally demonstrated in maintenance or patch
releases, which are often more stable and reliable than major releases of software because major releases inevitably introduce new defects along with new
features, while maintenance or patch releases focus on removing software
defects. Since new defects are seldom introduced when a software defect is
fixed, each critical defect removed is essentially one less residual defect to
cause a software failure in the field.

The next section defines operational profiles, describes software reliability growth theory, reviews several residual defect prediction techniques, and discusses how to evaluate prediction results.

1.9.1 Operational Profile

Operational profile characterizes how a system interacts with other elements in the enterprise's solution to deliver services to end users. A particular system can often be used in several different operational profiles, each of which may stress the system in slightly different ways, thus exposing somewhat different residual faults. For example, a four-door sedan automobile can be used both to carry passengers on paved roads and to haul bricks on dirt roads. Each of these profiles exposes the automobile to different shock, vibration, and mechanical stress, and thus the time to first failure of the automobile may be different in each of these two operational profiles. System testing should reflect the operation profile(s) that the deployed system will experience to assure that the vast majority of design and residual defects are discovered and corrected before field deployment.

Note that the operational profile of a deployed system can be changed by an enterprise after the system is deployed. For example, an enterprise (or perhaps even their end users) can change their policies and begin using names and strings containing Asian characters. While Western character sets such as ASCII can often be encoded as a single byte per character, Asian characters require two or more bytes per character, and thus the logic for manipulating and encoding Western and Asian character sets may be somewhat different. If Asian characters were not included in the system's test campaign, then there is a higher risk that residual defects will be encountered in field operations with Asian characters, such as importing and exporting system information via text configuration files. Hence, differences between *tested* operational profiles and *field* operational profiles present gaps in testing through which undiscovered software defects can escape to the field.

1.9.2 Software Reliability Growth Theory

When testing a system, residual defects are methodically exposed, so they can then be debugged and corrected. Discovery of residual defects generally progresses as shown in Figure 1.8. The X-axis shows the cumulative time system testers spend executing tests against the target system; the Y-axis shows cumulative number of defects discovered. Defect discovery often starts slowly as the test team progresses through a *"learning phase"* during which they become familiar with both the system and the test tools. As testers gain experience, their productivity increases and they enter a "linear phase" in which they discover defects fairly regularly as new test cases are executed and defects are exposed and recorded. This consistent defect discovery rate is shown as the

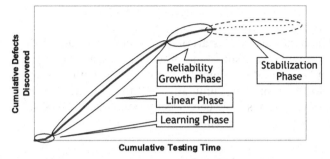

Figure 1.8   Canonical Software Reliability Growth

linear phase of defect discovery. Defects discovered throughout the test interval will generally be promptly fixed and new or patched software loads will be delivered to system test. These patched loads should enable system test to cover system functionality that may have been previously blocked by software defects. Thus, as more defects are discovered and removed, system test can verify more and more system functionality. Inevitably, a fraction of the defect corrections will themselves be defective, so some rework of defect correction (sometimes called "fix on fix") will be necessary. The rate of defective fixes should be very small, and thus the total number of residual defects should not increase significantly after software development is complete and formal system testing begins. After sufficient testing, debugging, and defect correction, the number of residual defects shrinks to the point that it becomes harder and harder for testers to discover previously unknown residual defects, and thus the previously linear discovery rate begins to flatten out. This transition from linear defect discovery rate to decreasing defect discovery rate characterizes the "*reliability growth phase.*" As the number of discovered defects asymptotically approaches the finite number of defects originally accessible to the piece of software in the particular operational profile, it takes more and more test effort to discover residual defects. At some point, the number of residual defects is so small that the system will operate with an acceptably low software failure rate, and the software enters the "*stabilization phase.*" As testing costs money and adds time to the schedule, a key business question is deciding when sufficient testing has been executed to assure that the system will be acceptably reliable.

Note that the X-axis in Figure 1.8 is labeled "*cumulative testing time*" rather than calendar time. This is because the independent variable that drives defect discovery during testing is actual test effort, rather than calendar time. The distinction between "testing time" and "calendar time" is important because test effort is rarely uniform across a 7-day week, and effort per week is rarely uniform across the entire test period. For example, test staff will take vacations and will have other work commitments like training and supporting other projects or releases that reduce their test time. System software failures may block some test cases and hardware failures may render test cells unavailable for testing. Also, testers may be more likely to work overtime toward the end of the test interval than they are in the start of the test interval. Normalizing defect discovery against cumulative testing time should factor real world variations out of the data, and thus produce a more accurate curve that is easier to interpret. A practical benefit of plotting cumulative test time on the X-axis is that it makes planning easier because one can directly estimate the test effort required between any two points on the curve.

1.9.3 Estimating Residual Defects

The number of residual defects can be estimated using a number of software quality methodologies, including [Demarco86], [Humphrey89], [Lyu96], or [Musa89]. Software reliability growth modeling [Musa89] has several advantages over some traditional software quality methodologies, including:

1. **It does not require deep knowledge of process performance of specification, design, and coding activities.** Importantly, this means that one can consider the behavior of software modules that were developed by others (e.g., third parties, open source, or reused modules) for which no process performance data is available.

2. **It provides an intuitive visualization that is easy for all members of a project team to understand.**

3. **Required input data is easy to acquire.**

Figure 1.9 shows a sample software reliability growth curve with a vertical line showing "system release" after hundreds, thousands, or more hours of cumulative testing time. The slope of the software reliability growth curve shows the rate at which critical software defects are discovered, often expressed as number of hours or days of testing estimated to discover the next previously

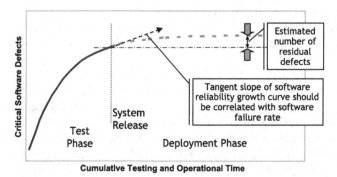

Figure 1.9 Estimating Residual Defects from Software Reliability Growth Model

unknown defect. As system testing is designed to mirror the operational profile of target customers, system testing should be a form of highly accelerated stress testing of the system because testers are deliberately trying to stress the system. Thus, the longer it is estimated to take dedicated system testers to expose a previously unknown residual defect, the longer it should take an enterprise or end user to encounter a previously unknown residual defect. The gap between the number of defects discovered at the time of system release and the asymptotic number of defects estimated by the software reliability growth curve estimates the number of residual defects.

The physics of hardware failure enables one to reliably estimate the failure acceleration factor due to elevated temperatures, and so on, in highly accelerated stress testing of hardware. Unfortunately, the "physics" of software failures is far messier than the physics of hardware failure, and thus there is far more uncertainty in estimating the "acceleration" or calibration factor between the defect discovery rate in lab testing and the critical software failure rate in field operation. Nevertheless, assuming system testing is mirroring the operational profile(s) of field deployments, one expects a rough correlation between the defect discovery rate at system release and the critical failure rate in field operation.

1.9.4 Calibrating Residual Defect Models

While it theoretically takes infinite time to activate all residual defects and perfect debugging to determine which are truly *new* residual defects versus activation of previously known defects, project teams generally can estimate the minimum effective asymptotic number of critical defects after about a year of field deployment by summing both the number of unique field-found defects and the number of additional, previously unknown defects that were discovered when testing maintenance and patch loads on the release. Depending on operational policies of enterprises operating the system and their support agreements with the system supplier, some or all of those failures may be reported back to the system supplier for analysis and corrective action. Thus, while a system supplier may never know exactly how many residual critical software defects were in a piece of software released to the field, the supplier often knows the minimum number of residual critical defects that were present based on what defects were subsequently detected by customers or while developing and testing maintenance releases or patches. This minimum effective asymptotic number of estimated critical defects can be compared to the number of defects predicted by the software reliability growth or other defect prediction model used. Since system testing inherently differs from actual field deployment in a variety of ways, there may be somewhat more observed residual defects than were estimated from modeling of system test data. Nevertheless, system testers should constantly strive to make their test configurations better reflect actual operational profiles to improve the

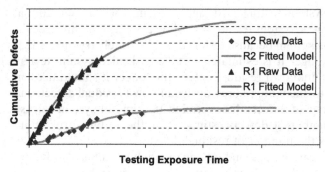

Figure 1.10   Comparing Software Reliability Growth of Different Software Releases

effectiveness of their testing, and thereby improve the expected prediction accuracy of residual defects based on system test data.

While it is often difficult to accurately and quantitatively extrapolate a single test or analysis result to likely field availability of a particular release, it is often insightful to compare and contrast test results from historic releases and current release against actual field performance of historic releases to triangulate a best estimate of reliability and availability. For example, Figure 1.10 overlays the software reliability growth analysis of two releases of a real system. Although R2 benefited from significantly more test time than R1, there appear to be far fewer critical defects and thus R2 should have a significantly lower software failure rate than R1. By combining this R2-versus-R1 comparison data with other R2 to R1 comparison data, one can estimate a range of how much lower the critical software failure rate of R2 is likely to be relative to R1. A software reliability growth curve, especially one that overlays previous release data like Figure 1.10, is often very useful to decision makers when evaluating software readiness for release.

1.10   PROBLEMS

1. Give three examples of fault activation that lead to service failure.

2. Give three examples of a failure cascade.

3. One 30-minute total outage and one 10-minute partial outage impacting half of a system's capacity occur across a population of 15 systems deployed in August; what is the service availability for the month?

4. What is the difference between MTBF and designed service life of hardware?

5. A particular FRU is predicted to have 10,000 FITs. What percentage of these FRUs is likely to fail per year during the unit's designed service life?

6. A system is built of five FRUs, each with 10,000 FITs. What is the annual predicted rate of hardware maintenance actions per system?

7. A particular FRU is predicted to have 10,000-hour MTBF. What percentage of these FRUs is likely to fail per year during the unit's designed service life?

1.11   FOR FURTHER STUDY

[TL9000] offers formal and rigorous guidance on quantitative measurement of service availability and hardware reliability. [Lyu96] and [Musa89] offer more information on software reliability and [O'Connor04] covers hardware reliability.

Chatper 2

System Basics

Systems are purchased by enterprises to deliver some valuable service to users. Obviously, the service has to be sufficiently valuable to some enterprise or user to justify spending time and money to acquire and integrate the hardware, software, and so on to produce an operational system. This chapter reviews how hardware and software are integrated into systems, how systems are integrated into solutions, how service quality and outages are assessed, and total cost of system ownership.

2.1 HARDWARE AND SOFTWARE

Modern computer-based systems are implemented in three general architectural layers:

1. **Hardware** includes processors, storage devices, and networking and input/output mechanisms that host the system's platform and application software. Figure 2.1 is an example of system hardware. Large systems are generally built from *field-replaceable units (FRUs)* of hardware like:
   - Single board computers or processor blades (Figure 2.2)
   - Hard disk drives (Figure 2.3)
   - Chasses that hold FRUs and provide connectivity to power and communications (Figure 2.4)

   Many systems today are built with so-called *commercial off-the-shelf (COTS)* hardware, and thus system suppliers have little or no control over the design for reliability diligence that was performed on the hardware. Careful quality and reliability assessment of sourced hardware is crucial before selecting COTS suppliers and FRUs to assure that quality and reliability diligence has been completed to make acceptable field performance likely.

Design for Reliability: Information and Computer-Based Systems, by Eric Bauer
Copyright © 2010 Institute of Electrical and Electronics Engineers

Figure 2.1 System Hardware

2. **Platform software** includes the operating system, drivers, databases, protocol stacks, and other middleware. The vast majority of platform software used in systems today is from third-party suppliers and/or open source. System suppliers may construct proprietary software platforms that integrate together "standard" third-party and open-source software with proprietary software to create a software platform that simplifies application development by reusing large amounts of non-application-specific code. Platform software often includes numerous failure detection mechanisms and should support rapid recovery from inevitable failures of application software, hardware, or platform software. Constructing and using appropriately rich software platforms can enable system suppliers to focus the majority of their scarce development and test resources on value-added, application-specific functionality.

Figure 2.2   Single Board Computer FRU

Figure 2.3   Hard Disk Drive FRU

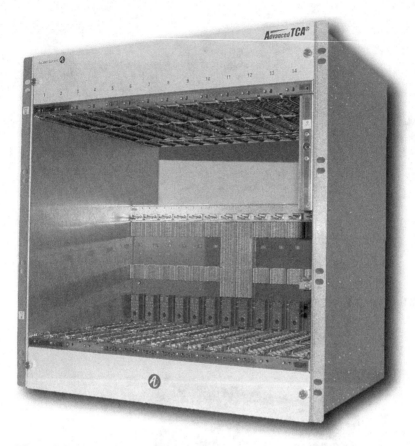

Figure 2.4   Chassis FRU

3. **Application software** implements the application or business logic that
   delivers valuable services to users or other systems in the solution.
   Although application software is typically much smaller than platform
   software, it typically has a higher density of residual defects than platform software because it has experienced less in-service time and thus
   fewer residual defects have been exposed and debugged. This is because
   the platform software may support many different applications, thus
   accruing many hours of exposure in a wide variety of operational scenarios. Hence, a substantially higher portion of critical software failures
   are often attributed to application software (including application integration with platform software) than platform software relative to what
   would be expected by simply comparing code size.

As shown in Figure 2.5, systems generally operate in the broader context
of a networked solution with human users and other systems connected

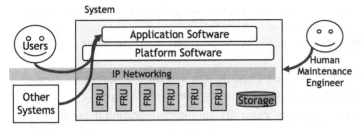

Figure 2.5   Canonical System Architecture

via IP networking. The application software is supported by platform software that executes on physical hardware that is organized into field-replaceable units (FRUs) that can be easily replaced; persistent storage—often arranged on FRUs—is generally included as well. Other network elements may be integral parts of the system's robustness architecture. For example, failure of adjacent systems (e.g., database servers, or authentication, authorization, and accounting systems) may impact a system's ability to deliver service. Interestingly, adjacent systems may also be part of the recovery architecture; for example, a domain name server or external IP switch might direct new service requests away from a failed element to a redundant element to restore service for end users. Human maintenance engineers are often the only people likely to physically "touch" the system's hardware itself, but operations, administration, and provisioning staff will also interact with the system over the network. The operations, administration, maintenance, and provisioning staff who support the system will rely on documented procedures, policies, training, and technical support from equipment suppliers.

2.2 EXTERNAL ENTITIES

Most systems operate in the broader context of a networked solution in which the system interacts with some or all of the following entities:

- **End users,** often via some client mechanism or device like a web browser or a set-top box for service delivery and self-care.
- **As a server for other systems.** Target system may offer services like authentication, authorization, and accounting for other systems that directly or indirectly support end users, maintenance engineers, or others.
- **Provisioning systems** provide the tools and mechanisms to add, configure, and support new and existing users. Provisioning systems often support batch operation for bulk provisioning.

- **Business and operations support systems** emit accounting, performance, and other data to business and operations systems to support accounting and billing, network and capacity planning, and other business operations.

- **Backup systems** regularly back up key system configuration, user, and other data to enable timely recovery from data failures.

- **Maintenance engineers** carefully monitor operational status of the system to detect, diagnose, and recover failures and anomalous behavior. Systems often support a console interface that gives maintenance engineers direct, interactive access and control of low-level system operation such as system boot, operating system startup, and loading applications. The console interface can be used by maintenance engineers to debug system startup problems, including hardware problems, and is often used for low-level maintenance activities like upgrading firmware.

- **Element management systems** monitor a system's alarms and operational characteristics, often via a version of IETF's Simple Network Management Protocol (SNMP).

- **Legal and regulatory systems.** Some services may be subject to legal or regulatory provisions such as lawful interception of communications (a.k.a., "wiretapping") or capturing compliance data, and these must be addressed according to applicable laws and regulations.

Figure 2.6 illustrates a sample system interaction context. Some of these interfaces deliver the primary functionality of the system (i.e., the service that justified purchasing the system itself), while other interfaces expose secondary or supporting functionality. Expectations and requirements for service quality will vary for the primary and secondary functionalities. Not all of these interfaces will be applicable to all systems. Note that the lines from

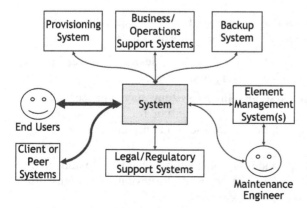

Figure 2.6 Sample System Interaction Context

different entities to the system are of different weight to signify that different entities often have different expectations for service quality. Typically end users enjoy the highest quality of service because they are generally paying for the service directly or indirectly and can often take their business elsewhere if service is not consistently very good. Interfaces that provide management visibility to support diagnostic, control, and recovery interfaces must also be reliable to enable maintenance engineers to deliver highly available service to end users. Business and operations support systems such as performance management reporting can often tolerate a lower grade of service; for example, scheduling real-time performance data to be unavailable for hours is often acceptable so long as the complete dataset can be made available at a later time.

2.3 SYSTEM MANAGEMENT

Systems require humans to operate, administer, maintain, and provision the hardware, software, and data that deliver valuable service to users. System management activities are often referred to as *OAM* for operations, administration, and maintenance (or sometimes management), or *OAM&P* for operations, administration, maintenance, and provisioning. The ISO Telecommunications Network Model [X.700] created a standard way of framing OAM&P activities by mapping systems management activities into five general management categories: *fault, configuration, accounting, performance,* and *security (FCAPS).*

1. **Fault management** concerns detection, isolation, and correction of system faults. Good fault management is essential to minimize the duration of service disruption when faults are activated. Since fault management is often critical to maintaining visibility into system operation and controlling manual recovery actions, its availability is likely to indirectly impact service availability observed by users.

2. **Configuration management** primarily concerns system configuration data that defines the linkage between modules within the system and between the system to other elements in the solution, and the versions of software and firmware running on a system.

3. **Accounting management** concerns usage and billing records.

4. **Performance management** supports network planning activities to assure the system can efficiently support offered traffic loads. Performance data is captured and analyzed to determine when and how the system should be reconfigured or grown to deliver acceptable quality of service to users.

5. **Security management** addresses security policy aspects of a system, including security authentication, authorization, and encryption.

User account management—such as adding, changing, and deleting users—is also a crucial function for many systems. Note that at least some management functionality will be accessible to end users as well as enterprise operations, administration, maintenance, and provisioning (OAM&P) staff. For instance, it is common for applications to provide a self-care interface to enable end users to manipulate the properties, behaviors, and preferences of their account. While exposing this functionality to end users (rather than solely to enterprise OAM&P staff) increases system complexity, it can improve end-user satisfaction by making it easier for users to tailor the service to meet their unique needs. In addition, self-care can reduce the operating expense of the enterprise because OAM&P staff need not be paid to execute the account changes that users perform themselves.

Changes to system hardware, software, and general configuration to address OAM&P can be executed in two operational contexts:

1. **Routine or nonemergency maintenance procedures.** The vast majority of maintenance procedures for typical systems can be carefully planned, scheduled, and approved weeks or days in advance. Days of preparation gives the engineer executing the work time to carefully review the written procedure, hints, and recommendations of colleagues; gather all necessary materials; assure that system's operational status is "perfect" before beginning the procedure; and gracefully drain traffic off of affected system modules. Routine procedures include:

   - Applying security, stability, and functionality patches to software
   - Upgrading application or platform software
   - Rebalancing or migrating subscriber traffic or data across systems, blades, hard disks, and so on
   - Growing hardware configuration to increase the system's capacity
   - Routine exercise of redundant hardware
   - Routine diagnostics
   - System or database backups

   Less common nonemergency procedures include:

   - Reconfiguring IP context or configuration of system (e.g., changing IP address or routing to system)
   - Physically relocating the system

2. **Recovery or emergency maintenance procedures.** Manual recovery procedures are sometimes required to restore the system to normal operation after failure, and to address emergency situations. Because recovery procedures are often executed on an emergency basis, staff will typically not have the luxury of time to carefully plan their actions in detail and they are likely to feel pressure to restore service as quickly as possible. Thus, manual troubleshooting and recovering of outages carries a somewhat higher risk of human error than routine or nonemergency procedures. Recovery procedures include:

- Diagnosing or troubleshooting failures not successfully automatically recovered by the system.
- Manual switchover to redundant blade or module.
- Manual restart of blade or module.
- Manual restart of system.
- Geographically redundant or site recovery.
- Restoring databases from backups.
- Replacing failed FRUs. Although FRU replacement is not usually required to restore service on high-availability systems configured with redundant hardware, FRU replacement is often completed as quickly as is practical to minimize the simplex exposure risk of catastrophic service disruption if the redundant unit fails before the failed FRU can be replaced.

Highly available systems will support in-service execution of all nonemergency and some emergency maintenance procedures. Systems are often at a higher risk of failure and service disruption when maintenance engineers are executing maintenance procedures than when the system is operating normally because the system may be deliberately placed into a simplex or special mode, or because of the risk of human error when executing a procedure, or for other reasons.

The following activities in OAM&P procedures are of particular concern because of increased risk of service-impacting errors:

- **Traffic migration.** To accommodate additional system hardware or shifting traffic patterns or to upgrade or update software or for other reasons, it is often necessary to migrate traffic from one instance or blade of a system to another. Some applications support sessions that can have a long duration, such as watching a streaming movie, and thus graceful traffic migration is essential to assure users have an acceptable quality of experience with the service. Practical systems often do not migrate "live" traffic; instead they wait for it to drain away naturally over a reasonable time. Migrating new sessions or traffic is often easily accomplished by directing new session requests to a different system instance or blade. An error in redirecting new sessions or traffic can cause service to become unavailable, and thus these procedures should be reliable and robust.
- **Manual switchover.** High-availability systems should expose mechanisms to maintenance engineers to enable on-demand switchover of every redundant module, as well as server or site switchover for systems supporting those levels of redundancy. Manual switchover is often used for emergency manual recovery when automatic failure detection, isolation, and recovery have not worked properly, or during software upgrade/update/patch/retrofit. Best practice for active/standby systems is to routinely perform manual switchovers every week in off-hours to assure

that all standby units are fully operational and properly configured to maximize the likelihood of successful switchover in an emergency situation. Manual switchovers are risky because:

- Software faults may prevent switchover from completing properly.
- There is the possibility of previously undetected (silent) hardware or software failure on the standby unit.
- The state of the previously active unit may have been compromised, and thus the standby unit has synchronized with compromised/inconsistent data.

- **Software update or patch.** System software is frequently patched or updated to fix reliability, security, or quality/stability problems. Activating new software often requires application processes to be restarted to activate new executable code, and may require restarting processors to activate updated operating system, platform, library, or other software. Note that in addition to updating or patching the application software, enterprises must be able to apply security and reliability patches to all platform software, including operating systems, databases, middleware, and drivers, as well as patches to included elements like shelf/chassis managers and Ethernet switches. All 24/7/365 systems should be designed so that software updates or patches can be applied and activated with minimal impact on user service, and complete written procedures should be provided so that maintenance engineers can reliably apply a software update or patch with minimal impact on user service.

- **Software upgrade or retrofit.** Major system releases add substantial new functionality, and may require changes to database schema, add new processes or libraries, and so on. Software upgrade or retrofit is substantially more complicated than software update or patch because:

  - Version of platform software components may change, including operating system, database, middleware, drivers, and so on.
  - Database schema may change, thus requiring the system's database to be changed prior to activation of new software. In addition, data records may have to be migrated or changed to support the new schema, such as adding default values for newly added data attributes and creating or updating linkages among entries.
  - Supported version of protocols for communications with other network elements may change, and this could change network interactions with other network elements. Different network interactions could activate previously unexposed residual defects in other network elements or in the system itself.
  - New processes, libraries, or configuration files may be added.
  - New or enhanced protocol messages may be used between different software modules within the system, such as new message types or logical states being added.

- Upgrade or retrofit may silently or implicitly write over some system configuration data, thus creating a configuration error or security vulnerability.

Given the elevated risk presented by software upgrade or retrofit, careful design, clearly written procedures, and thorough testing must be performed to assure that the risk of service disruption is acceptably low.

- **Rollback of upgrades, updates, and retrofits.** Installing and activating software upgrades, updates, retrofits, and patches is complex and there are many potential pitfalls from failures to migrate/convert a database due to unexpected data records, or countless other items. Best practice is to support a rollback mechanism to methodically revert an unsuccessful or undesirable upgrade, update, retrofit, or patch to the version of software previously used. Often, rollback is supported by permitting two installed application images to be stored on a system, possibly in different file systems to better contain any failures. The new software image is installed onto one file system without touching the currently executing "known good" image on the other file system. New software can be configured and data migrated or imported with minimal impact on running software. Then the new software can be started and service swung over to the new image to verify the new software, generally with test traffic. If software proves stable during initial verification and a subsequent "soak" period of initial operation (perhaps a week or two), then it can be accepted as a known good load. If the software proves unstable or toxic, then the system can be "rolled back" and restarted with the previously known good software instance on the other file system. As rollback may be executed from a less-than-perfect system state (e.g., an unsuccessful upgrade or new release that proved to be "toxic"), rollback must be very robust to revert from myriad possible upgrade-related failures.

- **FRU replacement.** Hardware will eventually fail, and the system should automatically restore service to redundant hardware. Maintenance engineers will typically replace failed FRUs on a nonemergency basis, thus reducing the risk of maintenance engineer's panic compromising the FRU replacement procedure. Some FRU failures may be catastrophic, meaning that system service will be impacted until the FRU is repaired or replaced. A FRU failure of a nonredundant hardware element or FRU failure when the system was operating simplex (e.g., previously failed FRU had not yet been replaced) would require emergency repair to restore service. Emergency hardware repairs or replacements carry an elevated risk of error that may expand or prolong the service outage. Physical manipulation of system hardware is inherently risky because:
  - The wrong FRU can be accidentally removed.
  - The wrong FRU type can be accidentally installed.
  - The FRU can be incorrectly configured.

- The FRU can be nonfunctional (often called an "out-of-the-box failure").
- The FRU boot code can fail to start up or load latest platform and/ or application software.
- The persistent storage on an FRU can fail to be configured or restored properly.
- **Hardware growth.** Traffic on systems often grows over time, and may grow very rapidly if the service supported by the system quickly becomes popular. All 24/7/365 systems should support in-service hardware growth, meaning that additional processor blades, database blades, hard disk drives, and so on can be added to the system to grow capacity without taking the system out of service. Since this procedure inevitably involves hardware manipulation of the system as well as changing the system's configuration, there is a risk of error that cascades into a service outage.
- **Online diagnostics.** Online diagnostic procedures permit maintenance engineers to diagnose operational impairments and failures to isolate the root cause of the trouble so that appropriate corrective action can be taken to restore full operations. Online diagnostics are inherently risky because they are executed on a system carrying live traffic (i.e., "online"). Risks include:
  - Bug in diagnostic code may impair some traffic scenarios or operations.
  - Resource conflict or exhaustion due to simultaneous diagnostic activities and nondiagnostic traffic.
  - Failure on unit being diagnosed may cause diagnostic code to cascade the failure into a more severe service outage.
- **Georedundant recovery/switchover.** Many highly available services are configured with redundant systems in geographically dispersed locations, commonly called *georedundancy*, thereby mitigating risk of site destruction or site denial such as from fire, flood, earthquake, tornado, tsunami, terrorist acts, or other force majeure. Best practice is to regularly perform disaster drills in which a site is abruptly taken offline to verify that disaster recovery procedures rapidly restore service onto the georedundant site. Georedundant recovery/switchover is risky because:
  - **Recovery actions of many elements must be coordinated.** IP infrastructure elements like routers and domain name servers must direct traffic away from the failed site toward the recovery site.
  - **Overload.** When all users who were active on the failed site switch over to the recovery site, there may be a flood of requests for reconnection/re-registration/reestablishment of service. Without robust overload control mechanisms to shape this surge of requests, the recovery site could collapse.

2.4 SYSTEM OUTAGES

As Section 2.2 explained, systems generally interact with several different external entities, often exposing very different functionality across different interfaces. These features range from end-user visible functions, to OAM&P, to performance enhancements, to installation and upgrade, to documentation, and even technical support and warranty arrangements. Complex systems, especially those with multiple independent processors on multiple field replaceable units of hardware, are more likely to experience failures that impair a particular function or a particular interface than they are to experience complete and utter loss of all functionality. Noncatastrophic failures often impact only a portion of a system's users or the system's capacity or functionality.

2.4.1 Classifying Service Disruptions

Chargeable outages are service-disrupting failures that accrue service downtime for availability calculations or metrics, such as for service-level agreement measures. It is important to have clear definitions of outage chargeability so system designers understand exactly how quickly fault tolerance mechanisms must perform to avoid accruing chargeable downtime. Likewise, the precise definition of the chargeable outage criteria enables system testers to establish precise pass criteria for robustness tests. Tolerance of brief service disruptions is influenced by three factors:

1. **Limitations of human perception.** If the behavior of robustness mechanisms is fast enough, then human senses may not even perceive the impairment caused by a failure and recovery.
2. **Robust design of adjacent systems and protocols.** Adjacent systems and protocols can be designed to mask the impact of brief failures.
3. **Nature of the service itself.** Non-real-time services are inherently more tolerant of brief service disruptions than real-time services.

Brief service outages are generally not crisply classified by enterprises or users. Rather, the impact of impairments ranges across a spectrum as shown in Figure 2.7. Figure 2.7 shows a service-impacting failure event on the left, and as time unfolds to the right one sees the categorization of the event increasing in severity. If the service impact lasts only a few tens or hundreds of milliseconds, then it may be considered a transient event and thus excluded from downtime calculations. If the event persists for hundreds of milliseconds to a few seconds, then service may be considered momentarily degraded but not formally recorded as a service outage. If the service disruption stretches beyond a few seconds, then users may deem that service is unavailable and enterprises are more likely to formally record service downtime. The latencies at which transient events evolve to degraded service events, and at which

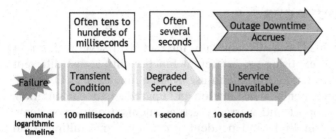

Figure 2.7   Sample Service Impact Classification by Event Duration

degraded service events escalate to service-unavailable (outage) events, will vary based on application, customer expectations and policies, statutory/regulatory requirements, and other factors.

For example, consider a voice-over-internet protocol (VoIP) application:

- A **transient condition** may cause a few voice packets to be lost, and trigger the digital signal processor rendering audio to activate a lost packet concealment algorithm to mask the lost packets. Most users will not notice the brief transient event.

- A **degraded service** event may cause loss of voice packets for a second or two, and this is likely to be recognized by users. Most users will say something like "Hello?" to confirm that they are still connected to the other party. If the other party responds and service returns to normal, then the call is likely to continue as usual.

- If voice packets are unavailable for approximately 4 seconds or longer, then most users will deem the call cut off (i.e., **service** is **unavailable**), and hang up.

A web application might have comparable impact classifications:

- A transient condition causes brief hesitation in displaying new web pages for users.

- A degraded service event causes noticeable delay in displaying web pages to users, possibly prompting users to cancel and reload web pages.

- Service is unavailable if the web page fails to display at all or if the server returns an explicit error, such as "`500 Internal Server Error.`"

A rigorous, measurable definition of service outage must explicitly address the following factors:

- **Primary functionality.** Every system delivers one or more primary functions. While a system's data sheet or marketing material often enumerates dozens of supported functions and features, there are generally only a small handful of primary functions that are crucial for service and thus would trigger a service outage if they were unavailable. For example, the primary function of a cable modem is to transmit Ethernet packets from the subscriber's home to and from the cable company's network; secondary functions for the cable modem include maintaining internal performance counters and statistics, exposing network management visibility and controllability to the cable company, and the glowing and flashing lights on the cable modem itself. Failure of performance counters, remote network management, or flashing lights on a subscribers cable modem may be an inconvenience, but those failures are vastly less impactful to the subscriber than failure to transmit and receive Ethernet packets from the public network and thus are not likely to be classified as service outages.

- **Define minimum chargeable outage duration.** Robustness mechanisms require time to detect, isolate, and recover from failures. Systems and solutions are often designed to withstand brief, transient service disruptions with little or no user impact. For example, lost IP packets will be retransmitted and the application may conceal the transient packet loss event from the end user, perhaps by filling in media for lost voice packets for a VoIP service, or via a slower, retried page load for a web-based service. System suppliers should work with their customers and applicable standards bodies to agree on acceptable service disruption latency for automatic failure detection, isolation, and recovery. Systems that meet this latency target for failure events should not be charged with outages and downtime.

- **Quantify partial functionality loss events.** The portion of functionality lost can be generally expressed as a percentage: number of primary functions lost divided by number of primary functions considered. For example, if a messaging system can both record and retrieve messages, then one might consider the loss of message retrieval but not message recording to be a partial outage of 50% functionality loss. Some systems offer service that doesn't make sense to divide into partial functionality loss events; for example, if a cable modem loses the ability to transmit Ethernet packets while retaining the ability to receive packets, the modem is incapable of offering the subscriber useful service, and thus a failure of transmission, reception, or both can be considered a total functionality outage.

- **Quantify partial capacity loss events.** Consumer electronics often serve a single logical user, and that single user represents 100% of the system's designed capacity. Thus, any event that impacts service delivered to that single logical user is a 100% capacity loss. Many enterprise, commercial, and industrial systems simultaneously serve many users, and are explicitly designed to contain failures to the smallest feasible number of users. For example, the users for a messaging system might be distributed across a pool of servers (or server pairs). If one of the servers (or server pairs) crashed and impacted all subscribers configured on that server (or server pair), then the event could be quantified either as the exact number of users impacted or as a percentage of impact by dividing number of impacted users by the total number of users on the system.

- **Define minimum chargeable capacity loss.** As some systems can scale very large, a minimum capacity loss for an outage event is often used. For example, a single messaging user being unable to access his or her messages is a problem, but that is fundamentally different from tens, hundreds, or thousands of users being impacted by a single failure. Enterprises may have different recovery policies based on capacity loss. For instance, events that impact dozens or hundreds of users are likely to attract vastly more attention from enterprise management than events that impact a single user; more aggressive emergency recovery procedures may be used to restore service to dozens, hundreds, or more users than would be used for single-user events. For example, if resolving an outage requires restarting software on a server, then an enterprise may perform an immediate server restart if most or all of the users served by that server are affected, but may defer the server restart to off-peak hours if only a single user is impacted.

All of these considerations can typically be blended into clear, crisp, and quantifiable outage definitions that can be agreed by all parties for classifying the subset of failures that will be deemed outages and determining the prorating of partial functionality or capacity loss events. For example, TL 9000 gives the following outage definitions for element management systems (described in Section 2.3, "System Management"):

- **Total outage of management system:** "*Complete loss of all FCAPS* [Fault, Configuration, Accounting, Performance, and Security] *functionality for more than 1 minute.*" [TL9000]

- **Partial outage of management system:** "*Loss of some FCAPS functionality for more than 1 minute. Partial outage time is weighted by % of users impacted and by amount of functionality lost by the outage.*" [TL9000]

Whereas total outages are often fairly easy to define, partial outages are more challenging to measure.

Individual outage events are often quantified by enterprises as *impacted user-minutes*. More sophisticated outage definitions may discount the downtime by portion of functionality lost. While every impacted user-minute is key to enterprises operating the system, system suppliers often find it easier to normalize outage events per *system instance*, such as with the five 9's expectation of 5.3 down-minutes per system per year.

A definition of total and partial outages enables a maintenance or support engineer from both the enterprise operating the equipment and the system supplier to clearly categorize each and every failure, trouble ticket, or network incident as either an outage or non-outage, and to quantify the capacity impact. A good outage definition enables architects, systems engineers, and developers to methodically identify which failures can cause service outages so they can focus their efforts on detecting, isolating, and recovering from those failures. Likewise, system testers can use this definition to clearly decide which failures produce service outages, and may earmark those service-impacting failures for special attention or analysis.

2.5 SERVICE QUALITY

Services offered to each type of user and adjacent systems have several relevant attributes:

- **Service functionality.** defines the functional characteristics of the service delivered across each interface, such as web service, voice, video, gaming, and so on. This service functionality defines the primary business value that is delivered by the system in normal operation and is generally fully specified in system requirements.
- **Engineered capacity.** Finite hardware resources such as CPU cycles, heap memory, and network bandwidth are required to deliver software-based service functionality. Real, and hence finite, system hardware is engineered to offer acceptable service to a specified capacity or traffic level. Exceeding this engineered capacity may result in resource contention and other factors that degrade the quality of service offered by the system.

The quality of service offered by a system to a user or other system can be assessed on the following dimensions:

- **Functional correctness.** How compliant is the actual service delivered relative to the specified service functionality? This is typically addressed as part of system testing and quality activities, and is not considered in this book.
- **Transactional latency** characterizes how long it takes the system to deliver service to an entity, such as return a webpage, complete a transaction, establish a session, switch IPTV channels, and so forth. The timesharing nature of popular operating systems and shared IP networks as well as other factors lead to variations in arrival rates of service requests as well as resource availability (e.g., CPU time), thereby producing variations in service delivery latency. Transactional or service delivery latency generally forms a probabilistic distribution with a fairly consistent minimum latency value, the bulk of the transactions centered around a "typical" latency, and a tail of longer latencies. The specific shape of the latency curve will vary with the architecture of the system

and networked solution. The two common figures of merit for transactional latency are the typical or median (50th percentile) latency, and a variance metric such as 95th or 99th percentile latency. Note that there is often a maximum acceptable latency beyond which even a logically correct response will be considered a failed transaction. This maximum latency value may be "hard" in that protocol or logic implemented in the client device explicitly aborts the operation and/or the session, or it may be "soft" in that the user typically abandons any attempt that has not succeeded within that time. For instance, if a webpage doesn't appear to paint fast enough, users may manually cancel and reload the page, or if a caller doesn't hear ring-back within about 5 seconds of dialing the last digit he or she will often hang up and redial.

- **Transactional reliability** characterizes the portion of transactions or interactions that are correctly delivered to the user or other entity. Impairments to this metric include "lost" operations (e.g., operations with no response, including those dropped due to proper operation of overload control mechanisms), errors processing transactions, and critical and subcritical failures, as well as transactions that were completed unacceptably late. Application-specific terms often exist for transactional failures, such as ineffective call attempts, aborted transactions, and so on. Transactional reliability can be measured from a negative perspective, such as 20 defects per million (DPM), or from a positive perspective as percentage successful, such as service accessibility of 99.998%. Note that 20 failed transactions in a million attempts are the same as a probability of 99.998% because $(1,000,000 - 20)/1,000,000$ equals 99.998%.

- **Service retainability** characterizes the portion of service sessions that are properly conducted to an orderly service disconnection. Cut off or dropped telephone calls are obvious failures of service retainability. Retainability metrics are applicable to session- or connection-oriented services.

- **Quality of experience.** Many popular services deliver some form of streaming content to users such as digitized video. The transmission and rendering of this content may be impacted by packet losses caused by failures or service disruptions, congestion, and other factors. For example, failures during delivery of audio content might be rendered as voice dropout and acoustic impairments; failures during video streaming may be rendered as pixelization or frozen or jerky images. In addition, service latency impacts the quality of experience or quality of service. For example, as one-way latency in voice packets used in VoIP service increases, natural conversations become awkward as parties are forced to alter normal conversational timing to avoid talking over each other. Forcing users to alter their patterns of behavior to accommodate degraded service characteristics adversely impacts the quality of experience.

2.6 TOTAL COST OF OWNERSHIP

Businesses invest in systems because they give them a good overall return on investment. The total cost of ownership (TCO) captures the overall cost to an enterprise of owning and operating a system over its entire service life. Total cost of ownership analysis is useful both in evaluating different system options and when trying to minimize enterprise expenses. As a simple example, one can compare the total cost of ownership of a traditional incandescent light bulb and a compact fluorescent light bulb; the incandescent light bulb is likely to cost less to purchase but require more electricity to operate. Estimating the cost to purchase each type of light bulb and price of electricity one can easily see why compact fluorescent bulbs generally save consumers money over time.

Real systems are vastly more complicated to own and operate than disposable light bulbs. Total cost of ownership of systems can be viewed as the sum of:

1. Capital expenses (*capex*) for system acquisition, installation, and startup
2. Ongoing operating expenses (*opex*), including incremental, failure-related expenses

Note that the total cost of ownership includes not only the cost of the target system that delivers the primary service, but other support systems that might be required to operate, administer, maintain, and provision that system. For instance, if an element management system is required to operate and manage the system, or a bulk or self-care provisioning system, or database backup system, for example, is required to properly operate the target system, then an appropriate portion of the capex, opex, and incremental failure-related expenses for those support systems should be included in the total cost of ownership as well.

System architecture, design, and other decisions directly impact these factors and can alter the capital expense–to–operating expense ratio. System design for reliability and quality diligence can reduce an enterprise's failure-related expenses.

2.6.1 Capital Expense

Although businesses and accountants have specific technical definitions of *capital expenses*, for the purposes of design for reliability the author considers the following to be system-related capital expenses:

- System hardware
- New or modified networking, power feeds, physical racks, cabinets, and related items to support system hardware
- System software, including upfront right-to-use license fees

- Documentation
- Initial stock of spare FRUs
- Training
- Costs for data migration
- System installation, configuration, and initial testing
- Consulting, professional services, or other expenses associated with integrating system into customer's business or operational support systems or processes

In addition to hard-dollar capex cost, there is the date first service will be available on the new system. Business cases justifying system purchase and deployment often assume specific in-service dates, and a slipping system-in-service date may impact the business case justifying the system's purchase and deployment. For example, a new system may be deployed to support business processes (e.g., ordering, customer care) for a new product or service launch, or even to offer a new service to customers. If the system in-service date slips, then the business may experience lower revenue (due to delayed product or service availability), higher expenses (because legacy systems or workaround processes must be used), poorer customer experience (because company cannot meet service quality goals), or other intangible costs. In some cases, schedule delays will cause an entire business case to collapse, such as if a critical system is not available to support a commercial launch in time for a holiday shopping season or competitive customer trial. To mitigate the business risk of delayed system delivery, installation, and commissioning, some customers will insist on contractual penalties against system suppliers tied to performance schedule, such as system in-service by a particular date.

2.6.2   Operating Expense

For purposes of design for reliability, the author considers three broad categories of opex:

1. Non-labor expenses
2. Labor expenses
3. Cost-of-poor-quality expenses

2.6.2.1   Non-Labor Expenses

Non-labor expenses include:

- **Real estate.** System hardware must be physically installed in an office, a data center, an outdoor location, a home, or elsewhere. While consumers and small businesses may not explicitly consider the floor space or rack space required by a system as an explicit expense, large customers often have crowded data centers and equipment rooms, and thus manage real estate in those locations carefully. In cases such as wireless base stations, system equipment may be installed in locations owned by others (e.g., antenna tower locations and tall buildings), and thus floor space for the equipment is explicitly billed to the system owner by the landlord.

- **Utilities.** Systems require electrical power to operate. Most of the electrical power consumed by a system is emitted as heat, and thus significant additional power must often be consumed for cooling to expel the waste heat.

- **Software licensing and maintenance fees.** System suppliers frequently offer maintenance releases to customers on a subscription basis. In addition, some system suppliers will also charge ongoing right-to-use fees.

- **Support fees.** Technical and product support may be available from system software and hardware suppliers via subscriptions or fee-for-service arrangements. To assure timely access to technical support in an emergency, many customers will purchase support agreements.

- **Hardware spares.** To enable hardware failures to be promptly repaired, customers often prearrange for rapid access to spare field-replaceable units of hardware. Some customers will maintain a spares pool on the site where the system hardware is installed, other customers will maintain a regional spares pool, and others will rely on third parties to provide rapid delivery of spare FRUs. Costs associated with maintaining access to this spares pool are often somehow covered by the customer.

2.6.2.2 Labor Expenses

Most systems require a significant investment of human effort by IT/IS or other operations staff to operate and maintain. Sophisticated customers carefully monitor the staff effort required to operate and maintain equipment, and take proactive steps to minimize these labor expenses. Labor-related expense covers loaded cost of the hours of human effort associated with each activity, which includes office space, computers, and benefits for IT/IS or operations staff. Note that some of these tasks require highly skilled staff with a higher labor rate.

- **System surveillance.** Someone is usually assigned to monitor system health and alarms during at least core business hours and often 24/7/365 for critical systems. One surveillance engineer in an operations center can often monitor many systems, but prompt detection and management of system alarms requires that the surveillance engineer not be overloaded through monitoring too many systems. Four or more staff is required to cover each 24/7/365 situation. For instance, nominally 4.2 shifts of 40-hour work weeks are required for 7-day schedules or nominally four 48-hour-in-8-day rotations. Vacations, holidays, training, and other factors will inevitably cut into this nominal schedule, and that time can be covered by overtime and/or with other staff.

- **Routine and preventative maintenance.** Systems require some degree of routine maintenance: system data must be routinely backed up, routine switchover testing should be performed periodically to assure standby hardware is fully operational, fan filters might need to be cleaned or replaced, and perhaps even landscaping must be trimmed around outdoor equipment to assure adequate airflow and physical access.

- **User provisioning and support.** Most systems provide at least some services that are user-specific, and thus some user information must be provisioned, configured, and maintained. In addition, users who are experiencing trouble must be assisted, and that assistance often ends with a human technical support engineer.

- **Performance monitoring.** Enterprises typically monitor performance and throughput of key systems to both assure that they are performing properly and delivering acceptable service to end users. This monitoring is often done weekly, monthly, and quarterly, and high-value systems may be monitored on a daily or hourly basis. This monitoring activity may include formal written reports to management. When performance degrades, it may be necessary to reconfigure the system, grow the hardware configuration, or both.

- **Configuration management.** Systems often permit users or services to be explicitly distributed across servers, clusters, network elements, or other physical hardware or logical software entities. In addition, resource management can often be configured to optimize resource allocation and sharing.

- **System growth and degrowth.** As system usage or data grows, it may become necessary to grow system hardware, such as by adding compute blades or servers, RAM, or hard disks. If traffic patterns shift or for other reasons, then the customer may opt to degrow hardware of lightly used elements and redeploy hardware assets into more heavily used elements.

- **Software upgrade.** In addition to occasional major feature upgrades to software, maintenance releases are often available every few months, and security patches may be available even more frequently. Customers must consciously decide which of these upgrades, maintenance releases, and patches should be applied, schedule the event, and successfully apply the new software. Sophisticated customers may evaluate some or all offered software upgrades in a lab to assure both that the software is nontoxic and that the documented procedure to apply the software is reliable and robust.

- **Hardware upgrade.** System hardware must occasionally be upgraded to apply hardware corrections, sometimes called "change notices" or perhaps even "recalls." While the cost of materials, and perhaps even shipping, may be paid by the hardware or system supplier, the customer's maintenance team must schedule, manage, and execute these hardware changes.

2.6.2.3   Costs of Poor Quality

In addition to well-known labor and non-labor operational expenses, system owners may experience direct and indirect expenses associated with poor quality or unacceptable system performance. These expenses include:

- **Noncompliance with service-level agreements.** Some end users enjoy formal *service-level agreements (SLAs)* that provide liquidated damage payments if service uptime commitments are not met. Thus, excess service downtime may trigger financial payments—often in the form of credits against future bills—by enterprises to end users.
- **Loss of revenue.** Unavailability of some systems prevent sales from completing, and thus can directly reduce revenue. For example, if an e-commerce website is unavailable, then potential customers can easily click to a competitor and take their business elsewhere.
- **Emergency repair.** When a system surveillance engineer detects a persistent alarm that requires further attention, the trouble may be assigned to a maintenance or support engineer for further troubleshooting, analysis, and repair. As emergency repairs are inherently unplanned events, they may result in overtime payments to staff maintenance engineers, and charges for system supplier's technical support.
- **Hardware repairs and returns.** When an FRU fails and is replaced with a spare, the failed FRU is either returned for repair or discarded. If the FRU is returned for repair, then there is a repair charge if the unit is outside of warranty and a logistics expense to ship back to repair center and return to the spares pool; if the FRU is discarded, then a replacement spare should be purchased.
- **Loss of brand reputation or customer goodwill.** Offering superior quality of experience to end users is essential for the success and growth of many enterprises. Failures that impact the service quality, reliability, and availability as perceived by end users often upset enterprises and devalue the enterprise's reputation for quality and reliability. In addition to end users directly impacted by any failure event, large service outages may become news items in either local news outlets or

trade/professional publications; very large outage events can even be reported by regional or national news outlets like CNN.

- **Regulatory or compliance reporting.** Failures or outages may trigger special reporting requirements to governmental bodies. Deliberately onerous governmental outage reporting requirements motivate enterprises to minimize the number of events that require reporting. "Too many" reports may trigger government inquiry and investigation, thus further distracting management's attention and increasing an enterprise's expenses.

Sophisticated enterprises have increasingly adopted business remedies to mitigate the risk of systems failing to meet availability and robustness expectations. Contractually binding service-level agreements (SLAs) or liquidated damage payments for failing to meet service availability or uptime expectations are becoming more common. The financial penalties for failing to meet the contracted service availability can be significant. The penalties due from system suppliers are often paid directly in cash, in the form of credits against future purchases, and indirectly in loss of goodwill and future business. Many customers will demand an explicit or implicit discount from suppliers of systems that have exhibited low service availability in the past, and may demand more aggressive contractual commitments and penalties to secure future business. Suppliers often consider the direct and indirect expenses associated with failing to meet customers' service availability expectations as a portion of the "cost of poor quality." Just as with warranty expenses, sophisticated suppliers will proactively manage this cost of poor quality to an acceptably low level that optimizes customer satisfaction, business expenses, and time-to-market; this book addresses how to do this.

2.6.3 How System Design for Reliability Affects Capex and Opex

The capex/opex tradeoff is a very common topic that is considered in many architecture and design—and eventually purchase—decisions. For example, consumers today decide between more expensive and energy-efficient compact fluorescent bulbs (higher capex, lower opex) and traditional incandescent light bulbs (lower capex, higher opex). Designers of complex computer-based systems have many similar technology, architecture, and design decisions that balance both the system's development expense and the cost of goods sold (e.g., the underlying cost of the system's hardware) against the overall operating expenses.

Quality activities explicitly strive to minimize failure-related expenses by minimizing the number of residual defects in a system and thus reducing the expected rate of failure. Reliability and robustness activities strive to minimize the failure-related expenses by minimizing the service disruption associated with inevitable failure events. Often, design for reliability and robustness involves increasing capex to reduce opex. Examples of common design for reliability and robustness areas that impact both capex and opex are:

- **Hardware redundancy.** Supporting and deploying configurations with either local or geographically redundant hardware can minimize risk of service unavailability caused by system failure or site denial/destruction.
- **Automation of procedures.** System development effort is required to automate manual procedures, yet this should reduce operating expenses by reducing the time required by maintenance staff (and perhaps the skill level) to execute the procedure. In addition, automated procedures have less opportunity for human error and hence a lower risk of service-impacting failures.
- **System diagnostics and troubleshooting tools.** System diagnostics can be crudely viewed as tools to automate much of the system surveillance task and to improve productivity of emergency repair by shortening the time to isolate inevitable failures, thus reducing both chronic effort by surveillance engineers and acute effort by maintenance engineers.
- **Automatic failure detection, isolation, and recovery mechanisms.** Failures that the system automatically detects, isolates, and recovers successfully have vastly lower failure-related expenses because maintenance staff is not required to execute emergency diagnostic and repair activities and because duration of service impact of successful automatic recovery is vastly shorter than for manual failure detection, isolation, and recovery.
- **Longer-life hardware components.** Just as automobile batteries are rated for months of expected service and tires are rated for thousands of miles of expected service, some hardware components like fans are rated for expected service life in a particular operational profile. Components that have a shorter expected service life than the designed service life of the system are likely to have to be replaced by the customer as an emergency or nonemergency maintenance action, thus increasing the customer's opex. For example, flash-based solid-state mass storage is generally more expensive than comparable hard-disk-based mass storage, but in many applications flash-based mass storage will be more reliable and last longer.

From a business perspective, it makes sense to invest in design for reliability to assure a system supplier's reputation for quality, especially for systems that will accrue with high incremental failure expense for the system's owner. Systems that are likely to be in service longer can also benefit from hardware design for reliability activities and design choices that reduce the risk of hardware components wearing out and failing during the system's in-service period.

2.7 PROBLEMS

The following problems consider a "target system" identified by the instructor:

1. What external entities does the target system interact with?
2. How can service quality be quantitatively measured for the interaction with two of the external entities?
3. What is the primary function of the target system?
4. How should *total outage* be defined for the target system?
5. How should *partial outage* be defined and quantified for the target system?
6. What factors drive the capital expense of the target system?
7. What factors drive the operating expense of the target system?
8. How can the operating expense of the target system be estimated?
9. What system features and design can reduce overall operating expense of the target system?

Chapter 3

What Can Go Wrong

Modern computer-based systems are complex, and they operate in an environment that is often unpredictable and sometimes hostile. While it is impossible to enumerate all the possible faults that can confront a system, one can usefully consider the types of errors that are likely to confront a system. This chapter begins with a few examples of real-world failures to illustrate breadth of failure possibilities. Systems are vulnerable to failure of one or more of broad ingredients that they depend on, such as hardware, software, networking, power, and environment. The eight-ingredient framework [Rauscher06] is a useful context for considering what can go wrong, and this is reviewed. As a practical matter, responsibility for assuring the reliability of each of these ingredients is split between the system supplier and the enterprise that operates the equipment. The remainder of this chapter details eight product-related error categories (FRU hardware, programming errors, data errors, redundancy failures, system power issues, network problems, application protocol errors, and procedures) that are generally recognized as the responsibility of the system supplier, and thus should be carefully considered when designing and testing a system.

3.1 FAILURES IN THE REAL WORLD

Murphy's Law says that anything that *can* go wrong *will* go wrong. While readers undoubtedly have observed many things going wrong in their personal lives, most will not be aware of the fundamental details of failure in the real world. There are an infinite number ways in which things can break or go wrong. Some hardware failures are clearly visible to the naked eye, such as the burned printed wiring board in Figure 3.1, corrosion in Figure 3.2, or hydrophilic dust accumulation that causes electrical short circuits in Figure 3.3. Some hardware failures have microscopic causes, such as Figure 3.4. Figure 3.5

Design for Reliability: Information and Computer-Based Systems, by Eric Bauer
Copyright © 2010 Institute of Electrical and Electronics Engineers

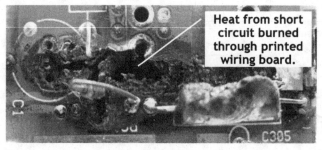

Heat from short circuit burned through printed wiring board.

Figure 3.1   Printed Wiring Board Burned by Short Circuit

Corrosion is caused by electrolyte leakage from electrolytic capacitors.

Figure 3.2   Failure Due to Corrosion

shows that early computer bugs could be directly observed, but modern software "bugs" sometimes produce clear signatures like Figure 1.7 the infamous 'Blue Screen of Death.' Other errors, like human mistakes, are easier to imagine than to capture in a photograph.

The point is that there is an infinite set of potential errors that can escalate to failures, and thus it is infeasible to consider each potential error and failure scenario explicitly. A more practical approach is to consider the classes of failures that a system is susceptible to, and then consider nominal or archetype errors that can occur. Section 3.2 frames the eight ingredients that systems critically depend on, and hence whose failure can cause service unavailability. Section 3.3 and the remainder of this chapter describe a set of product-related archetype errors that can be used to guide system design and testing. Focus on detecting, isolating, and recovering from these archetype errors should improve the probability that the system will also detect, isolate, and recover from many similar and related errors.

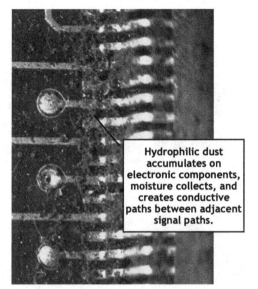

Hydrophilic dust accumulates on electronic components, moisture collects, and creates conductive paths between adjacent signal paths.

Figure 3.3   Dust Accumulation on Electronic Component

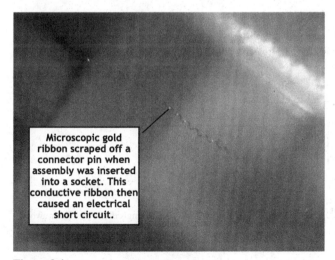

Microscopic gold ribbon scraped off a connector pin when assembly was inserted into a socket. This conductive ribbon then caused an electrical short circuit.

Figure 3.4   Microscopic Short Circuit

3.2 EIGHT-INGREDIENT FRAMEWORK

The **eight-ingredient framework (8i)** developed by Bell Labs [Rauscher06] is a useful model for methodically considering all potential system vulnerabilities. The 8i framework ingredients are: software, hardware, power, environment, payload, network, human, and policy. Systems are made from **hardware**

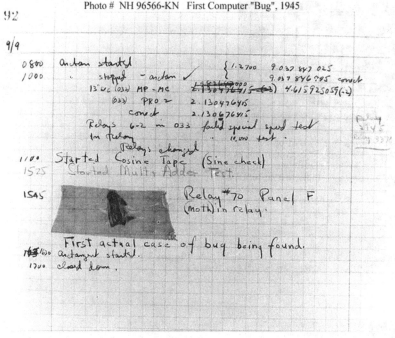

Figure 3.5   First Documented Computer Bug
Source: Figure taken from Wikipedia, http://en.wikipedia.org/wiki/File:H96566k.jpg, June 15, 2010.

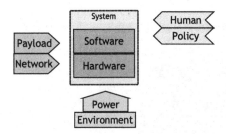

Figure 3.6   Eight-Ingredient (8i) Framework

that hosts application and platform **software**. The hardware depends directly on AC or DC electrical **power** and a suitable operating **environment** (e.g., acceptable temperature and humidity). Most systems interact with users and other systems via **networks** carrying **payloads** structured with standard or proprietary protocols. The systems are supported by **human** maintenance engineers or operators who follow documented or undocumented procedures and **policies**. Figure 3.6 graphically illustrates a typical system in the 8i context. Each of these ingredients plays a crucial role; each ingredient has vulnerabilities and is subject to faults, errors, and failure.

As a comprehensive approach, this framework considers product-attributable factors, as well as factors that the enterprise operating the system or others are accountable for, and external factors. By focusing on the error categories that system suppliers are responsible for, one can create a set of error categories that can be used to drive planning and analysis of the system's reliability requirements, design, analysis, and test plans. For example, the system supplier is accountable for assuring that the hardware operates correctly across a range of temperature and relative humidity, while the enterprise operating the system is responsible for assuring that the operational environment remains within the specified environmental parameters.

Now let's look at the ingredients in detail:

1. **Hardware.** Systems are built of physical objects made from electronic and physical components, cables, connectors, fasteners, and so on. Hardware is prone to well-known physical failure mechanisms and equipment suppliers are expected to deliver hardware with acceptably low hardware failure rates throughout the equipment's designed service life. Delivering hardware with acceptably low failure rates is achieved by following well-known hardware design for reliability and manufacturing quality practices. Inevitable hardware failures should be automatically detected by the system to minimize the risk of "silent" hardware failures. Hardware should be designed to give software visibility, and ideally automatic notification, of hardware failures so system software can promptly report the failure and activate automatic recovery mechanisms. Operationally, the system must rapidly detect hardware failures and isolate them to the appropriate field-replaceable unit (FRU) so that maintenance engineers can promptly replace the failed FRU to minimize simplex exposure time and restore the system to full operational status.

2. **Software.** Software enables the system's hardware to deliver valuable services to users. Software is prone to programming defects, as well as specification, architecture, design, and integration flaws that cause the system to behave incorrectly in certain situations.

The remaining six ingredients are external to the system itself, but are crucial in actual system operation:

3. **Power.** Power is required for electronic systems to function. The enterprise has primary responsibility for getting appropriate AC or DC electrical power to the system, and providing proper electrical ground. This category includes overvoltage and voltage spikes caused by lightning, power crosses, and short circuits for systems that are externally powered. Battery-powered systems are vulnerable to somewhat different hazards, such as battery exhaustion and wear-out.

4. **Environment.** Hardware systems are sensitive to ambient environmental conditions, including temperature, relative humidity, elevation

(because air density is critical for cooling), dust, and corrosive gases (e.g., the air pollution that causes acid rain). The system's physical design should assure that the system operates properly within its specified environmental parameters. The system must be properly located and installed so that there is sufficient physical clearance for maintenance engineers to work on and around the equipment to manipulate cabling and FRUs. The environment must be physically secured to prevent deliberate or accidental damage to the system, including physical security attacks and theft of hardware.

5. **Network.** Systems fit into a networked solution context in which IP packets are passed to other systems. The "network" ingredient transports the application "payload" ingredient. Crucial facilities (like optical transport fibers and copper cables) and elements (like routers and Ethernet switches) can fail, thus disrupting prompt and reliable delivery of application payloads.

6. **Payload.** Systems interact with users and other systems via messages or streams of application data passed via network facilities and infrastructure. As many of the elements that a particular system communicates with are likely to be different types of systems, often from other equipment suppliers, it is essential that network elements be tolerant of messages or data streams that might be somewhat different than expected. The information passed may be different because other elements interpret protocol specifications differently, or because they have enhanced the protocol in a novel way. The system supplier is, of course, responsible for assuring that its product can properly interoperate with other elements in the network.

7. **Human.** Human beings use, operate, and maintain systems. Humans who perform routine and emergency maintenance on systems present a notable risk because wrong actions (or inaction) can disable or damage the system. Wrong actions by humans can occur for many reasons, including:
   - Documented procedure is wrong, absent, or unavailable.
   - Man–machine interface was poorly designed, thereby making proper execution of procedures more confusing, awkward, or error-prone.
   - Person was not properly trained.
   - Person makes a mistake because he or she is under stress, rushed, confused, or tired.

   While the human beings operating a system are not typically employed by the system supplier and thus the actions of humans are not directly attributable to the system supplier, suppliers are accountable for correctness and completeness of written procedures and technical support they provide.

8. Policy. To successfully operate a complex system or run any large enterprise, it is essential to have business policies and processes that organize workflows and govern operations and behavior. Operational policies are required for all of the elements and interoperation with other systems and end users, as well as for employees and customers. These policies often include adopting industry standards, regulatory compliance strategies, service-level agreements, and so on. Enterprises define specific policies such as standards compliance and "profiles," which define discretionary values for protocols that permit multiple options that must be supported by system suppliers.

Several policies impact system failure rates, including:

- Policies for capacity planning and traffic shaping to assure that system typically operates within engineered limits
- Policies for deploying critical software patches and updates
- Policies for skills and training of maintenance engineers
- Security policies that assure networks and systems are hardened against cybersecurity attacks

Several policies impact outage recovery times, including:

- Emergency outage recovery policies
- Outage escalation policies
- Technical support agreements with hardware and software suppliers

3.3 MAPPING INGREDIENTS TO ERROR CATEGORIES

Each of the 8i ingredients is vulnerable to errors and failures. By methodically considering the errors and failures that are product attributable, fault-tolerant designs and appropriate robustness tests can be constructed to assure that systems meet their availability expectations. Other errors and failures will be enterprise or external attributable, and those risks can be managed and mitigated by the enterprise. Figure 3.7 shows a mapping of which ingredients are primarily product attributable, which are primarily enterprise and external attributable, and which are significantly affected by system supplier and enterprise. As this book is focused on system design for reliability, product-attributable errors are the primary focus.

The following list details the mapping of 8i ingredients into product attributable error categories:

- **Hardware ingredient** maps to error category **Field-Replaceable Unit (FRU) Hardware**, which assures that hardware failures are rapidly and automatically detected and isolated to the correct FRU. Failures of automatic recovery from that hardware failure are considered in the Redundancy category, described later.

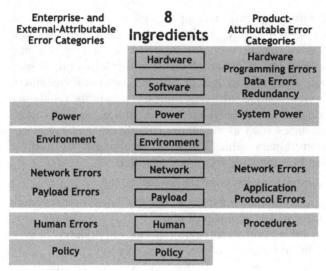

Figure 3.7   Mapping 8i Ingredients to Error Categories

- **Software ingredient.** From a product reliability perspective, it is convenient to consider the following error categories:
  - **Programming Errors.** The logic, construction, or implementation of software can contain flaws, oversights, or omissions that cause service disruptions.
  - **Data Inconsistencies and Errors.** Configuration, subscriber, and other data is required for systems to function properly; this data may become inconsistent, erroneous, or otherwise improper and cause service-impacting errors.
  - **Redundancy.** Software is often partially or totally responsible for detecting and isolating faults and errors to recoverable entities, then to trigger appropriate recovery actions and finally to recover service successfully. Errors in redundancy mechanisms can cause non-service-impacting errors to escalate to a service-impacting outage because recovery action failed or failure was not correctly isolated or detected.
- **Power ingredient.** The supplier is responsible for assuring that the system will tolerate a reasonably wide range of input voltage levels and power conditions, and that the system will automatically recover from power interruptions. The **System Power** error category considers automatic recovery from power fluctuations and disruptions. System power disruptions are often challenging for FRUs that have persistent storage devices because data may not be completely and consistently flushed to persistent storage before low voltages eventually cause hardware operations to cease. File systems and databases store both data and metadata

(control information), generally in separate data blocks. For example, file data is stored in one or more data blocks, and file metadata like file name, length, permissions, and so on are generally stored in other data blocks. Free (or used) data block information is likely to be stored elsewhere. If synchronized versions of data and all metadata are not successfully written to persistent storage before power is lost, then the file system will be inconsistent when power is restored, and thus the file system will probably require repair before the system is fully operational.

- **Environment ingredient.** Enterprises are responsible for the physical environment surrounding system hardware. For example, the enterprise must assure that the system hardware is qualified to operate reliably in the expected environment (e.g., temperature, humidity, shock, vibration, corrosive gases), and that the environment is maintained within the specified environmental parameters. Equipment suppliers must clearly specify the expected operating environment such as temperature, humidity, elevation, tolerance for shock and vibration, and limits of corrosive gases. These environmental requirements may be specified in appropriate industry standards such as Telcordia's GR-63-CORE National Electrical Building Standard (NEBS) [GR-63-CORE] for telecommunications equipment. Hardware should be properly tested to assure reliable operation within the specified range of environmental parameters. In addition to these classic environmental characteristics, the enterprise must also assure that the physical security of the environment is maintained so that hardware is not stolen, vandalized, or physically violated, thus compromising system availability or reliability.

- **Network ingredient.** The **Network Errors** category assures that elements robustly deal with network connectivity impairments. "Network" refers to IP connectivity, while the "payload" ingredient considers higher-level application protocols that are supported by the target system.

- **Payload ingredient.** The **Application Protocol** error category includes application signaling, bearer/media, and management/control payload from various elements, and assures that the system will robustly handle whatever application payload is presented. The Application Protocol error category also includes overload situations. Note that the Application Protocol category includes unexpected protocol sequences, structures, and content, such as from different interpretations of standards, as well as deliberate malicious acts by networked entities.

- **Human ingredient.** The **Procedures** error category assures that emergency and nonemergency procedures are documented, tested, and tolerant of likely errors, abnormal conditions, and failures that may arise during execution of the procedures.

- **Policy ingredient.** Enterprises that operate a system are obviously responsible for the policies governing operation and use of the system. To minimize the risk of enterprise-attributable as well as external- and product-attributable errors and outages, it is best for system suppliers to clearly articulate appropriate policy recommendations that are consistent with reliable and robust operation of the target system, such as:
  - Recommended protocol options and solution/network architectures/configurations
  - Recommended skills and training of maintenance engineers
  - Recommended routine, preventative maintenance schedules
  - Recommended redundancy and sparing policies

As a practical matter, suppliers are directly accountable for hardware, software, and payload, and for providing clear guidance on requirements/expectations for power, environment, network, humans, and policy. The enterprise operating the equipment is responsible for assuring that equipment is securely installed in a suitable environment, provided with power and network connectivity, and operated properly by qualified humans following appropriate policies. In summary, the eight product-attributable error categories that should be explicitly considered when creating system reliability requirements, when creating and analyzing system architecture and design, and when planning and executing robustness tests are:

1. Field-replaceable unit (FRU) hardware
2. Programming errors
3. Data inconsistency and errors
4. Redundancy errors
5. System power
6. Network errors
7. Application protocol errors
8. Procedures

3.4 APPLYING ERROR CATEGORIES

Having classified product-attributable failures into orthogonal error categories, one can consider the generally applicable error scenarios that can then be mapped to applicable modules of the target system. For any particular system there are myriad potential faults in each error category. For instance, any discrete component, integrated circuit, connector, and solder joint on an FRU can fail. Rather than focus on the myriad potential faults that a particular system is vulnerable to, one can consider the errors that are likely to result

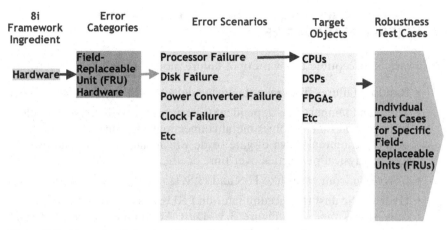

Figure 3.8   Example of Mapping 8i Ingredient to Error Scenarios

from potential faults, and then assure that those errors will be detected, isolated, and recovered with minimal service impact. For example, there are many solder joints that could fail, metallization that can electromigrate, and gates that could suffer dielectric breakdown, which could produce a failure of a microprocessor. So it is important to assure that various hardware failures related to a microprocessor can be rapidly and automatically detected. Figure 3.8 graphically illustrates the error linkage for hardware failures. The figure begins with the "hardware" 8i ingredient. As explained in the previous section, this is mapped to product-attributable error category "Field-Replaceable Unit (FRU) Hardware." FRUs are susceptible to myriad hardware failures; however, the most likely failures can be classified into broad error scenarios including processor failure, hard disk failure, board-mounted power module failure, and clock failure. One then considers how each of these scenarios can affect each FRU in the system. While compute blades in a modern system can contain hundreds or thousands of discrete components, there are typically a handful of components with higher predicted failure rates because they use leading-edge manufacturing processes or have high operating temperatures or other reliability-impacting factors. For instance, one can enumerate the components on each FRU that are at higher risk of failure, and then methodically verify that the system will rapidly detect, isolate, and recover from failure of each of those components. For instance, leading-edge microprocessors, digital signal processors, network processors, and so on often present elevated failure risk because they typically operate with high semiconductor junction temperatures to achieve high throughput and use advanced designs implemented in leading-edge manufacturing processes. One can use the error scenarios in each error category to methodically analyze system design and plan robustness testing.

3.5 ERROR CATEGORY: FIELD-REPLACEABLE UNIT (FRU) HARDWARE

Hardware is susceptible to a variety of failure modes including:

- Random failures from manufacturing defects such as poor solder joints
- Time- and temperature-dependent (aka wear-out) failures, such as electromigration that dissolves metal connections into surrounding silicon, or dielectric breakdown of gate oxide which causes the breakdown or loss of physical properties over time or use.
- Corrosion from gases like H_2S and H_2SO_4
- Hydrophilic dust that accumulates on FRUs, absorbs water, and electrically shorts pins (see Figure 3.3—Dust Accumulation on Electronic Component)
- Soft (i.e., nonpersistent) bit errors from cosmic rays or alpha particles
- Electrical or thermal overstress

Reliability qualification, electrical and thermal derating of components, robust design-for-manufacturing guidelines, highly accelerated life or design environmental stress testing, diligent factory testing, and other techniques should minimize the rate of hardware faults throughout the hardware's designed service life. Nevertheless, hardware failures will occur, and thus systems must rapidly detect and isolate hardware failures so that system software can activate appropriate recovery actions. Practical FRU hardware error scenarios to consider are:

- **Processor failure.** Complex and highly integrated devices like microprocessors, digital signal processors, network processors, field-programmable gate arrays, and so on are critical to FRU functionality and are often more susceptible to wear-out due to environmental-related effects. For example, weak thermal design and elevated ambient temperatures can cause a high-performance processor to run with excessive junction temperatures, thus accelerating time- and temperature-dependent failure modes that lead to premature failure.
- **Disk failure.** Hard disk drives are built around high-performance spinning platters and moving magnetic heads. Over time, moving parts (e.g., lubricated bearings) will wear and eventually fail. Although hard disks may have low random failure rates during their designed service life, their service lifetime is often shorter than the designed lifetime of the system electronics and thus hard disks may fail and require replacement before the system's electronics has reached the end of its useful service life.
- **Power converter failure.** Board-mounted power modules are used to convert voltages provided on the system's backplane to the voltages

required by devices on the board itself. As power converters often support a circuit on a FRU, disabling a particular power converter is often an effective way of simulating failure of a portion of the FRU.

- **Clock failure.** Oscillators drive the clocks that are the heartbeat of digital systems. Failing a clock will impact (and likely disable) the circuitry served by the clock, thus making it an effective fault simulation scenario.

- **Clock jitter.** In addition to hard (persistent) clock failures, the clock signal produced by an oscillator can jitter or drift. Clocks can drift as they age for a variety of reasons, including mechanical changes to crystal connections or movement of debris onto crystal. This jitter or drift can cause circuitry served by one oscillator to lose synchronization with circuitry served by another oscillator, thus causing timing or communications problems between the circuits.

- **Switching/Ethernet failure.** These devices enable IP traffic to enter and leave the FRU, and thus are critical.

- **Memory device failure.** Memory devices are typically built with the smallest supported manufacturing line geometries to achieve the highest storage densities. In addition, many systems deploy large numbers of memory devices to support large and complex system software. Dynamic RAM is susceptible to soft bit errors; FLASH memory devices wear out with high write voltages and over long time periods can lose data. Connector failure of memory modules can also be covered via this error category.

- **Parallel or serial bus failure.** High-speed parallel and serial busses are very sensitive to electrical factors like capacitance and vulnerable to crosstalk. Many connector failures can be covered via this error category.

- **Transient failure or signal integrity issue.** Weak electrical design or circuit layout can lead to stray transient signals, crosstalk, and other impairments of electrical signals. As these issues are transient rather than persistent, they are often difficult to debug.

- **Application-specific component failure.** Application-specific components like optical or radio frequency devices may be more failure prone because of small device geometries, high power densities, and newness of technology or manufacturing process. Components like fans, aluminum electrolytic capacitors (see Figure 3.2—Failure Due to Corrosion), and batteries are also subject to wear-out.

Many FRUs will include sensors for temperature, voltage, current, or other environmental parameters that will be carefully monitored by system software to assure power and environment remain within expected operational limits. Alarm and fault reporting requirements should clearly specify what alarm event should be raised when a sensor reports a value outside of operational limits. Testing of these sensor out-of-range scenarios is often covered as part of the functional testing of the alarm subsystem or during hardware integration activities to assure that software drivers properly integrate with FRU hardware. As such, sensor out-of-range is not considered as a robustness scenario.

3.6   ERROR CATEGORY: PROGRAMMING ERRORS

Software is susceptible to broad classes of acute faults that can immediately impact service, such as:

- Referencing uninitialized variables
- Accessing out-of-range array elements
- Omitted cases in switch statements
- Failing to check return codes from system and library calls that can fail, thereby enabling failures to cascade

Activation of critical programming faults often manifests one or more of the following error scenarios:

- **Memory leak, exhaustion, or excessive fragmentation.** Heap memory and buffers are routinely allocated, used, and deallocated by application and platform software. A common error mode is for memory to slowly "leak" because a design or programming defect prevents memory that is no longer needed from being deallocated. Over time, more and more of the memory will have leaked into this unused-but-not-deallocated state, and eventually memory allocation requests will fail, with potentially catastrophic consequences. A related problem is excess fragmentation of heap memory in which the pool of memory becomes so fragmented that requests for large, contiguous blocks of heap eventually fail.

- **Shared resource conflict.** Programming or logic faults related to sharing of a resource can lead to a resource never being released, and thus threads waiting for that resource block forever. Alternatively, an object or resource may not be correctly protected from concurrent access by different threads, and the object may behave incorrectly, become inconsistent, or otherwise produce an error.

- **Tight or infinite loop.** Programming errors, such as not limiting the number of retry attempts on a failed operation, can cause a thread to enter a tight or infinite loop that consumes CPU cycles and can prevent processes and threads of lower priority from running, or simply prevent the thread from returning control to the thread or object that invoked it.

- **Remote execution failures, including remote procedure call failures.** Remotely executed procedures and operations are inherently less reliable and are subject to variations in execution latency due to network reliability problems, failure of remote server, and quality of service variations.

- **Thread stack or address space corruption.** The stack or memory used by a thread is protected by the operating system only from corruption by entities outside of the process containing the thread. Software faults within the process itself, such as a thread writing past the end of an allocated array in the stack or heap, can cause heap or stack memory within the process's address space to become corrupted.

- **Referencing uninitialized or incorrect pointer.** Referencing an uninitialized pointer or otherwise attempting to read or write to a prohibited address will generally trigger a processor exception. If the read or write is into valid memory space, then the failure will not be instantly detected by the protected mode operating system, and thus must be detected by other failure detection mechanisms (e.g., checksums).

- **Logic errors.** Logic errors in threads or processes, such as incorrectly handling an error condition, can escalate into service-impacting conditions if design is not sufficiently robust.

- **Non-memory resource leaks.** Other finite operating system, platform, or application resources, such as open files, can also leak, eventually causing operations (such as file "open") to fail.

- **Process abort/crash/hang.** Processes can crash, hang, or abort by triggering processor exceptions (such as divide-by-zero) or for other profound failures.

- **Thread hang/abort.** Threads within a process can hang or abort due to programming defects.

In general, there is no correlation between the difficulty of debugging a problem and the severity of impact. A so-called "Heisenbug" that alters its characteristics or "moves" while being debugged is certainly harder to debug than ordinary software faults like wrong logic, but it is typically not any more or less likely to trigger or cascade into critical failures.

Robust systems will promptly detect software faults, properly isolate them, and automatically recover with minimal service disruption.

3.7 ERROR CATEGORY: DATA ERROR

Systems often rely on massive amounts of complex data as input and the data is susceptible to a variety of impairments. Robust systems must gracefully address data inconsistencies and errors with minimal service disruption. Faults in program logic, concurrency controls, lost IP packets, power disruptions, or other items can cause data inconsistency or error. Common data errors and inconsistencies to consider are:

- **File system corruption.** File systems may become corrupted due to disorderly power-down, FRU being physically removed while data was being written, or for other reasons. File system corruption can generally be repaired using the operating system's file system check and repair program. After checking and repairing the file system, it may be appropriate to check and repair application files. Recovery from severe file system corruption or unrecoverable file or data loss may require restoring data from backup.

- **Persistent storage device full.** Disks and other persistent storage devices are inherently finite and over time they may fill with temporary files, log files, core images, and so on.

- **Log file full.** Logs fill under normal or extraordinary circumstances. Verify that full log files are properly addressed by the system. Note that log file full is different from disk full because many operating systems will limit the maximum file size so a single log file could achieve this maximum file size (and thus not be capable of further writes) long before the file system fills. If the system creates new log files when one file fills, then persistent storage could easily become exhausted if an unexpected number of logged events occurs (perhaps from a security attack) or if enterprise staff fails to truncate or delete log files on a timely basis.

- **Checksum error.** Checksums are a convenient way to detect if a data record has been overwritten or corrupted after the checksum was computed and written. For example, if a software fault causes data to be written past the end of an allocated memory object, then the checksum of the object that was overwritten will reveal the error when checked. If checksums are altered to be invalid (e.g., set to a value known to be invalid) when the object is closed, released, or freed, then runtime checksum verifications will automatically detect if an object is used after being freed.

- **Inconsistency between multiple copies of data.** Redundant software instances generally maintain copies of some configuration and/or user data so service can be restored promptly after a failure. For example, information on active user sessions, and perhaps their transactions and other details, may be maintained on a standby or redundant FRU so that failure of the software module or FRU will not cause unacceptable service disruption to users. When multiple copies of volatile data are maintained, there is always the risk that a software defect, network error, or other issue can prevent a change in one copy from being properly replicated to other data instances, thus creating a data inconsistency fault. If redundant unit(s) is active, then erroneous results or faulty service may be delivered by the unit(s) with incorrect data. If redundant unit is standby, then recovery actions may fail to restore service successfully.

- **Database corruption.** Like file systems, databases can become corrupted via disorderly shutdown, and so forth. Will the system automatically detect a corrupted database?

- **Shared memory corruption.** Shared memory is often used for communications between different processes or threads on one or more processors. This memory may become corrupted due to a software bug, such as a synchronization defect that permits a thread to modify a portion of shared memory that is simultaneously being modified by another thread.

- **Linked list breakage.** Linked list control information like forward and backward pointers can be compromised by writing past the end of an allocated buffer, by synchronization problems, or by other programming errors. If a link in a list structure breaks and no longer points to the next element in the list, can this be detected and recovered?

- **File not found.** Does the system robustly respond if an expected file is not found?

- **File corrupted.** Does the system validate, check, and repair files to avoid inadvertently operating on corrupted file data?

- **Cannot access file.** If file system configuration, security, or other settings for a file do not permit it to be opened properly, will the system respond robustly?

- **Record not found.** Does the system gracefully deal with expected records not being found?

- **Record corrupted.** If the returned record is corrupted or inconsistent, will the system detect and handle it robustly?

3.8   ERROR CATEGORY: REDUNDANCY

Robust systems include redundancy mechanisms to automatically recover service rapidly following error. These mechanisms are complex and by design are executed when the system is not operating properly. Thus systems must be vigilant for faults of primary redundancy and recovery mechanisms so that these faults can be detected, mitigated, and properly alarmed to aid human operators in correctly debugging both primary and secondary faults. Error modes to consider:

- **Failed failover.** Failovers are complex operations that are often executed when the failed unit is in an ill-defined state. If the failover fails to complete promptly, then what is the secondary (and tertiary) error detection and recovery strategy?

- **Failure of high-availability process.** How are faults of high-availability monitoring and control processes promptly detected and automatically recovered?

- **Failover to failed (redundant) FRU.** What happens if the system attempts to fail over to a unit with a previously undetected hardware or software fault? By design, this situation will be triggered by routine switchover and execution of standby elements when standby unit has failed silently.

- **Site failure.** If the system supports geographically redundant deployment, then site-failure scenarios should be thoroughly tested.

3.9   ERROR CATEGORY: SYSTEM POWER

Electrical power is a basic requirement for hardware operation. In no case should any power disruption cause persistent data (e.g., configuration data, user records, usage records) to be compromised. In no case should power disruption cause hardware failure. Systems should automatically return to service after power is restored. To verify these behaviors, the following scenarios are appropriate:

- **Network element power failure** and restoration, including power feed failure.

- **Shelf power failure** and restoration for multishelf systems.

- **Single power feed failure** on systems with redundant power feeds.

- **Overvoltage.** Voltages delivered by commercial AC service occasionally surge or spike, and these events should not produce service disruptions or outages.

- **Undervoltage or brownout.** During periods of heavy electric power consumption (e.g., hot summer afternoons when air conditioning usage is very high), AC voltage may sag. As the voltage sags, incandescent bulbs dim, causing a brownout. Digital devices are inherently voltage sensitive (voltage differentiates logic "1" from logic "0"), so it is important for systems not to behave incorrectly during undervoltage or brownout periods. Typically, if the system can't supply specified DC voltage levels to system electronics, then the system will shutdown to avoid risk of unreliable processing.

- **Battery exhaustion** on systems that can operate on battery power.

- **Backup power generation.** If backup generators are configured, then they should be periodically tested to assure that they are in working order and that they will automatically pick up the load if power fails.

- **Fuse failure and replacement.** Fuses are designed to be field-replaceable units, so verify that any service disruption caused by fuse failure is acceptable. Fuse replacement should not produce a service disruption greater than that caused by the fuse failure itself.

3.10 ERROR CATEGORY: NETWORK

Network communications facilities and infrastructure can degrade or fail in a variety of ways; robust systems must detect and gracefully address these impairments. Error modes to consider are:

- **Failure of supporting system(s).** The system should gracefully address unavailability of other systems that it interacts with, such as authentication, authorization, and accounting servers; domain name system (DNS) server; element management systems; database servers; and so on. Unavailability of any of these systems should have the smallest practical impact on service availability.

- **Dropped IP packets.** Network congestion and overload control mechanisms of a router or other network element between two communicating parties can cause IP packets to be dropped. Dropped packets (e.g., release or session-disconnect messages) can put communicating parties into profoundly different states such as leaving one party unknowingly holding resources for a released or abandoned transaction, or a disconnected session.

- **Corrupted IP packets.** Electrical crosstalk and other factors can cause the physical flow of data to be disturbed, resulting in checksum errors that are detected by the receiving system. Practically, these differ from lost/dropped packets because corrupted packets are detected directly by the receiving system's hardware while lost/dropped packages must be detected indirectly.

- **IP packets out of sequence.** Networks with redundant paths can route individual packets over different paths with different latencies, and thus some packets might be received out of sequence.

- **Brief network outages.** Local, metropolitan, and wide-area IP networks use mechanisms like multiprotocol label switching (MPLS), spanning tree algorithms, and synchronous optical networking/synchronous digital hierarchy (SONET/SDH) to promptly detect and recover from failures of routers, switches, and transmission facilities. Some of these mechanisms may require 10 seconds or more to restore IP transmission after a failure. Robust systems will be designed so that successful network recoveries are given sufficient time to complete rather than prematurely triggering more impactful (and unnecessary) recovery actions like system reboot.

- **Regional power failure.** The 24/7/365 systems will typically be deployed with backup power so that commercial power failures will not directly impact system operation. However, some or all system users may be affected by a regional power failure. When commercial power is restored, users or systems in the affected region may automatically reconnect to the system, thus creating a surge in login/registration/setup requests. If client systems or devices automatically reregister (rather than requiring manual initiation), then power restoration may trigger a surge in traffic as most or all client systems or devices in the affected area attempt to login/register/setup. The system's overload control architecture should consider the login/register/setup spikes that can follow restoration of commercial AC power after a power failure.

- **IP port unavailable.** An IP port required by an application may be unavailable, perhaps because a failed or unexpected process instance is holding the IP port.

- **Inconsistent real-time clocks.** A networked element that is communicating with the target system might be configured with a somewhat different real-time clock value. Systems that assume clocks of other systems are synchronized with the system's clock may drift into inconsistent or erroneous states. Assuming that real-time clocks of all communicating systems are synchronized may cause apparent problems in temporal causality, like responses purporting to have been sent before requests have been received. Systems should not allow other systems' clocks to affect their processing logic.

- **Disruption of intrashelf IP infrastructure.** Most systems have a shelf- or chassis-level IP communications infrastructure that enables all blades in a chassis or shelf to communicate with each other. If the shelf- or chassis-level IP networking mechanism fails and some blades become inaccessible, will the system detect and robustly handle it?

- **Disruption of intershelf IP infrastructure.** Multishelf systems require a communications mechanism between shelves; this mechanism can fail. Will the system detect and robustly handle loss of communications between shelves?

3.11 ERROR CATEGORY: APPLICATION PROTOCOL

Computer systems often interact with other systems that may have flaws or errors in their protocol implementations, or that come from other suppliers that may have somewhat different interpretations of protocol specifications. In addition, variations in traffic and activity patterns will occasionally push service request volumes outside of engineered limits into overload, and thus trigger the system's overload control mechanisms. Also, malevolent individuals may attack the system with malicious packets or distributed denial-of-service (DDoS) attacks. Errors to consider include:

- **Unexpected protocol message structure or contents.** Protocols explicitly define a structure for encoding information into a sequence of octets. The protocol defines what data values are expected and permitted at what points in the message or stream, and how the various information elements relate, such as exactly what octets a computed "length" field includes and details of computing the message checksum. Robust systems will methodically check the validity and consistency of every field in every protocol message before processing it. Careful message checking is important to defend against different interpretations of protocol specification by different developers as well as from malicious attacks. For example, the well-known *ping of death* attack sent an Internet Control Message Protocol (ICMP) "ping" message to a system with the length set to 65532 rather than the normal length of 64; in the late 1990s, this attack caused operating systems that simply trusted the purported length to crash until this common vulnerability was patched.

- **Unexpected or illegal message sequences.** Because IP packets can be lost or delivered out of sequence, and malevolent individuals can deliberately attack systems, systems should be prepared to robustly accept protocol messages regardless of session state. While it may not be possible to successfully process unexpected (or illegal) protocol sequences, a session or context should never enter an undefined state and the software should never crash.

- **Overload, including denial-of-service attack.** Service request volumes will naturally fluctuate across day and night, and across the days of the week. In addition, unusual or extraordinary events of local, regional, or national significance—including power failures, earthquakes, terrorist acts, and deliberate denial-of-service attacks—can trigger spikes in traffic. Systems should be designed to gracefully accept and shed traffic volumes that are higher than engineered load.

- **Protocol version mismatch.** Large networks are never "flash cut" from one protocol version to another. This means that every system must gracefully interact with client, peer, support, and element management systems using older versions of any supported protocol. Systems should also be prepared to accept messages from any of those systems in newer versions of protocols; while the system is not expected to support more advanced protocol versions than it was designed for, it should correctly negotiate to a supported version of the protocol.

3.12 ERROR CATEGORY: PROCEDURES

Performance of humans can be affected by many factors such as training, knowledge, circadian rhythms, state of mind, physical health, attitude, emotions, and their propensity for certain common mistakes, errors, and cognitive biases. These factors lead to four general classes of errors:

1. Errors in **planning and preparation**, such as failing to take required training or prearrange for emergency technical support or spare FRUs

2. Errors in **problem detection**, such as not noticing that an automobile's fuel gauge is on empty or that the oil pressure or tire pressure warning light has illuminated

3. Errors in **problem diagnosis**, such as making hasty assumptions about the root cause of a failure without properly confirming the diagnosis

4. Errors in **action execution**, such as inadvertently skipping a step in a procedure or accidentally removing the operational FRU instead of the failed FRU

TL 9000, the telecommunications industry's quality standard, offers the following definition of *procedural error* [TL9000]:

An error that is the direct result of human intervention or error. Contributing factors can include but are not limited to

a) *deviations from accepted practices or documentation,*
b) *inadequate training,*
c) *unclear, incorrect, or out-of-date documentation,*
d) *inadequate or unclear displays, messages, or signals,*
e) *inadequate or unclear hardware labeling,*
f) *miscommunication,*
g) *non-standard configurations,*
h) *insufficient supervision or control, or*
i) *user characteristics such as mental attention, physical health, physical fatigue, mental health, and substance abuse.*

TL 9000 offers the following examples of procedural errors [TL9000]:

a) *removing the wrong fuse or circuit pack,*
b) *not taking proper precautions to protect equipment, such as shorting out power, not wearing ESD* [electrostatic discharge] *strap, etc.,*
c) *unauthorized work,*
d) *not following Methods of Procedures (MOPs)*
e) *not following the steps of the documentation,*
f) *using the wrong documentation,*
g) *using incorrect or outdated documentation,*
h) *insufficient documentation,*
i) *translation* [system or user configuration] *errors,*
j) *user panic response to problems,*
k) *entering incorrect commands,*
l) *entering a command without understanding the impact, or*
m) *inappropriate response to a Network Element alarm.*

Procedural error scenarios are inherently messier than other error scenarios because they often manipulate multiple system ingredients simultaneously. At the highest level, one can consider the following broad procedural error scenarios:

- Written procedure is wrong, ambiguous, or unclear.
- User interface is wrong, ambiguous, or unclear.
- Defect in OAM&P script or command, including not requiring confirmation prior to executing service-impacting commands (for instance, including a confirmation step like *"Are you sure? Y or N"* and having *"yes"* or *"continue"* be the default choice).
- Human error in execution of procedure.
- Flawed business processes or policies that compromise the ability of humans to successfully execute procedures, such as not assuring that staff is appropriately trained, or not having escalation policies defined and support agreements in place so emergencies can be addressed without elevated risk of panic responses.

In addition to direct procedural errors, execution of some routine and recovery procedures will put the system into a nonredundant or simplex configuration, and thus the system may not be able to recover properly if a non-procedural-related failure occurs while the procedure is being executed. For instance, if the software on the "standby" side of a system is being upgraded when a failure occurs on the "active" side, then the system will be incapable of automatically recovering service because the standby side was not in normal operation.

3.13 SUMMARY

Ishikawa diagrams (sometimes called *fishbone diagrams*) are used to visualize cause and effect. Figure 3.9 is an Ishikawa diagram of the errors presented in this chapter. Each of the error categories can act as a cause to produce the effect of a failure. One can create an Ishikawa diagram for the expected causes of system failures with the error scenarios listed in order of likelihood or observed frequency. This visualization is a convenient reference to use in system design and system reliability analysis and when planning robustness testing.

In addition to random hardware failures, activation of latent software defects, or accidental external events, there are criminal and malevolent parties who actively seek to compromise systems. Their aggressive attacks deliberately seek to exploit defects and weaknesses in a system's architecture, design, coding, configuration, or other opportunity. The product-attributable defects that can be exploited are covered in the error categories presented in this chapter. For instance, denial-of-service attacks can occur as application protocol overload or as overload of lower-layer network protocols, and

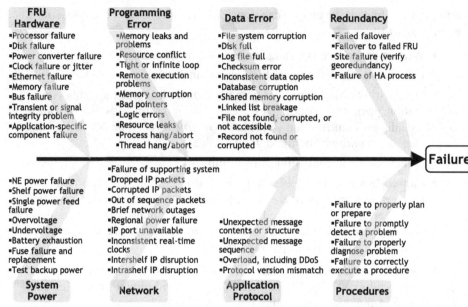

Figure 3.9   Ishikawa Diagram of Common Product-Attributable Error Scenarios

attackers can exploit errors in handling of application protocol messages to cause systems to crash. Architects and developers should always remember that malevolent individuals will sometimes deliberately attempt to coerce a system to fail, and thus must proactively design robustness mechanisms to withstand these attacks. Testers should aggressively work to expose weaknesses in the lab because criminals may methodically attack the system once it is deployed.

3.14   PROBLEMS

The following problems consider a "target system" identified by the instructor:

1. Give five critical hardware error scenarios for the target system.

2. Give five critical software error scenarios for the target system.

3. Give five critical data error scenarios for the target system.

4. Give five critical network error scenarios for the target system.

5. Give five critical application protocol error scenarios for the target system.

6. Give five critical procedural error scenarios for the target system.

3.15   FOR FURTHER STUDY

[Rauscher06] gives a complete treatment of the eight-ingredient framework. As part of quality management systems, most enterprises and suppliers will maintain detailed records of outages and complete root-cause analyses for most or all service outages, which can be reviewed to understand historic failures. In some industries, formal incident or accident reports must be filed with the government, and learning from the mistakes of others is wise. In addition, customers can often ask their suppliers for failure mode analyses for events than impacted their equipment. Even if a system supplier or enterprise sources a hardware module or software package from the industry, understanding exactly how and why that module failed in the past can be useful. Careful review of historic root-cause analyses offers valuable insight into likely opportunities for future failure.

Part Two

Reliability Concepts

Chapter 4

Failure Containment and Redundancy

Systems are designed by mapping interconnected software objects, modules, and components onto hardware with appropriate application logic to fulfill the system's requirements. Good architectures have well-defined interfaces between the objects, modules, and components that comprise a system, and robust architectures will contain failures to the smallest feasible object, module, or component, and support rapid service recovery onto a redundant object module or component to minimize service disruption to end users. This section discusses units of design, failure containment, recovery groups, redundancy strategies and techniques, and considerations for architecting recovery groups and redundancy into systems.

4.1 UNITS OF DESIGN

Modern systems contain millions of lines of platform and application software executing on integrated circuits containing millions of logic gates. To manage this complexity, hardware and software are organized into smaller components or modules that are connected together. System architecture and design defines how components or modules come together to form the system. Each of those components or modules used in the design had their own architecture and high-level design, and so on, until we get to discrete hardware components or individual lines of code. These units of design can generally be thought of as logical containers or objects as shown in Figure 4.1. The container object accepts input parameters and logical state information, and on success produces correct output. If input parameters, logical state, and object logic are inconsistent with the object's specifications, then the object will return an error or exception. If there is a major fault activated in the object, then the object may hang or be nonresponsive, and thus return neither success

Design for Reliability: Information and Computer-Based Systems, by Eric Bauer
Copyright © 2010 Institute of Electrical and Electronics Engineers

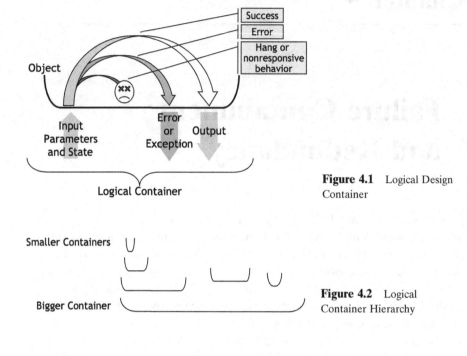

Figure 4.1 Logical Design Container

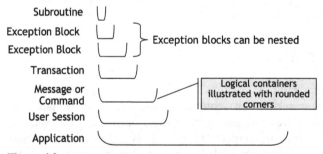

Figure 4.2 Logical Container Hierarchy

Figure 4.3 Logical Containers in Sample Network Application

nor error to the larger object or entity that invoked, accessed, or contains the object.

Containers are often organized into hierarchical designs. To describe this hierarchy, we will use the everyday notion of physical size; smaller containers fit into bigger containers. This is illustrated in Figure 4.2.

An example of logical container hierarchy for a sample network application is illustrated in Figure 4.3. Logical containers from biggest to smallest (bottom to top) are:

- **Application.** The application process itself is the biggest logical container in this example.

- **User sessions.** Multiuser applications often support multiple simultaneous logical sessions with different users. By design, sessions should start,
operate, and end independent of each other, so faults or fault recovery
of one session should not affect another.

- **Message requests.** Protocol messages or requests generally represent
formal units of error containment because the system can gracefully
return an error to the requestor. Systems are expected to methodically
validate input parameters, and return an appropriate error if those
inputs are not sufficiently complete or consistent to permit the
requested operation to move forward acceptably. If any failure is
detected during processing of the message request, then the application
returns an error to the requestor. By design, any failure detected during
processing of a message request should be contained to the processing
of that message request, although it is possible that profound message
failures will cause the next containment level (i.e., user session) to
abort.

- **Transactions.** Databases often support explicit transactions that start
with *begin* and either conclude successfully with *commit* or gracefully
terminate with *abort*. Message requests may map to one or more
transactions.

- **Robust exception handling.** C++ and Java enable programmers to
explicitly contain blocks of code within *try* and *catch*; any failure detected
within that block of software can *throw* an exception, which can be
methodically addressed to avoid cascading the failure to other modules.
Even if the programming language does not formally support try/throw/
catch blocks, good programming will structure the code so that return
codes from all subroutine calls are checked, failures are contained, and
appropriate error mitigation actions are taken.

- **Subroutines.** Subroutines are a natural fault container because:
  - They have well-defined inputs that facilitate careful validation of
  input parameters, which can limit propagation of errors in calling
  routines.
  - They generally return explicit status codes indicating success or
  failure.

  The calling routine is expected to appropriately address failures returned
  from any subroutines.

Hardware and platform software generally offer the physical container
hierarchy illustrated in Figure 4.4. From biggest to smallest (bottom to top),
these containers are:

- **System.** The entire system itself is the largest physical container. To
recover catastrophic application failures and to bring up new software
releases, it is occasionally necessary to restart entire systems.

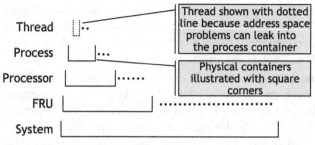

Figure 4.4   Typical Physical Container Hierarchy

- **FRU.** FRUs are convenient physical hardware objects that are designed to be easily installed and replaced in the field. For example, blade servers support modular computer FRUs, or *blades*, that can be installed and removed in the field to grow (or degrow) system capacity and to replace failed hardware.

- **Processor.** FRUs that execute software must contain a processor of some kind. Note that many FRUs will host several processors that work together. Often there is a host processor running application software and one or more digital signal processors, graphics processors, or network processors to offload some compute-intensive operations. These processors may support independent software resets, meaning that one processor can be reset and reinitialized without requiring other processors on the FRU to be reset.

- **Process.** General operating systems often support discrete software processes, each of which executes in its own address space. The process is the basic unit of physical containment for software, primarily enforced by the operating system's address space protection, which prevents an application's address space from being altered by another application. The operating system also controls processes individually, such as starting them, tracking resource usage, and if necessary killing them.

- **Thread.** Operating systems often support multiple threads of execution within a single process's address space. Application logic must synchronize access to memory and resources within the process's address space to prevent simultaneously executing threads from inconsistently or erroneously manipulating shared memory objects or resources.

Systems are built by mapping the logical containers of an application's architecture onto the physical containers supported by the platform's hardware, operating system, and middleware. Figure 4.5 shows the highest-level architecture of a sample network application server. The physical system container hosts two types of FRUs: a "front-end blade" that processes network traffic and a "database blade" that hosts the application's database management system. Each of these blades hosts a high-performance multicore CPU

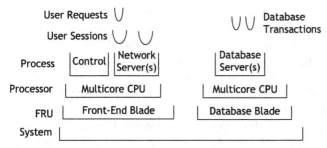

Figure 4.5 Sample High-Level Mapping of Logical and Physical Containers

with RAM, hard disk drive, and so on. Each of these processors runs a pro-tected-mode operating system that supports multithreaded processes running in private, protected address spaces. There are three primary processes:

1. Control process that controls startup and execution of the application itself, as well as offering management visibility and controllability to OAM&P staff via an element management system.

2. Network server process that interfaces to client applications. Each network server process hosts logical client sessions; each logical session contains pending user requests.

3. Database server process performs formal database transactions on behalf of requests of the network server process in support of specific user requests.

Each of these processes is implemented with multiple threads, objects, try/throw/catch blocks, subroutines, and so on.

The visualization in Figure 4.5 makes the basics of fault containment apparent. For example, if an error occurs while processing a specific user request, then the user request can be aborted and an error message returned to the client from the user session container. If that is insufficient, then the user's session can be aborted and a disorderly disconnection returned to the client. If that is insufficient, then the network server process instance can be killed and restarted. If that is insufficient, then the operating system on the processor can be restarted. If that is insufficient, then the FRU can be reseated (producing a hardware reset) or replaced. If all of these actions are inadequate, then the entire system can be restarted. Note that practical systems may auto-matically support only a subset of these possible automatic recoveries to simplify recovery logic.

While failure detection by a logical or physical container is usually straight-forward, recovering service is often complicated because state information must be synchronized between the recovered container and other containers within the system. Given finite development and test resources, it is best to pick specific layers of containment that will efficiently support automatic recovery and then design those layers to rapidly recover from a broad range of error conditions and thoroughly test automatic recovery mechanisms to assure that they are highly reliable. For example, while it is physically possible to kill and restart threads within a process or restart a single processor on a FRU hosting multiple processors, system architects may opt to focus on process- and FRU-level recovery instead because it is generally easier to completely reinitialize an entire process or restart an FRU than to resynchronize all of the threads and shared resources within a process or all the interprocess communications facilities and shared resources across several tightly coupled processors. However, if simpler coarse-grained recoveries like processor restart will not meet the application's recovery latency budget or will cause unacceptable collateral impact to otherwise unaffected users, then it will be necessary to support finer-grained recoveries that are faster and have less collateral impact. Having decided which units of design will be recoverable, architects and designers can focus on making recoveries as fast as possible with minimal service disruption.

The goal of robust design is to promptly detect and isolate a failure to the smallest logical or physical container and automatically take correct action to recover from that failure, such as to abort processing of a malformed message and return a suitable error status to the client. If the fault or subsequent error is more severe (e.g., an error that triggered a memory access to an invalid memory location, and thus a processor exception), then more severe recovery actions may be required such as:

1. Killing the errant process
2. Cleaning up pending or lost work
3. Restarting or promoting another process instance
4. Synchronizing the restarted or promoted process with the running process instances
5. Directing client traffic onto the restarted or promoted process

If the attempted automatic recovery action fails to restore service, then a more severe automatic recovery action can be attempted. The automatic escalation of recovery actions will continue to a point defined in the system's architecture and requirements; for example, most systems will automatically restart an application process that raises a processor exception and dumps core, but few applications will automatically restart the entire system without explicit confirmation from a human maintenance engineer.

Units of design also offer failure containment, and thus represent architectural firewalls. The failure of a smaller container should never cascade to cause the failure of a larger container. Rather, the larger container should treat the failure of a smaller container as an error that is methodically addressed rather than cascading the failure to the underlying container. Considering Figure 4.5, a failure of a user request should be treated as an error by the user session container (which may cause the user session to be terminated by the network server process), but that user request failure should not cascade into a failure of the network server process or impact the multicore CPU hosting the network server process or the FRU or the system.

4.2 FAILURE RECOVERY GROUPS

Detecting failures within logical containers is conceptually simple: Either the unit explicitly reports a failure to the containing unit (e.g., return code indicating error or failure), or the containing unit implicitly detects the failure from errant behavior (e.g., failing to respond within specified time) or via some asynchronous failure indication (e.g., processor exception). By default, PC software typically supports two failure recovery groups: One can restart the errant application, or one can restart the entire operating system. Highly available software may also support smaller failure recovery groups such as database transactions that can be aborted, user requests that can be failed, user sessions that can be aborted, and process instances that can be restarted. For example, some platform library or subroutine calls can simply be retried if failure was caused by a transient event (e.g., a lost IP packet), or a database transaction can be aborted, or the system can respond to a user request with a suitable error response, or (for connection-oriented services) the system can even gracefully terminate a user session.

Failure recovery groups are suites of logical entities that are designed and tested to be recoverable while the remainder of the system remains operational. The most common failure recovery group is the software process, such as a browser, word processor, or e-mail application process on a personal computer. If a browser, word processor, or other PC application crashes, then one can often restart a process instance and continue working without impacting other applications and services that are running simultaneously on the PC. This is because modern operating systems are explicitly designed to treat an individual application process as an independently recoverable failure group. The operating system completely cleans up a failed process so that it can be restarted without having to restart the operating system itself. Well-designed application processes can be restarted from failure without having to disrupt (e.g., restart) any other running processes. For instance, consider the sample application in Figure 4.5 that had both "control" and "server" processes running on one blade; ideally, each "server" process is a distinct failure group so that server process instances can be executed and terminated independent of other "server" or "control" processes. Thus, if a critical failure (e.g., a processor exception for illegal memory access) occurs in one instance of a "server" process, then the failure will be contained to that one "server" process instance, and the system can be restored to normal operational status by simply starting another instance of the "server" process with no impact on users served by other instances of the "server" process. This level of recoverability is possible because the system has been explicitly designed and tested to support independent failure recovery of "server" process instances. Communications, synchronization, and sharing mechanisms must be designed to clean up after failure of a recovery group instance and appropriately resynchronize with a new recovery group instance.

Processes are the most common unit of software recovery, but complex applications may also support recovering groups of processes and/or hardware units like FRUs. Restarting failed processes or groups of processes is an efficient way to recover from broad classes of errors not related to hardware failures. Database transactions, user requests, user sessions, and similar logical objects may be recovery units for subcritical failures. The obvious strategies to reduce the overall user impact from a critical failure are:

- Design small failure recovery groups that permit the smallest practical unit of design to be impacted by recovery action.
- Assure that failures are rapidly detected within the smallest failure recovery group to minimize the failure cascade risk.
- Assure that service can be rapidly restored onto redundant or restarted failure group.

4.3 REDUNDANCY

Systems sometimes deploy redundancy to increase throughput or capacity, such as adding multiple processor cores to an integrated circuit, or memory modules to a processor board. Redundancy can also be used to increase service availability, such as having two headlights on an automobile or multiple engines on an airplane. Unfortunately, networked systems rarely offer services as simple as illumination via headlamps or thrust via engines. Networked systems implement state-dependent services that often rely on context and massive amounts of configured, stored, and real-time data; improving throughput and reliability is more complicated than bolting another headlamp to the front of the automobile or mounting another jet engine under the wing of the airplane.

Redundancy in computer-based systems is most often implemented at three levels:

1. **Process.** Protected-mode operating systems like Linux make processes excellent recoverable units. For a system to support process-level recovery, it must be able to integrate a new process instance with preexisting process instances on-the-fly so that preexisting process instances properly work with the new, recovered process instance. A redundant process is instantiated and ready to accept traffic as soon as the system shifts traffic to it. Having redundant processes ready to accept traffic often shortens recovery times because process startup and initialization is performed in advance rather than as part of the failure recovery action.

2. **FRU.** As the primary unit of hardware repair, it is common to use the FRU as the primary unit of hardware redundancy as well. For instance, compute blade FRUs in blade servers are convenient units of redundancy, especially if blade FRUs can be removed, replaced (or simply reseated to diagnose hardware versus software failures), and restarted while the system is operational.

3. **Network element.** Some services are provided across a cluster or pool of individual network elements (aka *systems*) with a mechanism to balance or direct the traffic load across the pool of individual systems. For example, any operational Domain Name Server network element can respond to a DNS query request. Deploying more DNS servers on a network increases the probability that at least one DNS server will be available to serve user requests.

Multiple instances of the same thread type are often implemented within processes to improve throughput and performance, especially on multicore processors. While these threads are technically redundant, they are not generally useful for robust recovery because critical failures are rarely contained to a single thread.

Redundant hardware, such as a pool of processors or an array of storage devices, may also be implemented on a single FRU (or even integrated circuit) for cost, density, or other reasons. While the system may continue to operate in a "limp" along mode after one element in the pool has failed, highly available systems are designed to permit each FRU to be replaced while the system is in service and to then restore service onto the replaced FRU gracefully without requiring a system reboot. Thus, highly available systems should support FRU-level redundancy to maintain service while a FRU is being replaced and reinitialized, and is gracefully accepting service.

Redundant units are typically organized into one of two common arrangements:

1. **Active standby.** As the name suggests, one of the units is actively serving users at a time, and the redundant unit is in a standby state, not serving users. The redundant unit is typically powered on with platform and application software booted to a predefined state. Depending on the application and software platform architecture, the redundant unit may be ready to take over for a failed active unit in seconds or longer. The terms *hot*, *warm*, and *cold* are often used to characterize the readiness of the application software on the standby unit:

   • **Cold standby.** Application software (and perhaps operating system) needs to be started on a processor to recover service after failure of active unit.

   • **Warm standby.** Application software is running on standby unit, but volatile data is periodically (rather than continuously) synchronized with active unit so time is required to rebuild latest system state before standby unit can recover service after failure of active unit.

- **Hot standby.** Application is running on standby unit and volatile data is kept current so standby unit can recover service rapidly after failure of active unit.

Since standby units are not actively delivering service, there is a risk that a hardware or software failure has occurred on the standby but has not yet been detected by the monitor software that runs when the unit is in standby. Hot and warm standby systems should periodically execute diagnostic self-test software to verify that hardware and software remains in full working order. The best practice is to routinely switch over service to standby units to assure that standby units remain fully operational and ready to recover service from a failure of an active unit. This should expose any previously undetected hardware or software problems when the previously active unit is fully operational to recover service if necessary.

2. **Load shared.** In load-shared redundancy arrangements, all operational units are actively serving users. By convention, "N" refers to the number of units required to carry the full engineered service load of the system and "K" refers to the number of redundant units configured, and hence this configuration is often called "**N + K load sharing.**" The smallest load-shared configuration has a single unit capable of carrying the full engineered load (N = 1) and a single redundant unit (K = 1); this minimal "1 + 1 load-sharing" arrangement is typically referred to as "**active-active.**" By keeping the "redundant" unit active, there is a lower probability of undetected or "silent" failure of the redundant unit in active-active configurations compared to active-standby arrangements. For example, commercial airplanes are designed with N + 1 engine redundancy so that if one engine fails on takeoff the airplane can successfully take off, maneuver, and land.

Hybrid redundancy arrangements are sometimes used for applications with titles like primary/secondary or master/backup, in which some functions (e.g., queries) might be distributed across any operational element but other operations (e.g., updates) are served only by the "primary" or "master" instance. If the primary or master fails, then an automatic selection process designates one of the secondary or backup instances to be the new primary or master.

4.3.1 High-Availability Middleware

Recovering service onto a redundant unit after failure is complex; requiring failure recovery to be fast with minimal user impact makes the task even harder. As with other hard yet common problems, a variety of common high-availability mechanisms or middleware options are available. These mechanisms range from coarse-grained strategies for redundant network elements to very fine-grained strategies. Practical systems may use several of these general mechanisms.

- **IP networking mechanisms** that distribute or balance network load across a pool or cluster of servers. Virtual IP addresses, load-balancing Ethernet switches, and managed Domain Name Server responses (e.g., responding with multiple or round-robin IP addresses) can be used.

- **Clustering.** Clustering enables two or more individual computers to be arranged into a pool. Clustering middleware and mechanisms can share the load over all the units in the pool to maximize performance and throughput, or can set aside one or more units as standby. Cluster middleware is frequently offered by both operating system suppliers and third parties

- **High-availability middleware** provides infrastructure to support robust synchronization, data sharing, monitoring, and management of application processes to facilitate highly available services. The Service Availability Forum (SAF) has defined standard programmatic interfaces for high-availability middleware, and several compliant implementations are available. There are also proprietary and open-source high-availability middleware platforms available. Note that general middleware platforms like message-passing middleware often support mechanisms and configurations that enable highly available application services and may be sufficient for many applications.

- **Application checkpoint mechanisms** enable the system to create a "checkpoint" snapshot of system state that can later be restored to recover from a failure by restarting service with the system state from the snapshot. Various checkpoint packages are offered on different operating systems.

Several technology or device-specific high-availability middleware options are also available, including:

- **Virtual machines.** Virtual machine instances represent a natural failure container and recoverable unit. Java virtual machines, VMware, and other virtualization technologies enable software to execute in a protected environment that contains any critical errors. This enables redundant virtual machine instances to be used to enable high availability.

- **Redundant array of inexpensive disks (RAID).** As the name implies, RAID is a mechanism of arranging multiple hard disks to improve availability or throughput or both. Hard disks have historically been one of the most failure-prone hardware elements because the lubricated bearings wear out and other moving parts are likely to fail long before solid-state devices wear out. RAID replicates data across multiple hard disks so that a single disk failure does not cause catastrophic data loss. Since all data is replicated, read throughput can be increased by parallel access to multiple drives, such as reading even data blocks from one drive and odd data blocks from a second drive, and having the RAID driver assemble these blocks for the operating system. There are various RAID configurations that are often identified with numbers. RAID1 replicates (aka *mirrors*) identical information onto two or more disks, thus providing protection from hard disk failure. RAID0 divides the data across two drives (aka *stripes*) to increase throughput but does not replicate the data, and thus offers no availability benefit. Other RAID mechanisms provide different balances of throughput, availability, cost, and complexity.

- **Database redundancy and replication.** Many database management systems support a variety of database redundancy and replication options that can be used to support failure recovery.

- **File system replication.** Various file system replication mechanisms exist and can be used to facilitate synchronization of data across redundant systems or FRUs.

General high-availability middleware options can be complemented by application-specific mechanisms such as:

- **Multiple process instances.** Many multiuser server applications are inherently multithreaded, and can be easily partitioned into multiple processes communicating via interprocess communications mechanisms like remote procedure calls or message queues in shared memory. These multiprocessor architectures often can be configured with multiple instances of each process, often with the load shared across all or most process instances. Multiple process instances give the twin benefits of reducing the impact of a critical process failure, because only users served by the failed process instance are impacted, and shortening recovery time, because a redundant process instance is available to serve traffic at the time of critical failure.

4.4 SUMMARY

High-availability systems should support the smallest practical number of recovery mechanisms so that development and testing efforts can focus on optimizing a small number of recovery mechanisms to be reliable and fast. As a practical matter, the goal of minimizing the number of supported recovery mechanisms is balanced against:

- **Minimizing collateral impact of recovery.** Coarse-grained recovery actions may impact users who were not impacted by the failure event itself, and thus the recovery action may cause greater user impact than the failure event itself.

- **Minimizing recovery latency.** Redundancy and recovery strategies should be chosen to minimize recovery latency for end-user service. Smaller failure/recovery groups with simpler state information are generally faster.
- **Minimizing system and software complexity.** Some redundancy options are inherently more complex than others. Higher complexity implies higher development and testing effort and lower reliability. For instance, aborting a transaction that experienced a failure, returning an error to the user's client application, and letting the user and/or client application retry the operation is often much simpler than attempting to continue processing a transaction that experienced a critical failure.

4.5 PROBLEMS

The following problems consider a "target system" identified by the instructor:

1. Give an example of the failure containment hierarchy of software failures in the target system.
2. Give an example of the failure containment hierarchy of hardware failures in the target system.
3. Give an example of three failure recovery groups for the target system.
4. What redundancy is included in the target system?
5. Give three architectural or design characteristics of the target system that prevent critical failures from cascading.
6. Give three architectural or design characteristics of the target system that shorten automatic recovery time from critical failure.

4.6 FOR FURTHER STUDY

Failure containment and redundancy are generally fundamental architectural capabilities of the programming languages and middleware used to build the system. Readers should carefully study the documentation and training materials for the languages, middleware, hardware, and other underlying components that will be used to build the system to assure that the system architecture and design appropriately leverages the failure containment and redundancy mechanisms that these tools support.

General books on fault tolerant system design like [Hanmer07] should be consulted for more information on failure containment and redundancy.

Chapter 5

Robust Design Principles

There are architecture and design techniques beyond failure containment and automatic recovery that facilitate robust system operation, including:

- Robust application and communication protocols
- Optimized retry strategies
- Overload controls
- Process and throughput monitoring
- Data auditing
- Hardened cybersecurity

Each of these techniques is discussed in the following sections.

5.1 ROBUST DESIGN PRINCIPLES

While architecture and design of specific systems will vary, several design principles or patterns are applicable to a wide range of systems. A proposed architecture or design can be evaluated against these principles, and gaps may highlight opportunities to improve system robustness. Robust design principles to consider are:

- **Redundant, fault-tolerant design.** All critical components should be redundant with automatic failure detection, isolation, and recovery mechanisms to continue or restore service after failure.

- **No single point of failure.** No single hardware device or logical point in the design should be in the critical service delivery path. Note that platform or application software may be required to activate a *switchover* to move traffic from the "failed side" to the "operational side". By having redundancy built into the system design, service can be restored rapidly following failure via a rapid and automatic switchover from the

Design for Reliability: Information and Computer-Based Systems, by Eric Bauer
Copyright © 2010 Institute of Electrical and Electronics Engineers

failed unit, rather than requiring a much slower manual hardware replacement or repair activity.

- **No single point of repair.** Systems should be designed so that any FRU can be replaced without impacting service. While this is fairly straightforward to achieve for blades and hard disks, it is often infeasible for the backplane or midplane of single-shelf or single-chassis systems. Many systems include backplanes or midplanes with pins that accept FRUs with matching connectors. Systems with multiple chasses (and presumably one backplane or midplane per chassis) should be designed so that a single chassis can be down without producing an unacceptable service disruption so that repair or replacement of backplane or midplane can be completed without impacting service. Systems with a single chassis (and thus a single backplane or midplane) must be powered off to permit repair or replacement of backplane or midplane to be completed safely; thus the backplane or midplane is a single point of repair in single-chassis systems.

- **Hot-swappable FRUs.** *Hot swap* refers to the ability to replace hardware while the system is powered on ("hot") and delivering service; the alternative to hot swap is to require some or all of the system to be powered down to replace a failed FRU. By design, hardware failures should be contained to a single, hot-swappable FRU, especially high-failure-rate blades and hard disk drives. Backplane buses and interface circuitry must be carefully designed so that replacement of a FRU cannot electrically impact any other FRU.

Systems that are not permitted to have scheduled downtime for planned activities should consider the following principles:

- **No service impact for software patch, update, and upgrade.** Systems should be designed so that application and platform software can be patched, updated, and upgraded without impacting user service. Systems with redundant hardware can often minimize service disruption by upgrading redundant hardware units separately. On active-standby or active-active architectures one can gracefully drain traffic off one hardware unit and upgrade it; migrate traffic from the active unit to the upgraded unit; upgrade the previously active unit; and restore the upgraded system to normal redundant operation. Systems with load-shared pools of redundant units should permit each element in the pool to be upgraded individually. While not all applications will support this upgrade model, it is essential to carefully design the strategy for upgrading the application as well as operating system, databases, middleware, firmware, and all other programmed logic. At some point in a system's useful service life virtually every piece of software or firmware will be upgraded at least once, and the system's redundancy and recoverability architecture determines the extent of service disruption for those inevitable software upgrades.

- **No service impact for hardware growth or degrowth.** Popular systems will grow over time as traffic volume increases. Growing the hardware configuration is a special case for recovery groups to consider because the system configuration, such as number of blades or disks, actually increases after the system is booted. Highly available systems will accept and use additional hardware that is properly configured without requiring system restart. Less common is hardware degrowth, such as relocating FRUs from one system to another system to support changes in traffic patterns or replacing FRUs with higher-capacity or performance units.

- **Minimal impact for system reconfiguration.** As system usage and traffic patterns change it is often necessary to rebalance workloads across blades, disks, systems, and other limited resources. In some cases, the easiest way to activate system reconfiguration is to restart a recovery group so that it boots with the new configuration.

5.2 ROBUST PROTOCOLS

Application protocols can be made more robust by well-known techniques such as these:

- **Use reliable protocols** that retransmit lost or dropped packets, segment and reassemble large messages, and resequence messages delivered out of sequence. Transmission Control Protocol (TCP, RFC 675, 793, etc.) and Stream Control Transmission Protocol (SCTP, RFC 4960, etc.) are common examples of reliable protocols.

- **Use confirmations or acknowledgments.** All requests should have explicit acknowledgments so the requestor can verify that the other entity received and acted on each request.

- **Support atomic requests or transactions,** so that requests or transactions that are compromised by failure can be retried against a recovered component

- **Support timeouts and message retries.** If the client does not receive a response from the server to a message within a defined timeout, then the client will often resend the request. If the server's response was lost rather than the client's request, then the server will have received the same request message twice. The protocol should recognize this duplicate message and resend the original acknowledgment rather than naively executing the same request twice. The asynchronous and multiuser nature of many applications and networks makes it likely that bursts of activity will cause congestion that will occasionally overwhelm buffers or networking facilities, thus causing messages or IP packets to be discarded or lost. If an acknowledgment or reply is not received by the time the timeout expires, then the element will retransmit its request. The requestor should establish a small maximum retry count, after which the requestor will deem the other party to be unavailable. This simple strategy is employed by people making telephone calls. People generally expect a reply from a statement on a timely basis when they are speaking with someone. When speakers are on a telephone call, they expect a natural flow of conversation with one party's statements being acknowledged with some audible response from the other party. If one party speaks and hears no audible reply within a brief period, that party will ask, "Hello?" If the person hears no reply to the first "hello," then he or she may ask a couple more times. If there is no audible reply to any of the "hello" statements, then the speaker will deem the call to have been cut-off and will disconnect and perhaps call back the other party. This is how people detect cut-off telephone calls in a matter of seconds; systems can follow a similar strategy of establishing reasonable response timeout expectations and a small maximum number of retry attempts. Ideally, this means that the maximum failure detection latency to verify a communications failure will be the retry timeout period times the maximum retry count plus one (the initial message that was not acknowledged). Mathematically, this is expressed as follows:

$$NominalFailureDetectionLatency \approx RetryTimeout * (1 + MaximumRetryCount)$$

Given the system's failure detection latency budget (discussed in Section 10.5, "Robustness Latency Budgets"), it is straightforward to establish feasible maximum retry counts and timeouts to meet the budgeted latency.

- **Use heartbeat or keep-alive mechanisms,** so that user applications and system components can actively monitor the availability of key entities that they communicate with. Ideally, if another system becomes unavailable, then this can be detected before service is required from that entity. This enables a system to proactively detect and recover from unavailability of a supporting system without impacting user service, thus reducing the risk that unavailability of the remote system will be detected when servicing an end-user request.

- **Use stateless or minimal-shared-state protocols,** thereby minimizing the risk that one of the communicating parties will get out-of-sync with the other party. Stateless protocols are generally easier for servers to recover and reduce the risk of data inconsistency because all or most state information is controlled by the client, rather than shared by both communicating parties.

- **Support automatic reconnection,** so that if a connection or session is lost due to software, hardware, or network failure, then the client will automatically restore the session or connection when the failure is cleared.

5.3 ROBUST CONCURRENCY CONTROLS

Concurrency controls enable applications to efficiently share resources across many users simultaneously. In addition to processor time, the system may also share buffers and other resources on behalf of the users. Platform mechanisms like semaphores and mutual exclusion locks should be used to serialize access to critical sections controlling shared resources to avoid different application threads or processes from simultaneously allocating, manipulating, and accessing the same portion of shared memory or resource pool, and so on. Without proper concurrency controls a resource can inadvertently be left in an invalid or inconsistent state (e.g., two different threads each believe they have exclusively allocated the same resource), or with one or more threads or processes having an inconsistent view of the resource's state. It is essential that robust concurrency controls protect all shared resources, including work queues and message pools. In addition, applications should be designed so that concurrency controls that may have been held by a process that failed can be recovered without having to restart the entire system. Ideally, a monitor process will periodically scan semaphores, locks, and other concurrency control mechanisms to assure that programming or timing errors have not compromised any concurrency controls such as leaving dead locks standing.

5.4 OVERLOAD CONTROL

Systems are implemented on physical hardware that is constrained by real physical limits on processing power, storage, and input/output bandwidth; these physical limits translate to capacity limits of the volume of service that can be delivered with acceptable quality of service. Because physical hardware has real costs, business decisions must be made for exactly how much physical hardware is deployed for a particular system; thus systems capacity is generally engineered for the expected maximum busy day, busy hour, or busy minute traffic load rather than the largest theoretical traffic load (e.g., the load carried by the full wire speed of the IP connection to the system itself). Occasionally, demand for service will exceed the engineered capacity, and thus the system may be unable to deliver acceptable quality of service to all users; under extreme situations like a denial-of-service attack, a poorly designed system's software may even crash. Overload control enables a system to gracefully manage traffic that exceeds the engineered capacity of the system.

System congestion or overload is often caused by one or more of the following:

- **Unexpected popularity.** Unexpected media attention, viral marketing, service popularity, or simply pessimistic demand forecasts can cause service demand to outstrip engineered capacity, thus causing chronic overload.

- **Underengineered system.** Incorrect assumptions about traffic and usage patterns, inadequate capital investment, or deferred hardware growth plans can cause insufficient hardware to be deployed to support the offered load.

- **Incorrectly configured system.** Operating systems, software platforms, and applications often require configuration of system resources, such as allocating system memory into buffer pools and mapping logical databases onto physical hard disk drive partitions. If the system is incorrectly configured, then bottlenecks will develop, thereby causing the system to perform below what would otherwise be expected.

- **External events** prompt many end users to request service more or less simultaneously. Some of these external events are fairly cheerful, such as marketing, promotional, sporting, and entertainment events, or caused by local or regional customs around celebrations and holidays like New Year's Eve or "Black Friday" (the day after Thanksgiving holiday in the United States, which is traditionally the busiest shopping day of the year). Events of national significance, including terrorist attacks, earthquakes, tsunamis, and major news events may also trigger spikes in traffic.

- **Power outage and restoration.** While regional power outages may prevent end users in affected areas from accessing a system, power restoration may trigger most or all affected end users to promptly reconnect. If reconnection is automatic, then the spike in reconnection requests could be significant because affected computers will be synchronized by the power restoration event.

- **Network equipment failure and restoration.** Failure of key networking equipment, such as a router failure that isolates the system from most of its end users, will cut off traffic. Eventually, service will be restored and those end users will reconnect. If reconnection is automatic, then there could be a spike in traffic synchronized to the network restoration event.

- **System failure.** If service is distributed across several instances of the system in a load-shared pool or cluster, then failure of one of those systems will cause workload to be shifted to system instances that remain operational. If the failed system was operating at or above engineered capacity, then there could be a large surge in offered traffic as service fails over to the operational system(s).

- **Denial-of-service attack.** Criminals may deliberately attack and attempt to crash a system to extort payment to cease their attack, to commercially advantage a competitor, for terrorist reasons, or simply as cybervandalism.

Overload control has two facets:

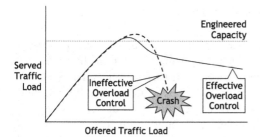

Figure 5.1 Overload Control

1. **Control mechanisms,** which shed load or otherwise shape the traffic.

2. **Control triggers,** which activate control mechanisms when congestion occurs and deactivate those mechanisms after congestion event has ended. Note that different criteria or thresholds should be used to trigger deactivation of congestion controls than are used to activate the controls. This hysteresis should minimize the risk of activation and deactivation oscillations of overload control mechanisms.

Figure 5.1 graphically illustrates the operation of congestion control. The X-axis shows the offered load such as message arrival rate; the Y-axis shows the served load such as successful message response rate. When the offered load is below the engineered capacity of the system, all traffic should be successfully served. Thus behavior is linear up to the system's engineered capacity; the slope of the line should be 1 (45 degrees) because 100% of the offered traffic is successfully served. The system's hardware resources will begin to saturate at some point above the engineered capacity of the hardware configured for the deployed system. An initial sign of saturation is often slower system response times as more requests have to queue for longer times because threads are competing for CPU or other resources. Without effective overload controls, internal queues and buffers will eventually fill, and the software platform or application will block waiting for resources or fail outright. As more software platform system and library calls block and/or fail, the application will become unstable until it eventually fails catastrophically.

Best practice is to detect congestion as traffic climbs above the engineered capacity and the system shows signs of saturation, such as an unacceptably low percentage of CPU idle time or overflowing work queues, and then activate congestion control mechanisms. Congestion control mechanisms gracefully shed load to minimize the going-forward load on the system. Specific load-shedding techniques are application specific but typically include failing new connection, logon, or command requests with a "too busy" error. Other systems attempting to access the target system that receive the "too busy" error response should avoid quickly retrying their service request to the target system, thereby smoothing the spike in traffic.

5.4.1 Congestion Detection Techniques

Modern systems are generally constructed of several application processes with many threads built on rich software platforms, often with queues of messages or work requests between different software modules. The system's architecture assures that work can be appropriately sequenced and scheduled so that resources are shared across all of the entities that are competing for CPU cycles, access to persistent storage, I/O bandwidth, or other system resources. The operating system scheduler executes runnable threads based on priority and configured scheduling rules. Thus, overload may manifest differently across the system: however, one or more of the following symptoms are generally observed:

- **Slower system response times.** Systems typically process several different transaction or request types that often have fundamentally different response times. As these different transactions often demand somewhat different system resources, overload may manifest differently on different transactions. For example, if disk I/O has saturated, then transactions requiring database access will be queued but transactions that can be served from cached or in-memory data will be completed promptly.

- **Longer work queues.** Work queues are used to smooth inevitable variations in workload and to facilitate sharing of CPU and other system resources. Under normal operating conditions with moderate-to-heavy load, many work queues will have some pending work, thus enabling the operating system to efficiently switch between many runnable threads to maximize throughput. As the system saturates, the queues will fill with a backlog of work, and eventually some queues may overflow and presumably discard work requests (rather than blocking, which is more likely to cascade the overload condition).

- **Higher CPU utilization.** As the workload increases, the CPU may spend more time processing application-level tasks, as well as context switching and synchronizing access to shared resources. Thus, high CPU utilization is often an indicator of system stress, but may not indicate overload. For example, routine maintenance activities like system backups and data integrity audits will often run at lower priority than tasks serving end users in off-hours, and although the operating system may take the CPU or hard disk drive to full utilization while these operations execute, the operating system will readily preempt these tasks to serve end-user requests that arrive.

Significantly slower response times and overflowing work queues are usually signs that a system is saturated and in overload. Sustained high CPU utilization is a less reliable sign of overload because well-designed systems will enable the operating system to gracefully schedule tasks to fully utilize whatever resource is the bottleneck at any particular time.

5.4.2 Congestion Control Mechanisms

Ill-conceived overload control mechanisms can cause a simple overload to avalanche to catastrophic failure. As the system enters overload, response times to end users will slow. As the response latency increases with no indication of overload from the system, end users and/or client software are likely to assume that their request was lost (e.g., IP packet was dropped by a router somewhere), and will thus retry their request. The retry attempt can further push the system into overload; as more and more clients retry their requests the workload builds and eventually causes a poorly designed system to crash.

Well-conceived overload control mechanisms proactively shape traffic rather than simply make a best effort to address whatever happens to arrive. Systems can shape traffic via:

- **Rejecting new sessions** when the system is overloaded with a "too busy" error so the client or end user won't immediately retry to start a session. A variety of rejection policies are possible: Systems can reject all new sessions, or every nth new session, or sessions from certain types of users (e.g., lower-priority or grade-of-service subscribers), and so on.

- **Rejecting new message requests** when the system is overloaded with "too busy" errors so the client or end user won't immediately retry the request. Various message rejection strategies are possible: round-robin rejection of new messages, or rejecting all traffic from some users, or rejecting certain types of messages, and so on.

- **Disconnecting active sessions.** This is obviously an extreme measure, but orderly disconnection of some (presumably lower-priority) users is preferable to crashing the system for all (or higher-priority) users.

- **Disabling servers or services.** If the system implements multiple services, perhaps running on multiple IP ports, then it may be possible to disable some or all services and close some or all IP ports experiencing overload. This is a very extreme measure, but it should keep the host system from crashing and thus may protect other applications that may be co-resident on the host system.

These overload control mechanisms should operate as close to the network connection and as early in processing network requests as possible so that the system uses minimal resources to reject overload traffic, thereby freeing resources to address the backlog of pending work and recover. For example, if new sessions will be rejected when the system is in overload, then reject the sessions in the frontend process before consuming scarce system resources to authenticate and validate the user.

5.4.3 Architectural Considerations

Systems should be designed with processes or threads running in three broad classes:

1. **Low-priority** maintenance and background tasks that do not directly impact end-user experiences, including system backup, routine audits, gathering performance management information, and so on
2. **Medium priority** for tasks that directly or indirectly interact with end users
3. **High priority** for management visibility and control tasks, including overload control

As the system begins to saturate, the operating system scheduler will preempt or defer low-priority maintenance and background tasks to make more resources available to the medium-priority tasks that directly and indirectly interact with end users. Typically one of these background maintenance tasks will post a timestamp of the last time it ran so control tasks and maintenance engineers can use the latency since that background task last executed as a rough indicator of the load on the system. As the system further saturates, medium-priority tasks will begin to be deferred, thus impacting end users. By running control tasks at high priority, tasks controlling automatic congestion control will always be able to run even when medium-priority service delivery tasks are being deferred. In addition, processes and tasks supporting management visibility and control by human maintenance engineers must also be run at high priority to enable human maintenance engineers to identify and isolate overload conditions in real time, and take appropriate corrective actions such as disconnecting users or disabling services. Thus, even if the system is enduring a denial-of-service attack on the user service interface (which is supported by medium-priority processes), the high-priority management visibility and controllability process should preempt the overloaded user service processes to enable maintenance staff to take actions to protect the system.

5.5 PROCESS, RESOURCE, AND THROUGHPUT MONITORING

Some errors like resource leaks are not immediately manifest in normal system operations. To rapidly detect these errors before they cascade into critical failures, robust systems will actively monitor critical processes, resources, and throughput. Monitor processes can proactively monitor system health via mechanisms including:

- **Heartbeat checks of critical processes** to assure that they are sane enough to respond within reasonable time
- **Resource usage checks,** such as monitoring process sizes, free space on file systems, and CPU usage

- **Data audits** (described in Section 5.6)
- **Monitoring system throughput, performance and alarm behavior.** If system throughput drops or performance degrades or alarms are posted and not automatically cleared, then the system may be experiencing errors and at risk of cascading into failure.
- **Health checks of critical supporting systems,** such as periodically verifying operational status of supporting systems via hello, keep-alive, or status queries

While most of these resource checks can be run in a lower-priority process or thread, it is important to assure that the application's master control process runs at a higher priority than other application processes and that the master control process (or companion process at high priority) is designed to detect and recover infinite loops in application processes that might prevent lower-priority process monitoring mechanisms from being run. Many of the techniques presented in Chapter 6, "Error Detection," are conveniently implemented in periodic system integrity scans.

5.6 DATA AUDITING

Applications maintain volatile data on the state of shared resources, sessions, and contexts with other systems and end users, and other information. Some of this data may be maintained by two or more entities, such as state of active sessions or transactions being maintained by both client and server processes. Over time, this data may drift out of sync because a design or programming error may fail to record a relevant change in volatile data, or a synchronization error may cause a change to be accidentally overwritten, or because of some other problem. Robust systems will periodically audit volatile state data to assure that it is consistent, and correct any detected errors. Data integrity checks may be implemented as lower-priority threads within a process, or a separate process to check shared memory. Data integrity logic can verify and correct the following:

- Verify consistency of data within each record to assure that all data values are within acceptable limits and are consistent with the schema.
- Verify consistency between data records, such as that all pending work is associated with an active user record.
- Verify timer and timeout values to assure that no "dead," "stuck," or "hung" records remain.
- Verify checksums on data records.
- Verify forward and backward pointers in linked lists.
- Verify consistency of elements in queues and other resource pools.

Audit processes can generally be set to lower processing priority and the operating system will run them whenever there are available cycles.

Systems can also run similar integrity checks of persistent data storage such as databases and files. Because checks of persistent storage may consume significant I/O bandwidth, persistent storage integrity checks must be scheduled into low system usage times.

5.7 FAULT CORRELATION

Typically, failures trace back to a single fault that was activated, and that initial fault may have cascaded to cause detectable errors in several parts of the system. In ordinary consumer and commercial systems, a human must manually sift through the error indications and alarms to debug the failure and take appropriate corrective action (often simply rebooting the system to force a restart of all software). In highly available systems, the debugging and recovery should be performed automatically by the system. Given the maximum acceptable service disruption latency requirements of highly available systems, the debugging and recovery must be performed quickly to minimize service downtime. In addition, the least severe recovery action should be executed to minimize overall service impact of both failure event and recovery action. For example, one doesn't want to simply reboot a multiuser system (rather than restarting an individual process or shifting users to another process instance) on every software problem because a system reboot is likely to impact all active system users while the primary failure may have impacted only a portion of the system users, or perhaps only a single user.

Therefore, robust systems must automatically perform the following tasks:

1. **Assess fault persistence.** Some faults are caused by transient events that will correct themselves without explicit recovery action by the system, while other faults are persistent and require recovery action. Transient faults may be perceived for any one of various reasons, such as:

   a. An IP packet is dropped somewhere due to proper actions of overload control mechanisms.

   b. A spike in traffic or system workload causes some system tasks to stall.

   c. A failure (e.g., cable cut or router failure) occurs in the local or wide area network that produces a brief network disruption while the networking infrastructure reconverges on an alternate traffic routing arrangement.

   Automatic retry mechanisms designed into software are often sufficient to "ride over" many transients. The challenge is to decide when the fault is persistent enough that automatic retry mechanisms are insufficient to ride over the fault. A false-positive decision (deeming fault to be persistent when automatic retry mechanisms were sufficient to ride over the fault) can trigger the system to take an unnecessary recovery action that is likely to extend the duration of service impact while the recovery mechanism executes. In addition, the unit of recovery may include other users so the recovery action may impact service delivery to others who may not have been affected by the transient event itself. A false-negative decision (deeming a persistent fault to be a transient event that requires no recovery action) creates a silent or sleeping failure. Eventually that false negative will be detected either by the system properly detecting a secondary fault that cascaded from the primary failure, or manually by the human maintenance engineer.

2. **Isolate primary fault to appropriate recoverable unit.** Directly detected faults like processor failure are generally easy to isolate, but indirectly detected faults such as nonresponse from processes on other FRUs are harder to isolate. Fault management systems should collect and correlate enough indirectly detected failures to isolate the true failure if direct failure detection doesn't occur quickly.

3. **Activate correct recovery mechanism.** Appropriate recovery action should be automatically triggered after failure is isolated to a recoverable unit.

4. **Assure successful recovery.** System performance and throughput is restored to the same level as before the failure.

5.8 FAILED ERROR DETECTION, ISOLATION, OR RECOVERY

Error detection, isolation, and recovery is more likely to fail than "normal" functional software because error detection, isolation, and recovery software operates when the system is in an unpredictably degraded state, and thus one cannot assume that the system's hardware, software, configuration data, network infrastructure, physical environment, power, users, or OAM&P staff are all behaving as expected. In addition, high-availability systems strive to recover from failures rapidly, and thus are biased to automatically initiate recovery actions as quickly as possible rather than waiting longer to be absolutely certain of a failure diagnosis before taking action or waiting for a human maintenance engineer to detect and diagnose the failure and manually select and initiate a recovery action. Therefore, a small percentage of system failures are likely to experience one or more of the following secondary failures:

- **Detection (or silent) failure,** in which the system's primary failure detectors do not notice, the failure and thus robustness mechanisms are not activated.

- **Isolation failure,** in which the system indicts the wrong recoverable module, initiates automatic recovery action for a module that had not failed, and thus the action cannot recover the primary failure.

- **Recovery failure,** in which the recovery action does not successfully recover service onto a redundant or restarted module.

Thus, robust systems must include layers of failure detection to assure that if a failure escapes detection by primary failure detectors, a secondary or tertiary detector will notice it before end users start calling in complaints to the system's support organization. Process, resource, and throughput monitors (described in Section 5.5) are a secondary layer of failure detection that should mitigate the risk of failed failure detection, isolation, or recovery.

5.9 GEOGRAPHIC REDUNDANCY

Disasters like fires, floods, tsunamis, hurricanes, tornadoes, earthquakes, and terrorist attacks can destroy or render a physical office or data center temporarily inaccessible or unavailable. While conventional hardware failures can generally be recovered in hours by replacing an individual FRU, replacing a destroyed or damaged system is more complicated and takes longer. To mitigate the risk of prolonged unavailability of critical services due to disaster, enterprises often deploy a second system in a geographically remote location, thus minimizing the risk that a single disaster would damage both sites. Each of these geographically redundant systems is engineered to operate standalone for an indefinite period, as would be necessary if one site were destroyed or rendered unavailable or inaccessible by a disaster.

Geographic redundancy is fundamentally different from redundant deployment of systems on the same site (called *colocation*) because:

- **Communications bandwidth is inherently lower between geographically separated systems.** Physical factors like signal loss, dispersion, and interference become more significant as distance increases, thus making long-haul transmission far more complicated than communications within a single room or office. To maintain acceptable transmission reliability, bandwidth is limited as distance increases. Even when high-bandwidth links are available between distant geographic locations, the monthly charges can be very expensive, and thus communications charges can impose a practical financial limit on the maximum afford-able bandwidth. In contrast, very-high-speed local-area networks are cheap.
- **Communications latency is inherently higher.** It takes light 3 milliseconds to travel 1000 kilometers and 5 milliseconds to travel 1000 miles. In addition to the physical propagation latency due to the speed of light, data must pass through more intermediate systems like routers, multiplexors, and long-haul transmission systems than for local-area communications within a single room or office. This communications latency directly contributes to service latency seen by users, thus affecting the quality of experience.

Lower communications bandwidth and higher communications latency constrain and complicate design of georedundant systems. For example, while real-time data mirroring can work well for colocated systems, mirroring data across a bandwidth-limited communications link quickly becomes impractical as system usage grows. Likewise, the higher communications latency to a geographically remote system can reduce throughput of synchronous transactions and communications. While periodic data updates can be carried over more affordable long-haul connections than real-time data updates, non-real-time data synchronization creates a window of vulnerability in which data changes that occur after the data synchronization but before the disaster will be lost when the georedundant system is activated. This window of vulnerability may be similar to the window that exists between scheduled database backups. If a database is restored, then any changes since the time of the last backup will be lost.

Since lower-bandwidth connections and higher communications latency often prevent georedundant systems from maintaining the real-time state and status necessary to switch over with minimal service disruption, a georedundant switchover is likely to have a significant—and hopefully brief—service impact. Thus, enterprises will want to be sure that less-impactful recoveries are ineffective before triggering a georedundant switchover.

Enterprises will often deterministically assign traffic to georedundant systems (e.g., 100% of traffic to active system at site A and 0% of traffic to standby system at site B) to simplify network operations, management, and troubleshooting of issues. When a georedundant switchover is activated, 100% of the traffic would be moved from the system on site A to the promoted system on site B. If this switchover impacts stable traffic on site A, then enterprises will be reluctant to consider a georedundant switchover for partial outages as a georedundant switchover might impact users who were not impacted by the primary failure. In addition, if the georedundant switchover means implicitly rolling back or expunging data and service changes made since the last resynchronization, then the switchover risks delivering an unacceptable quality of experience to users.

Also, activating a georedundant recovery is likely to add to the enterprise's cost because all staff costs associated with executing the georedundant switchover and eventual switchback are in addition to the cost of repairing the failure of the active system. If the georedundant site is not staffed 24/7/365, then staff might be required to deploy to the site before georedundant recovery can begin. Once the georedundant site is operational and the georedundant system must be made fully operational, if the georedundant system is in "hot" standby, this may be simple, but if the system is in "warm" or "cold" standby, then a complex manual procedure may be necessary to bring the system to operational status. The network must then be reconfigured (e.g., by updating DNS) to direct service requests to the newly active georedundant system rather than the previously active system. Finally, any residual traffic associated with the previously active system must be cleared, either by eventually timing out or via manual or automatic actions. The georedundant switchover can take minutes to hours to complete, and after the repair of the previously active system is completed a georedundant switchback must be performed.

Thus, while georedundant recovery makes sense when a disaster occurs which destroys a system—and perhaps an entire office or site—it is not generally worth the incremental expense and expense to recover from hardware or software failures that can be resolved automatically or promptly via manual actions. Typically it is more efficient to focus effort of maintenance engineers on promptly recovering from hardware or software failures than defer system failure recovery actions with georedundant switchovers. Hence, georedundancy does not typically improve product attributable service downtime.

5.10 SECURITY, AVAILABILITY, AND SYSTEM ROBUSTNESS

In addition to random hardware and software faults or accidental human errors, modern systems must withstand deliberate attack by criminals and malevolent parties. These malevolent parties often work methodically to find and exploit vulnerabilities to achieve their criminal goals. Potential criminal motivation to compromise a system's ability to deliver service is to extort money from the enterprise to suspend the attack, or unscrupulous competitors can seek to disadvantage a competitor by disrupting business operations or stealing trade secrets, or cyberterrorists attack to advance their political goals. Robust design, along with the system's comprehensive security architecture, assures that the system can withstand security attacks. This section considers the subset of security hazards that affect availability using a standard end-to-end security framework. This section does not purport to address cybersecurity in general, and readers are strongly advised to methodically address system security; [USCERT] or [CERT] provide excellent starting points to consider overall system security.

Note that the U.S. Department of Defense [DoDD8500.1] uses the term *robustness* in the context of security with a different meaning from what has been used in this book:

> *E2.1.37. Robustness. A characterization of the strength of a security function, mechanism, service or solution, and the assurance (or confidence) that it is implemented and functioning correctly. The Department of Defense has three levels of robustness:*
>
> > *E2.1.37.1. High Robustness: Security services and mechanisms that provide the most stringent protection and rigorous security countermeasures.*
> > *E2.1.37.2. Medium Robustness: Security services and mechanisms that provide for layering of additional safeguards above good commercial practices.*
> > *E2.1.37.3. Basic Robustness: Security services and mechanisms that equate to good commercial practices.*

This book considers general system robustness, rather than narrowly focusing on robustness of a system's security functions.

5.10.1 X.805 Security Architecture

The International Telecommunication Union's Recommendation X.805, *"Security Architecture for Systems Providing End-to-End Communications"* [X.805], characterizes the linkage of security to service availability and other system characteristics. The standard defines eight security dimensions:

1. **Access control** assures that only authorized users and systems are permitted to access system services and resources.

2. **Authentication** assures that humans and nonhumans interacting with a system are correctly identified.

3. **Non-repudiation** assures that entities cannot deny that operations have been actually performed. For example, this prevents situations in which a person falsely claims that she did make a purchase or cash withdrawal.

4. **Data confidentiality** assures that data is not divulged to unauthorized parties, such as revealing personal details that enable identity theft.

5. **Communications security** assures that information packet flows are not diverted.

6. **Data integrity** assures that correctness and accuracy of data are not compromised.

7. **Availability** assures that service is not compromised by deliberate attack or malicious acts. *Distributed denial-of-service (DDoS)* attacks by armies of infected computers, called *botnets*, is one example of availability threat. Computer viruses or malware that consume CPU or other system resources, or compromise configuration or other data, can also impact a system's ability to deliver service.

8. **Privacy** assures that general information about patterns of communications like user's geographic location, IP address, and usage history are not divulged.

X.805 recognizes that systems offer services across three generic service planes:

1. **End-user plane** carries application payload, such as digitized video like MPEG-4.

2. **Control plane** controls traffic on the end-user plane using protocols like SIP. For example, the control plane of an IP television service selects programming to view, as well as negotiating video codec and other service delivery details.

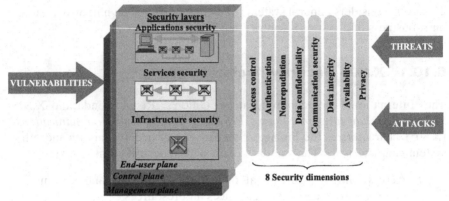

Figure 5.2   X.805 Security Dimensions, Planes, and Layers
Source: Recommendation ITU-T X.805 (2003), *Security architecture for systems providing end-to-end communications (Fig.2).*

3. **Management plane** provides system visibility and controllability to maintenance engineers and systems responsible for system operations, administration, and maintenance.

The end-user plane generally carries far more traffic than the control plane, and the control plane generally carries more traffic than the management plane. Although traffic in all three planes is carried via IP, traffic is often separated onto different physical or virtual local-area networks to prevent problems on one plane (e.g., security attacks) from impacting other planes.

Each of these service planes is protected by three security architectural layers:

1. **Application security layer** covers security of both basic application-enabling mechanisms like web servers and SNMP agents, as well as application-specific network protocols and interfaces.

2. **Services security layer** covers enabling services like Domain Name Service (DNS), which maps domain names to IP addresses; authentication, authorization, and accounting services; and so on.

3. **Infrastructure security layer** covers network communications facilities and modules.

The relationship between security dimensions, layers, and planes is illustrated in the X.805 standard in Figure 5.2.

5.10.2   X.805, Availability, and Robustness

Robust system design assures that a system continues to offer service despite inevitable failures and unexpected events in field deployment. Robust design should also address security threats to availability that can compromise reliable service delivery. The X.805 standard recognizes two distinct security threats to the availability security dimension:

1. **Interruption of services.** Primary security risk of service interruption is from distributed denial-of-service attack in which a system is deliberately attacked by perhaps thousands of computers in an attempt to overload and crash the target system. The thousands of attacking computers are typically personal computers with broadband connections that were compromised via malware that was surreptitiously installed without the PC owner's knowledge. These compromised PCs are covertly herded into botnets that participate in coordinated attacks against targets selected by the criminal who controls the botnet. The criminal can use this botnet for commercial gain by attacking a target system and then extorting payment from the owner of the system to stop the attack, thus permitting service to be restored. Botnets can also be used in the context of cyberterror and cyberwarfare.

2. **Destruction of information or other resources.** If malevolent individuals or malicious software compromises a system, then critical data can be damaged or destroyed, or resources can be misused (e.g., malware that consumes CPU). Rigorous security design, reviews, testing, and scans should be performed to assure the system provides robust security to guard against this threat.

Unavailability due to security threats is primarily caused by malevolent individuals who proactively work to attack systems. Availability attacks often take one of the following forms:

- **Malformed packets** (e.g., ping-of-death) that cause application or platform to crash. Robust system design should assure that no malformed or malicious message should ever cause an application to fail.

- **Distributed denial-of-service** (DDoS) attacks that overload the system with application requests or IP traffic with the goal of causing the application or platform to crash. Ideally, overload control mechanisms should prevent the system from crashing even under a wire speed DDoS attack that saturates the system's network interface or connection to the public network. Automatic overload detection and controls will typically be complemented with external intrusion protection systems or firewalls to limit malicious traffic volumes reaching the system, and by emergency actions of maintenance engineers, including explicitly blocking malicious traffic and perhaps even disabling the system until the attack can be suppressed. Note that overload controls should be included on all network interfaces that are externally accessible, because malevolent individuals will probe to find vulnerable protocol interfaces to attack.

- **Penetration and vandalism** or reconfiguration of the system, thus compromising the system's ability to properly deliver service. While a system's security policy and architecture should minimize risk of penetration and vandalism, troubleshooting and emergency recovery procedures (e.g., data restoration) should be useful in recovering from vandalism.

- **Attacks with invalid login attempts** to fill audit or other log files, or cause valid user accounts to be "locked" due to excessive failed login attempts. While locking accounts due to failed login attempts is purely a security issue, proper management of overflowing log files is a system robustness concern.

5.10.3 Product Hardening

A number of good design practices can minimize a system's vulnerability to security attacks, and collectively these practices are often referred to as *product hardening*. Security-related product hardening techniques that will improve robustness and availability include:

- Disable all network services on the system that are not directly or indirectly required by the application, such as telnet, rlogin, rcp, and so on. Network services that aren't running aren't susceptible to attack.
- Block remote access for privileged accounts; require key system-impacting commands and actions to be initiated from the system console. Requiring commands to be entered from the system console implicitly requires any attacker to have physical access to the system, thus preventing many attacks from cyberspace.
- Verify security permissions on all directories, especially directories in the search path, so that attackers can't install hacked commands. Scrutinize any file-sharing mechanisms like NFS, FTP, TFTP, and so on to minimize the risk that an attacker can install, delete, or manipulate a file on the system that can compromise system operation.
- Monitor third-party suppliers and open-source communities to promptly identify applicable critical security and stability patches for sourced software included in the application or platform; integrate critical fixes into application or platform patches, and push to enterprises promptly.
- Use least-privilege access controls to minimize damage that can be done if user accounts are compromised.
- Provide an explicit list of expected software processes that should be running on each processor so that maintenance engineers can audit running processes both for troubleshooting and to verify that unexpected processes have not been added.

Security references like [CERT], [USCERT], [CWE], and [NIST] provide more complete security hardening guidance. Product teams should research and apply the security hardening techniques that are recommended for the operating system and middleware, and carefully consider how to harden their application itself. Recognize that applying software patches, updates, and upgrades creates a risk that the hardened system will be compromised when new software is installed or configurations are changed; system test should verify that installing software patches and upgrades, including those from third-party suppliers, doesn't revert the system's configuration to a more permissive default state, thereby opening windows of vulnerability for attackers.

5.11 PROCEDURAL CONSIDERATIONS

Procedure-related errors arise due to one or more of the following:

- Documented or undocumented procedure executed by human was wrong, ambiguous, or misleading.
- User interface was ambiguous, misleading, or wrong.
- Human erroneously entered wrong input.
- Human executed wrong action, neglected to execute correct action, or executed actions out of sequence.
- System failed to check input or system state prior to executing requested operation.

Best practice for designing highly reliable procedures is to focus on three broad principles:

1. Minimize human interactions.
2. Help humans to do the right thing.
3. Minimize the impact of human error.

Each of these principles is detailed below. Procedures are executed in the context of policies established by the enterprise operating the equipment, and these policies influence both the rate of procedural failures and the duration of manually recovered outages. Robust operational policies are also covered.

5.11.1 Minimize Human Interactions

Systems experience maintenance procedures in two ways:

1. **Via command interface** on local or remote command line or graphical user interface. These commands issued by maintenance engineers often run with highly privileged authorization, which permits system configuration and operation to be profoundly impacted.
2. **Via direct manipulation of system hardware,** such as insertion or removal of a FRU or network connection. Maintenance engineers can physically insert and remove FRUs or cables at any time. Occasionally they accidentally remove the wrong FRU (e.g., the operational FRU rather than the failed FRU). Systems must anticipate this behavior and deal with it as well as possible.

Any human procedural action to manipulate or alter a system's hardware, software, or operational configuration, or an action that might inadvertently alter them, presents a risk of triggering an outage. Reducing the rate of human procedural actions is a primary strategy for reducing the risk of procedural outages. Manual emergency recoveries have a higher risk of human error than nonemergency procedures because of:

- **Uncertainty about state of the system** and exactly what actions are most appropriate.
- **Time pressure to rapidly restore service.** Stress of emergency recovery can lead to poor human judgment that may prompt panic actions that compromise automatic recoveries (e.g., manually rebooting system rather than waiting for automatic recovery to succeed) or lead to taking hasty and desperate recovery actions (e.g., manually replacing FRUs in a system one at a time rather than thoughtfully troubleshooting the problem).
- **Limited preparation or practice time.** While nonemergency procedures can be carefully planned and rehearsed, and not initiated until all prerequisites are complete, failures that require emergency actions happen without warning, regardless of how prepared the maintenance engineers are.

One minimizes human maintenance interactions by automating both nonemergency and emergency procedures. Automation can lead to two direct availability-related benefits:

1. **Automated mechanisms that eliminate manual procedures also eliminate the risk of human failure.**
2. **Automated procedures have fewer steps to execute, and hence fewer opportunities for human mistakes.** After all, procedures not executed by humans are not at risk of human errors like entering wrong input parameters or executing actions out of sequence.

In addition to reducing risk of procedural downtime, increased automation should reduce the workload on maintenance engineers and thus should reduce the enterprise's operational expenses via reduced labor expenses.

5.11.2   "Help-the-Humans" Techniques

One helps the human maintenance engineers do the right thing via:

- Well-designed procedures
- Well-written and thoroughly tested documentation
- Good troubleshooting tools
- Technical support
- Training

5.11.2.1 Well-Designed Procedures

Well-designed procedures are:

- **Simple.** Every procedure should be as simple as possible, but no simpler. Automation and minimizing the number of tasks per procedure contribute to simplification. A Golden Rule of constructing good *methods of procedure (MOPs)* states no more than seven distinct steps should be present in a module. Anything more than seven steps should be grouped into a subprocedure. Each additional task and decision point in a given procedure creates another opportunity for a mistake. Making each procedure have a minimal set of tasks and decision points reduces the risk of error. Fewer steps also speed up the execution of the procedure, potentially resulting in less downtime or reduced simplex exposure (depending on the procedure).

- **Clear.** Ensure that procedures will be understood by the staff who will execute them. This includes use of clear language, list formats, and whitespace. Step-by-step instructions and pointers to key things to watch for, such as the state of a particular LED, also improve procedural clarity.

- **Intuitive.** Procedures should be intuitive so staff executing the procedures will be biased to execute the procedure correctly. This may be accomplished through software, user interface, and physical design, labeling, and marking. It includes keyed connectors; appropriate labeling and marking; using color codes, size, or shape to differentiate system elements such as fuses; and designing uniform circuit-pack craft interfaces (LEDs, switches, marking). All these are aimed at guiding the maintenance engineer toward the proper action.

- **Similar to each other.** Similar procedures reduce the procedural failure rate by letting maintenance engineers become familiar with the procedures more quickly. Examples include common power-up and power-down procedures for FRUs, common location of controls and indicators on FRUs, and consistent terminology and documentation.

- **Require confirmation before service-impacting operations (e.g., asking "Are you sure?").** Explicitly requiring human maintenance engineers to confirm critical actions via a second step that they actually want to impact service is a best practice. This will prevent a single human error from causing a service-impacting failure.

- **Clearly report system's operational state.** All alarms should be collected and displayed together. Alarm messages must be clear, simple, and consistent. Alarm-reporting algorithms must make it easy to understand the system state under various conditions. Clear communication of the system state is very important because this information becomes the basis for further action.

- **Include "safe stop points."** Clearly identify points within the procedure where it is safe to interrupt or stop the procedure temporarily. Build these safe stop points into the construction of the procedure. For example, each point in a multistep procedure where the system is duplex (i.e., full system redundancy) might be a safe point. This allows technicians to leave the system in a known safe state when they have to suspend execution of the procedure, such as to respond to higher-priority issues. Ideally, the safe points should allow the procedure to be rolled back if necessary.

5.11.2.2   Well-Written and Tested Documentation

All procedures needed for system operation, maintenance, and recovery should be clearly documented and methodically tested. Documentation should reflect the system release it applies to; text messages and screenshots should accurately reflect what maintenance engineers are likely to see. Documentation should be available electronically, thus making it easier to ensure the documentation is up to date and is available with the system (it is less likely to get lost than a paper manual), and also allows enhancements like interactive help, and so forth.

In addition to documenting maintenance procedures, best practice is to provide both a planning and installation guide and capacity planning information, all of which may be consolidated into a single document.

5.11.2.2.1   System Planning and Installation Guide   As 24/7/365 systems are intended to operate continuously, it is best to install the system properly in the network to minimize the need for planned reconfiguration events after the system enters service. The system's planning guide should give enterprise staff information necessary for them to:

- Select the proper hardware configuration to serve the planned load.
- Select a physical location with adequate clearance to permit maintenance engineers to access and repair the system.
- Provide adequate power and cooling.
- Provide necessary IP connectivity, including appropriate network security arrangements such as firewalls.
- Plan for spare hardware to enable prompt recovery from inevitable hardware failures.
- Plan settings for all configurable parameters and options.
- Understand what skills and training are appropriate for staff who will operate, administer, maintain, and provision the system.
- Plan appropriate schedule for routine and preventative maintenance.

The system's installation guide should give instructions on physically installing the system written in language appropriate to the skill and training of the staff.

Note that the staff installing the equipment may have much less training than the staff that will operate and maintain the equipment. For example, while IT or data center staff know that electrical ground wires should be connected to *metallic* cold-water pipes, inexperienced installers have been known to ground electronic systems to plastic cold-water pipes because the installation guide assumed that installers would implicitly know that metallic cold-water pipes are necessary to assure proper electrical grounding. (Poor electrical grounding will cause operational problems with power and hardware.)

5.11.2.2.2 Capacity Planning Guide   Useful and effective systems often see traffic grow over time as users gain experience with the system and seek to fully leverage the value of the system. This may eventually cause traffic to grow beyond the engineered capacity of the installed hardware, causing the system to become saturated and overloaded. Extended periods of overload cause poor experiences for some or all users and increase the risk of critical software failure because the system is operating outside of engineered limits. To support optimal capacity planning by enterprises, system suppliers should provide the following:

- **Dimensioning data.** How the system should be configured to properly support various traffic loads.
- **Performance and throughput metrics.** Systems should provide complete and easy-to-understand performance and throughput measures so enterprises can easily determine the actual traffic level and service mix on the system. Enterprises should routinely compare the observed performance and throughput metrics to the recommended and maximum throughput capacities that the configured system was dimensioned for.
- **System growth and reconfiguration procedures.** As system traffic grows and eventually exceeds recommended traffic capacities, enterprises should execute documented and tested procedures to grow the system's hardware configuration and/or to gracefully migrate traffic to other (possibly new) systems. Ideally these growth and reconfiguration procedures can be executed without impacting user service.

5.11.2.3 Troubleshooting Tools and Technical Support

Inevitably, some problems will require manual troubleshooting and recovery by maintenance engineers on an emergency basis. These manual actions might be required because the true failure is not correctly isolated by the system (and thus the wrong recovery action is initiated), or because the automatic recovery action was unsuccessful, or perhaps because automatic recovery is not supported for this failure, or possibly even because the system failed to detect the failure at all.

In these cases, maintenance engineers rely on:

- **Appropriate alarms.** Critical and major alarms provide maintenance engineers with their primary insight into operational impairments. Alarms should identify both explicit failures (e.g., crashed processes) and abnormal events (e.g., threshold-crossing alarms). The alarm mechanism should include logic to prevent excess alarm events from filling logs. In an emergency, excess alarms will obscure the true failure and force the maintenance engineer to wade through too much information to determine true root cause before they can consider appropriate recovery action. Ideally, systems will be properly configured and maintained so that there are no "standing alarms" in normal operation; thus any alarm present when maintenance engineers start emergency recovery actions are abnormal and thus are likely to be related to the failure.

- **Performance monitors.** Appropriate performance measures should be provided by the system to enable maintenance engineers to understand how the system and major modules are actually performing. Examining error counts, throughput statistics, and other performance counters helps characterize current operational performance and can be used to troubleshoot failures and bottlenecks in the system.

- **Visual status indicators on FRUs.** Including LEDs on FRUs to indicate failure facilitates rapid troubleshooting and reduces the risk of the wrong FRU being pulled from the system.

- **Online diagnostics.** Online diagnostics enable maintenance engineers to troubleshoot failures without further impacting service. While restarting a system is a logically easy way to test if a failure is caused by software rather than hardware (hardware failures typically persist after restart while software failures often clear) it is likely to impact all system users, and thus it should be a maintenance engineer's last resort. Ideally, maintenance engineers have a rich set of online diagnostic tools that make service-impacting diagnostic techniques unnecessary. It may, of course, be necessary to take service-impacting actions to clear a failure, but these should be taken deliberately to restore service rather than as desperate diagnostic actions.

- **Documentation of required software processes.** Providing a checklist of required processes enables a maintenance engineer to rapidly confirm that all processes are in fact running. Note that this can also be used to verify that no malicious processes have been installed on the system.

- **Documented emergency recovery procedures.** Clear and complete written procedures should help maintenance engineers rapidly troubleshoot failures and execute emergency recoveries.

- **Technical support.** When maintenance engineers are not able to promptly troubleshoot and restore service, they should contact the equipment supplier's technical support team for emergency assistance to diagnose and recover service as quickly as possible.

5.11.2.4 Training

System suppliers should provide training materials and opportunities for OAM&P staff that are offered in a language and written at a level that is appropriate to the enterprise staff. Certification programs can help formalize training programs, and further encourage OAM&P staff to diligently complete appropriate training.

5.11.3 Minimize the Impact of Human Error

Like all humans, operations, administration, and maintenance staff make typographical errors, accidentally select the wrong option with their mouse or pointing device, and make other mistakes. Systems should anticipate that such errors will occasionally be made, and thus take proactive steps to minimize the risk that such errors will escalate into service-impacting failures. Specific actions that well-designed systems will take to minimize the risk of human errors escalating into service-impacting failures are:

- **Check input parameters** to ensure valid parameters and commands have been entered. This includes checking that all input parameters meet syntax and semantics rules of the application. When possible, the input should be cross-checked against other data for reasonableness, and the user prompted to correct or confirm inconsistencies.

- **Confirm service-impacting and profound requests.** Prompt user with a confirmation question like "*This command will impact service; okay to continue? (y/n).*" It is even common to confirm simple yet impactful actions like asking the user, "*Do you want to save changes to <filename> before exiting?*"

- **Provide documented backout, undo, or rollback mechanisms** whenever possible. Undoubtedly, all readers have personal experience with the "undo" feature of a PC application clearing a mistake they made; the same sort of undo feature that makes it easier to use a word processor is valuable on critical systems.

5.11.4 Robust Operational Policies

Robust system and procedural design must be complemented by robust operational policies of the enterprises operating the systems to enable 24/7/365 system operation. Operational policies influence both the rate of critical failures and how rapidly service is restored following critical failures. For example, a timely security or reliability patch from a supplier does not help if the enterprise operating the system does not bother to install it. While system suppliers have minimal control over the actual operational policies followed by the enterprises operating the systems, suppliers can provide guidance, documentation, training, and tools that encourage robust operational policies. This section considers the context of operational policies, relevant business policies, and operational policies.

5.11.4.1 Context of Operational Policies

The key is that there is an infinite set of potential errors that can escalate to failures, and thus it is infeasible to consider each potential error and failure scenario explicitly. A more practical approach is to consider the classes of failures that a system is susceptible to, and then consider nominal or archetype errors that can occur. Section 3.2 frames the eight ingredients that systems critically depend upon, and hence whose failure can cause service unavailability. Section 3.3 and the remainder of this chapter describe a set of product-related archetype errors that can be used to guide system design and testing. Focus on detecting, isolating, and recovering from these archetype errors should improve the probability that the system will also detect, isolate, and recover from many similar and related errors.

The eight-ingredient framework identified six ingredients *external* to the system's two internal ingredients (hardware and software). Those six external ingredients frame the context that the system operates within and are controlled by the enterprise operating the system. The enterprise has explicit and implicit policies that govern or influence each of these six external ingredients; this section considers what system suppliers can do to help enterprises deploy policies that assure the lowest critical failure rate and shortest outage durations possible. The six external ingredients are:

1. **Power.** The installation guide should specify the electrical system's power and grounding requirements, and the enterprise should assure that these requirements are met.

2. **Environment.** The installation guide should specify maximum and minimum operating and storage temperatures and relative humidity, as well as limits for corrosive gases, altitude, shock, vibration, electromagnetic interference, and any other environmental risks that the system is susceptible to. Essential details on physical installation should also be specified, such as whether the system is expected to be installed in a physically secured location like a locked data center, or if it can be safely installed in an unsecured location, like an office, or end user's home office, or even outdoors. The enterprise must assure that these environmental expectations are met.

3. **Network.** IP infrastructure requirements should be specified in the installation or planning guide such as: maximum packet latency; maximum packet loss ratio; maximum latency to recover from router or other network element or facility failure; and recommended network architectures and options. Assumptions about what network security devices such as firewalls and intrusion detection and prevention devices

should be installed to protect the system should be stated. The enterprise must assure that these expectations are met.

4. **Payload.** Maximum throughput and service loads for each supported configuration should be clearly specified in capacity planning documents so a deployment can be properly engineered. Recommended application and protocol option settings should be stated in planning documents.

5. **Human.** Skills and training expectations of installation, operations, and maintenance engineers should be clearly specified in planning documents. Documentation and training should be offered to staff that will interact with the system early enough so that they can minimize the risk of mistakes when planning, installing, activating, and operating the system.

6. **Policy.** System supplier should clearly document assumptions, and best practice for policy-related items, including:
   - **Recommended system and network engineering rules:** how the system should be configured to minimize risk of overload, and at what service thresholds the system should be grown or reconfigured.
   - **Recommended redundancy and sparing strategy:** how much hardware redundancy should be installed to meet particular availability targets. Which hardware elements should be spared on-site for immediate access, versus accessible in, say, hours (e.g., at a local depot) or days (e.g., at a regional, national, or international depot).
   - **Recommended maintenance schedule:** what routine preventative maintenance actions should be performed, and when.

5.11.4.2 Relevant Business Policies

Enterprises operating the equipment should establish and execute good business policies, including:

- **Skills and qualifications of maintenance engineers.** Assure that maintenance engineers operating the system have the skills and qualifications recommended by the system supplier. For example, if maintenance (e.g., emergency recovery) manuals are written in English, then the maintenance engineers should be fluent in English.
- **Appropriate training.** Maintenance engineers should have completed appropriate training to minimize the risk of error while executing both emergency and nonemergency procedures. If certification programs are available, then the enterprise should consider requiring certification for maintenance engineers and others.
- **Security skills assessment.** Enterprises should assess the security knowledge of OAM&P staff and provide training to address gaps.

- **Maintenance policies.** Best practice is to perform maintenance actions that may or will impact user service in off-peak hours, often called *maintenance windows*, such as between midnight and 4 A.M. or on weekends. While scheduling maintenance actions to off-hours is less convenient for maintenance engineers and may accrue overtime expenses for the enterprise, it minimizes the user impact of the maintenance action. As businesses become global, there are fewer off-peak hours because of the geographic arrangement of the Americas, Europe, Africa, Asia, and Australia around the planet. Thus tolerance for planned service downtime in maintenance windows is likely to decrease over time.

- **Bonus Policies.** Management and employee incentive or bonus payment policies are deliberately designed to focus the attention of staff on specific metrics and drive achievement of defined targets. For example, if bonus payments for operations staff and management are tied to measured service availability performance, then they are likely to make a bit more effort to minimize the impact and duration of any outage events that do occur. To encourage careful planning and preparation, one large enterprise considers the number of unscheduled equipment "touches" on the hypothesis that well-run equipment should rarely require actions that are rushed and not carefully planned. The fewer times a human being touches the equipment, the lower the risk of human-attributed or procedure-related outages. Equipment is considered "touched" if a maintenance engineer takes any action to the system that was not formally approved and scheduled in advance. Appropriately designed bonus metrics and targets around service availability or service quality can focus an enterprise on operating its systems at peak availability.

5.11.4.3 Operational Policies

The organization operating the system within an enterprise will have a variety of formal or informal operational policies for both general behaviors and system-specific policies. Well-designed and thoughtful operational policies reduce the rate of critical failure events and shorten outage durations compared to ad-hoc policies. While system suppliers have no direct control of the operational policies deployed by enterprises operating their systems, encouraging enterprises to deploy best practice operational policies reduces the risk of critical failures and prolonged outages. Some specific operational best practices to encourage are:

- **Deploy security and reliability/stability patches promptly.** The longer an enterprise waits to deploy patches, the larger the window of vulnerability to risks that have been corrected in the patch.

- **Establish technical support arrangements with system supplier.** It is much easier and less stressful for operations staff and suppliers to reach agreements on technical support arrangements before a critical failure occurs than it is to establish business arrangements in the midst of an emergency outage recovery.

- **Prearrange for spare FRUs.** Hardware failures are inevitable and spare FRUs may not be routinely stocked items at local distributors or supplier offices. As device technology advances, one generation of FRUs will be discontinued and another generation will replace it. Thus, the FRUs in a system may no longer be manufactured a couple of years (or less) after the system is brought into service. Thus, to assure timely access to necessary spare parts, arrangements should be made before the spare is required to assure spares will be promptly available to restore the system to redundant (and hence highly available) operation.

- **No standing alarms.** Over time various minor, major, and critical alarms may accumulate in system logs. While these alarms may (or may not) be a minor annoyance during normal operation, they can obscure and confuse the true root cause of a new critical alarm and delay or confuse emergency recovery actions. Enterprises should minimize the number of standing alarms so maintenance engineers can promptly diagnose the true root cause of an outage event and quickly decide on the proper emergency recovery action.

- **Outage escalation policy.** Maintenance engineers will diligently work to recover an outage as long as they believe they are making progress before asking for help. If an event occurs in off-hours when few others are on duty, then maintenance engineers may be reluctant to contact managers or staff on their mobile phones or at their homes. To minimize the risk of outage recovery being delayed out of polite courtesy, best practice is to establish formal outage notification and escalation policies. For a high-value system, the policy might be that the manager on-duty or on-call must be notified of a total capacity loss outage if service is not restored within 15 minutes and an executive must be notified if service is not restored in 30 minutes. This relieves both uncertainty and further stress from the maintenance engineer working the emergency recovery on when to call for help, and assures that enterprise leadership has the opportunity to engage additional resources to accelerate emergency recovery.

- **Frequent routine execution of standby elements.** Standby elements in systems with active-standby redundancy should frequently be checked by routine switchover and execution on standby FRUs. This minimizes the risk of a silent or previously unknown failure of the standby element, thereby increasing the probability that an automatic recovery onto that standby FRU will complete successfully.

- **Frequent data backups.** System data should be frequently backed up so that minimum information is lost if data restoration is required.

- **Periodic disaster recovery drills.** If a system is deployed in a geographically redundant configuration, then the enterprise should periodically test disaster recovery procedures to assure that service is properly restored onto geographically redundant unit using the documented disaster recovery procedure.

5.12 PROBLEMS

The following problems consider a "target system" identified by the instructor:

1. Identify three robustness features of one communications protocol supported by the target system.
2. Identify three external interfaces to the target system that can be overloaded.
3. How can overload be detected for the three identified interfaces?
4. How can overload be controlled for the three identified interfaces?
5. Identify five process, resource, or throughput monitors that can be used by the target system.
6. Identify three data audits that can be used by target system.
7. Is the target system subject to security attacks against system availability? Why?
8. What design features of the target system can be used to minimize human interaction?
9. What design features of the target system can be used to help OAM&P staff reduce the risk of error?
10. What operational policies should be recommended to users of the target system to maximize service availability?

5.13 FOR FURTHER STUDY

[Lyu95] and [Hanmer07] provide details on architectural and design of fault-tolerant systems. In addition, The Network Reliability and Interoperability Council[1] Best Practices [NRICBP] provide hundreds of brief concrete recommendations across the entire spectrum of service-impacting factors, from buildings and physical security, to human resources and training, to emergency procedures and policies, to hardware and software design, and more.

---

[1]Network Reliability and Interoperability Council "*partner[s] with the Federal Communications Commission, the communications industry and public safety to facilitate enhancement of emergency communications networks, homeland security, and best practices across the burgeoning telecommunications industry*" [NRIC].

Chapter 6

Error Detection

Having designed a system with appropriate fault containment and rapid failure recovery mechanisms, developers must now assure that errors and failures are promptly detected. This chapter methodically reviews common failure detection techniques for each error type in the eight error categories defined in Chapter 3, "What Can Go Wrong." Many of the techniques given in Chapter 5, "Robust Design Principles," are referenced as common failure recovery techniques for each error type.

6.1 DETECTING FIELD-REPLACEABLE UNIT (FRU) HARDWARE FAULTS

Most advanced integrated circuits have mechanisms for detecting common hardware failures like parity or CRC (cyclic redundancy check) errors. Circuits should be designed so that all of these errors are visible to software drivers. Ideally, a hardware failure will trigger an interrupt or directly detectable failure, such as a parity error or error status in response to a device command from a software driver. The software platform will push this failure notification to the high-availability mechanism so an appropriate recovery action can be activated.

Beyond these primary failure detectors, highly available hardware should also include:

- **Processor watchdog.** Hardware watchdog mechanisms are frequently deployed in which the expiration of a hardware timer automatically triggers a hardware reset of the target processor. In normal operation the platform or application software will reset the timer every time a periodic sanity check routine completes successfully. The hardware timer is reset to a value nominally twice the normal interval between these regular sanity checks. If the regular sanity check does not complete successfully and reset the watchdog timer before it expires, then the processor will be hard reset by the watchdog. This mechanism both

Design for Reliability: Information and Computer-Based Systems, by Eric Bauer
Copyright © 2010 Institute of Electrical and Electronics Engineers

detects "insane" software and automatically recovers from various critical software failures.

- **Bus and other hardware watchdog timers,** so nonresponsive hardware elements can be promptly detected and reset.
- **Power, temperature, and environmental monitors** to explicitly detect and alarm unacceptable conditions so proper corrective actions can be taken.
- **Power-on self-test** (POST) to verify basic hardware sanity and operability before application software is booted. Note that removing and reinserting FRUs (often called *reseating*) is a common troubleshooting technique. Theoretically, hardware problems will persist after reseating an FRU but software problems will vanish. Ideally, the power-on self-test should provide sufficient test coverage to rapidly detect the majority of hardware failures in seconds to minimize the risk that a maintenance engineer is misled to believe that a hardware failure that is not exhibited in normal application startup and typical operation is a software failure. In this case, a second service disruption is inevitable when the application or platform software attempts to use the failed circuitry. The power-on self-test should be automatically executed when the FRU is reinserted and should detect and report the hardware failure (often via a red "error" LED); maintenance engineers will quickly recognize an illuminated red "error" LED on an FRU as indicating that an FRU should be replaced.

Hardware and platform software are generally configured to detect some failure conditions in real time, and raise an interrupt when such an event occurs. Interrupts for illegal memory access, illegal instruction, overflow/underflow on mathematical calculation, and so on, will be raised by the hardware and platform operating system, and can activate exception processing software. Platform or application software should catch these major signals and take prompt actions to recover from the failure, such as cleaning up pending work and starting another instance of the failed process. (See Table 6.1.)

6.2 DETECTING PROGRAMMING AND DATA FAULTS

Input parameters should be validated and errors should be immediately reported back to the invoking routine/object so they can isolate the failure that almost cascaded into the detecting process, object, or subroutine. Return codes should be checked on all subroutine and library calls, and proper status codes should be returned by each object method. In addition to checking for gross input errors like null pointers, routines can verify checksums or consistency of input data structures.

Table 6.1 Detection Technique for FRU Hardware Failures

	Field-replaceable unit (FRU) hardware	
Error category	Common failure detection technique	Common failure recovery technique
Processor failure	• Heartbeat with processor on controlling or redundant FRU • Hardware watchdog timer • Processor exception	• Switchover to redundant FRU
Disk failure	• Failure reported explicitly by disk controller, possibly with hardware interrupt • Timeout • Periodic read of all disk blocks	• Redundant array of inexpensive disks (RAID) can automatically detect and mask disk failure • Switchover to redundant FRU
Power converter failure	• Timeout or error detected by device interacting with component powered by failed power converter • Failure reported explicitly by failing power converter	• Switchover to redundant FRU
Clock failure	• Failure reported explicitly by failing clock device component • Failure detected via timeout or aberrant behavior of device(s) fed by failing clock device	• Switchover to redundant FRU
Clock jitter	• CRC, framing, or other communications failures • Aberrant behavior of device fed by jittering clock device, or by devices communicating with devices fed by jittering clock device	• Switchover to redundant FRU
Switching/ Ethernet failure	• Failure reported explicitly by networking component, possibly with hardware interrupt • Timeout expiration or improper interaction with device detected by software driver on processor	• Link aggregation across redundant network interfaces • Switchover to redundant FRU
Memory device failure	• Parity error • Timeout • Processor exception (e.g., illegal instruction)	• Switchover to redundant FRU • Error checking & correcting (ECC) RAM for soft errors

Table 6.1   Continued

Field-replaceable unit (FRU) hardware		
Error category	Common failure detection technique	Common failure recovery technique
Bus error/ failure	• Parity or CRC failure • Timeout	• Switchover to redundant FRU
Transient failure or signal integrity issue	• CRC or parity failure • Timeout • Miscellaneous behavioral failures detected by hardware components or processor	• Switchover to redundant FRU
Application-specific component failure	• Failure reported by component or device to software driver, possibly with hardware interrupt • Timeout detected by processor or other component interacting with failed device	• Switchover to redundant FRU

Software that requires exclusive access to a shared resource can block waiting for resource access, and software that communicates with another processor or other system can hang if the request or response gets lost or garbled, or if the other processor or system is unavailable. Guard timers should be set by an entity when it makes a request of another entity. If the requesting entity has not received a response when the guard timer expires, then the request can be retried a small number of times. One or two retries is generally sufficient to recover from lost requests. Note that the total latency of guard timeout times across the maximum try count should be less than budgeted failure detection time. It is acceptable for software to have an infinite loop on input (e.g., reading an input queue); all other loops should have finite maximum iteration counts. (See Tables 6.2 and 6.3.)

6.3 DETECTING REDUNDANCY FAILURES

High-availability infrastructure generally controls secondary failure detection mechanisms and most recovery actions. This infrastructure is vulnerable to failure because it is activated when the system is in a degraded state, and because successfully restoring operational status of an application is inherently complex because many objects must be rapidly resynchronized to minimize service disruption. Therefore, robust mechanisms should be deployed to detect and recover from failures of the high-availability infrastructure. Note that recovery from a high-availability infrastructure failure could be as profound as a complete system restart. (See Table 6.4.)

Table 6.2 Detection Techniques for Programming Error Failures

Programming errors		
Error category	Common failure detection technique	Common failure recovery technique
Memory leak or exhaustion (including excessive fragmentation)	• Checking return codes from all memory allocation and reallocation operations • Critical resource monitoring of heap, including alarming when available heap drops below a minimum threshold	• Switchover to redundant FRU • Restart affected software platform
Buffer overflow	• Auditing stored data length against allocated data length • Verifying presence of data value terminator within allocated data length • Verifying buffer header, including tattoo,[a] if used	• Repair compromised data structures • Abort transactions associated with compromised data structures • Restart process(es) associated with compromised data structures
Shared resource conflict	• Resource monitoring of lock latency • Monitoring of threads waiting for locks	• Abort transaction • Break lock • Restart application process(es) • Switchover to redundant FRU
Tight or infinite loop	• Heartbeat or keep-alive mechanism with all processes by a monitor process running at higher operating system priority • Monitor CPU usage of processes • Program counter monitoring	• Kill and restart looping process • Switchover to redundant FRU
Remote execution failures and hangs, including remote procedure call failures	• Expiration of guard timer • Heartbeat with key remote servers	• Retry operation, possibly to a different server • After a small number of retries, fail the operation (rather than infinitely looping)
Thread stack/ address space corrupted	• Processor exception for invalid memory access, segmentation violation, or illegal instruction	• Kill and restart affected process • Switchover to redundant FRU

Table 6.2 Continued

Programming errors		
Error category	Common failure detection technique	Common failure recovery technique
Reference uninitialized or incorrect pointer	• Processor exception for invalid memory access, segmentation violation, or illegal instruction	• Kill and restart affected process • Switchover to redundant FRU
Logic errors	• Error returned by subroutine, method, command, or application • Error returned by operating system or platform subroutine or object • Processor exception for invalid memory access or segmentation violation	• Kill and restart affected process • Switchover to redundant FRU
Other, non-memory resource leaks	• Critical resource monitoring • Checking return codes from all resource allocation and related operations	• Kill and restart affected software platform • Switchover to redundant FRU
Process abort/ crash/hang	• Operating system signal • Heartbeat or keep-alive mechanism with all processes to a monitor process running at higher operating system priority	• Kill and restart affected process • Switchover to redundant FRU
Thread hang/abort	• Operating system signal • Audit of thread throughput, performance, CPU usage, etc.	• Kill and restart affected process • Switchover to redundant FRU

[a]A simple yet effective technique to detect buffer corruption or use-after-free is to "tattoo" signatures onto specific types of data structures, buffers, and other in-memory objects. For instance, a simple system might use a handful of types of data structures and could use the following "tattoos" in the first four bytes of these objects:

• 'U,' 's,' 'e,' 'r'—for user object/data structures.
• 'S,' 'e,' 's,' 's'—for session object/data structure.
• 'R,' 'q,' 's,' 't'—for transaction request object/data structure.
• 'F,' 'r,' 'e,' 'e'—when object/data structure is closed or otherwise made inactive/invalid.

It is then trivial to verify that a parameter provided as input is actually an active User object, rather than a Session or Request object, and that it has not been freed.

Table 6.3 Detection Techniques for Data Inconsistency Errors

Data inconsistency or error		
Error category	Common failure detection technique	Common failure recovery technique
File system corruption, including from disorderly disk write on power down	• Check that file system was properly unmounted before remounting	• Journaling file system automatically recovers intent log to make file system consistent when remounting file system after reboot • Run file system check and repair
Disk partition/ file system full	• Critical resource monitoring checks available free space on all file system partitions and raises alarm when free space drops below threshold • Monitor return codes on all file creation and writing operations	• For file systems capturing security-related data (e.g., login attempts, logs of administrative commands), security policy may dictate that system suspend all operations rather than risk compromising security-related data • For non-security-related data, system wraps around, overwrites, or automatically truncates files, or writes to an alternate file system, or simply discards the data
Database corruption	• Detect via database check on opening database • Detect in real time when executing database operation • Detect during periodic integrity scan	• Run check-and-repair program • Restore from backup
Database mismatch between active and standby	• Detect during periodic integrity scan • Detect during routine or emergency switchover	• Force one instance to resynchronize with the other instance • Restore from backup
Shared memory corruption	• Runtime consistency check of buffer prior to use • Checksum error • Periodic integrity scan discovers inconsistency	• Run check-and-repair routine • Switchover to redundant FRU • Restart software on processors accessing compromised shared memory

Table 6.3   Continued

Data inconsistency or error		
Error category	Common failure detection technique	Common failure recovery technique
Linked list breakage	• Invalid pointer discovered during linked list operation • Periodic integrity scan discovers inconsistency	• Run check-and-repair routine • Restart process or software platform hosting linked list
File not found	• Failure detected in real time when file cannot be opened • Periodic integrity scan	• Create new file • Restore file from backup
File corrupted	• Real-time checksum or integrity check fails • Periodic sanity scan fails	• Create new file • Restore file from backup
Record not found	• Failure detected in real time when record cannot be found or opened • Failure is detected via periodic audit/ integrity scan	• Restore record or complete dataset from backup • Use repair to delete dangling references to nonexistent record
Record or object corrupted	• Checksum or tattoo error • Record integrity/ consistency check failure • Failure is detected via periodic audit/ integrity scan	• Restore record or complete dataset from backup • Use repair program to correct corrupted record • Delete corrupted record, and use repair to restore referential integrity
Corrupted executable	• Operating system reports executable or library cannot be executed or loaded • Failure is detected via periodic audit/integrity scan	• Reinstall corrupted file • Reinstall application
Checksum error	• Failure detected in real time when failed object is accessed • Failure detected by periodic audit scan	• For volatile data, switchover to redundant FRU • For persistent data, run repair program or restore from backup
Cannot access file or write protected	• Operating system file operation (e.g., open) fails • Periodic audit scan detects wrong access permission bits	• Restore file from backup • Reinstall file or application

Table 6.4   Detection Techniques for Redundancy Failures

Redundancy failures		
Error category	Common failure detection technique	Common failure recovery technique
Failover to failed (redundant) hardware	• Run application or platform software on warm or hot standby element that periodically exercises/tests all hardware to promptly detect failures on redundant unit • Regularly scheduled routine switchover	• Report duplex failure to element management system so manual recovery can be initiated
Failed failover	• High-availability monitor software detects that service is not restored within expected time	• Manual recovery • Restart software on unit that failed failover
Site failure or unavailability	• Site unavailability detected manually • Heartbeat failure of several systems at a single site	• Site failover is typically performed via a detailed Method of Procedure involving several manual actions
Failure of high-availability process(es)	• A second instance of high-availability process or a platform mechanism monitors key high-availability processes, possibly hosted on a different FRU	• Promote standby high-availability process to active • Switchover to redundant FRU • Failed high-availability processes are automatically restarted when possible

6.4 DETECTING POWER FAILURES

Electrical power can be abruptly lost to an entire system, a single frame, a single shelf/chassis, or even a single FRU (e.g., when a maintenance engineer physically removes it from the shelf/chassis). FRUs with persistent storage devices like hard disk drives, flash memory, and nonvolatile RAM should be designed so that power failures are detected via a power failure interrupt, and software has sufficient time to flush data from system memory into persistent storage and properly stabilize the persistent data by properly writing checksums and so on to minimize risk of data inconsistency or corruption. When power is reapplied to the FRU, shelf/chassis, frame, or system, the hardware should automatically execute power-on self-tests to assure hardware has not been damaged and boot platform software. The operating system should always verify that the contents of persistent storage devices are in a consistent state as part of boot up. Typically this is done by verifying that file systems are marked as having been gracefully closed and unmounted previously and that checksums over nonvolatile storage devices match their contents. If any persistent storage device is in an inconsistent or inappropriate state, then check-and-repair mechanisms should be activated prior to starting application software. (See Table 6.5.)

Table 6.5   Detection Techniques for System Power Failures

	System power	
Error category	Common failure detection technique	Common failure recovery technique
Network element power failure (and restoration), including power feed failure	• Power fail interrupt to host processors triggers rapid stabilization of persistent data	• Element automatically restarts when power is restored • Journaling file system automatically recovers intent log to make file system consistent when remounting file system after reboot • All persistent storage is checked to assure data is intact and sane; if not intact and sane, then check and repair if possible
Shelf power failure (and restoration)	• Software on one shelf completely loses connectivity to processes on another shelf • Intershelf IP switch on unaffected shelf detects failure via hardware mechanisms	• Software on operational shelf promotes itself to active and recovers traffic previously served by unavailable shelf • Software on operational shelf polls for other shelf to return to operational status, and then automatically reconnects with it
Battery exhaustion	• Battery voltage sensor	• Gracefully flush and unmount persistent storage to avoid corrupting data store • Journaling file system automatically recovers intent log to make file system consistent when remounting file system after restart

6.5 DETECTING NETWORKING FAILURES

Network errors may be detected by hardware, platform software, or application software. Hardware will detect some profound failures of local network facilities (e.g., physical disconnection of LAN connectivity) and link layer problems such as framing, message length, and cyclical redundancy check (CRC) errors. Protocol stacks in platform software will automatically retry some unacknowledged protocol packets, and resequence packets that arrive out of order. Application software is often responsible for monitoring message timeouts and sending periodic "keep-alive" or "hello" messages to verify that remote systems are both accessible over the network and nominally operational.

Since networking and remote systems can become unavailable for many reasons, applications should not block with synchronous network I/O because this would cause the local system to cascade a remote failure. Application software should be designed so that unavailability of any nonlocal (or local) resource can be gracefully addressed. Application or platform software should periodically recheck availability of key nonlocal resources so that when they are restored the system can resume normal operation. (See Table 6.6.)

Table 6.6   Detection Techniques for Network Errors

Network errors		
Error category	Common failure detection technique	Common failure recovery technique
Failure of adjacent/ supporting network elements	• Absence or failure of heartbeat or keep-alive messages • No acknowledgment or response to messages sent to a particular network element	• Explicitly reconnect to alternate elements • Requery DNS for IP address (hopefully of an alternate element) and reconnect • Make best-effort attempt to continue delivering service (e.g., using cached data or operating in a limp-along mode). For example, locally save usage, billing, and other records that normally would be sent to failed element; push the records to the element after it is restored to service
Corrupted IP packets	• Detected via Ethernet or networking hardware via CRC failures • Detected via network drivers that parse IP packets	• Corrupted packets should be negatively acknowledged, and thus should be retransmitted by the sender • Explicitly reconnect to an alternate element • Requery DNS for IP address (hopefully of an alternate element) and reconnect • Make best-effort attempt to continue delivering service, such as engaging lost packet concealment algorithms when rendering streaming media

Table 6.6   Continued

Network errors		
Error category	Common failure detection technique	Common failure recovery technique
Dropped IP packets	• Gaps in packet sequence numbers detected • Expiration of some protocol timeout	• Dropped packets should be negatively acknowledged, and thus should be retransmitted by the sender • Make best-effort attempt to continue delivering service, such as engaging lost packet concealment algorithms when rendering streaming media • Explicitly reconnect to alternate elements • Requery DNS for IP address (hopefully of an alternate element) and reconnect
IP packets/ messages out of sequence	• Directly detected by platform or application software	• Platform or application software resequences packets • Discard stale (late) packets • Make best-effort attempt to continue delivering service, such as engaging lost packet concealment algorithms when rendering streaming media
Disruption of (external) IP infrastructure	• Protocol timeout	• Retry/retransmit • Make best-effort attempt to continue delivering service, such as engaging lost packet concealment algorithms when rendering streaming media • Explicitly reconnect to alternate elements • Requery DNS for IP address (hopefully of an alternate element) and reconnect
Restoration following regional network or power failure	• Spike in traffic detected by processes accepting network requests	• Overload control architecture supports huge volumes of simultaneous session initiation, (re)registration or connection requests

6.6 DETECTING APPLICATION PROTOCOL FAILURES

Application protocols and messages can be complex and highly dependent on context or state information that is maintained by communicating entities. Applications should carefully validate message integrity and correctness before processing it. This validation should verify syntax and semantics, and perform whatever application-specific consistency and policy checks are appropriate. Applications must be vigilant for deliberately malicious messages that seek to exploit wrong behaviors; no received parameter should be presumed to be correct without proper validation.

Table 6.7   Detection Techniques for Application Protocol Failures

	Application protocol	
Error category	Common failure detection technique	Common failure recovery technique
Invalid protocol syntax	• Unrecognized message or protocol mismatch • Unexpected parameters received	• Reply to invalid message with the appropriate protocol error • Terminate session • Renegotiate to a different protocol version supported by system and other entity
Invalid protocol semantics	• Protocol/message parser detects error	• Reply to invalid message with the appropriate protocol error • Renegotiate to a different protocol version supported by system and other entity • Terminate session
Unexpected or illegal message sequences	• Protocol/message parser detects error • Unsupported commands or messages received	• Reply to invalid message with the appropriate protocol error • Terminate session
Out-of-range parameters (including illegal command codes)	• Directly detected by platform or application	• Reply to invalid message with the appropriate protocol error • Terminate session
Malicious messages	• Directly detected by application or platform software	• Reply to invalid message with the appropriate protocol error • Terminate session
Overload, including denial-of-service (DoS, DDoS) attack	• Detected by message arrival rate • Detected by workload or activity monitor • Detected by CPU or resource monitor	• Overload controls shape traffic • Firewall or intrusion detection system blocks traffic • Reply to invalid message with the appropriate protocol error • Terminate session(s) • Suspend account • Block IP addresses

Message overload is another hazard to vigilantly detect and manage. Overload can come from occasional traffic spikes, external events (including activation of recovery action of a sister server that has failed-over traffic), and deliberate distributed denial-of-service (DDoS) attacks. Application logic should detect overload conditions rapidly and reject packets as logically close to the receiving network interface as possible. Since malicious overload could drive traffic to saturate the IP connection to the Ethernet switch or router, it is essential that overload traffic be shed efficiently without crashing the system. After the overload condition clears, the system should automatically return to normal operation. (See Table 6.7.)

6.7 DETECTING PROCEDURAL FAILURES

Systems should carefully design their man–machine interfaces to minimize the risk of human error when nonemergency and emergency OAM&P procedures, as well as end-user activities, are executed. This is discussed in Section 5.11, "Procedural Considerations."

System software should verify the correctness, completeness, and reasonableness of all human inputs and gracefully fail or question dubious requests. Note that procedural errors can appear as hardware, software, or other errors. For example, a FRU that is improperly seated and thus has incomplete or unreliable electrical connections to the midplane, backplane, or carrier board can appear as a hardware failure; skipping a required step in a maintenance procedure might cause the software to block or hang, thus appearing as a software failure. Thus techniques for detecting hardware, software, and other failures in this chapter should also detect the effects of various procedural failures.

6.8 PROBLEMS

The following problems consider a "target system" identified by the instructor:

1. Identify three mechanisms that the target system could use to rapidly detect hardware failures.
2. Identify three mechanisms that the target system could use to detect activation of programming faults.
3. Identify three mechanisms that the target system could use to detect data inconsistencies or corruption.
4. Identify three mechanisms that the target system could use to detect failures in high-availability or redundancy infrastructure.
5. Identify three mechanisms that the target system could use to detect network errors or disruptions.
6. Identify three mechanisms that the target system could use to detect application protocol errors.
7. Identify three mechanisms that the target system could use to detect procedural errors.

6.9 FOR FURTHER STUDY

[Lyu95] provides further information on fault detection and fault tolerance.

Chapter 7

Analyzing and Modeling Reliability and Robustness

This chapter reviews qualitative and quantitative techniques to assess the likelihood and feasibility of a system meeting its reliability requirements.

This chapter covers:

- Reliability block diagrams
- Qualitative model of redundancy
- Failure mode and effects analysis
- Overview of architecture-based availability modeling of unplanned hardware and software failures
- Algebraic modeling of planned downtime.

While creation of architecture-based Markov modeling is beyond the scope of this book, this chapter gives the reader a clear understanding of how Markov modeling works and how it can be used to assess feasibility and likelihood of meeting availability requirements.

7.1 RELIABILITY BLOCK DIAGRAMS

A reliability block diagram (RBD) is a visualization that illustrates the simplex and redundant arrangement of critical modules that are required to be operational to deliver service. The premise is that for service to be up (available) there must be at least one path across the diagram through modules that are all up. Thus, modules that are redundant are shown in parallel, while modules that are simplex are shown in series. This simple visualization is surprisingly powerful because it enables one to gradually expose the complexity of a system to analysis. Figure 7.1 illustrates this by logically expanding a "black-box" system into a simple RBD showing "computer hardware," "platform

Design for Reliability: Information and Computer-Based Systems, by Eric Bauer
Copyright © 2010 Institute of Electrical and Electronics Engineers

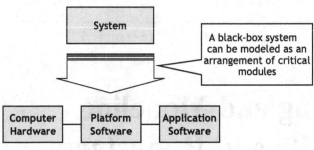

Figure 7.1   Sample Reliability Block Diagram

software," and "application software" logically arranged in series to highlight the fact that this particular system has no redundancy and depends on these three logical modules to deliver service. Each of these modules could be further diagramed to enumerate the critical modules within them. Generally one will construct RBDs down to the level that a design is being analyzed so reviewers can clearly understand what modules are critical to service delivery, and whether those critical modules are configured with any redundancy.

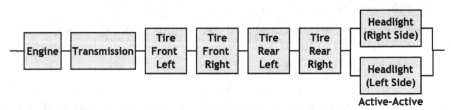

Figure 7.2   Simplified Automobile Reliability Block Diagram

Figure 7.2 gives a simplified reliability block diagram of an automobile. The engine and transmission are simplex elements, and thus they are shown in series. Interestingly, automobiles include four identical tires and two identical headlights, yet the system's dependency on the multiple instances of these modules is very different. Each of the four tires must be operational for the car to be available, and hence the four tires are shown in series with the engine and transmission. Both headlights illuminate the forward path of the automobile and are engineered so that the light from a single headlight is sufficient to safely operate the automobile at night, and hence the headlights can be shown in parallel in the RBD. Technically, automobile headlights are active-active because both lights are normally on together; there is no special action required by one light to deliver illumination when the other light fails. Other redundancy arrangements, such as active-standby, N + K load sharing, and M-out-of-N, can be represented in RBDs, generally with a comment noting the redundancy model alongside the parallel modules.

The primary analysis value of an RBD is that it highlights the single points of failure in a design; any nonredundant module in the critical path is, by definition, a single point of failure. Since RBDs highlight the modules critical for service delivery, they are naturally very good first steps in reliability analysis because they clearly capture the modules that should be considered in failure analyses and in architecture-based availability modeling.

7.2 QUALITATIVE MODEL OF REDUNDANCY

Highly available systems are designed to automatically detect, isolate, and recover from failure. To achieve the fastest possible recovery, service is often restored onto redundant modules that are either active or in hot standby and ready to rapidly accept service from a failed module. In some cases, the entire element may be duplicated, such as having two identical jet engines on an airplane. In other cases, each type of field-replaceable hardware unit may be duplicated, such as arranging compute blades in pairs or load-shared pools. Simple redundancy is visualized in Figure 7.3 as a reliability block diagram by showing a pair of elements in parallel; if at least one of the systems is available (up), then a request can traverse across one of the systems to deliver service. Real high-availability systems may be built by architecting redundant arrangements of all critical modules so that no single unit failure will produce a service outage.

Fundamentally, redundant pairs can either share the load across both elements (called active-active) or have one unit actively serving load while the redundant unit waits in standby (called active-standby). In both of these cases, failure of a unit actively serving load (i.e., active unit in active-standby arrangements, or either unit in active-active arrangements) will impact service availability. The service impact can be simply modeled by considering four factors, as shown in Figure 7.4. While the example in Figure 7.4 gives an active-standby pair, the model is similar for load-shared or active-active redundancy arrangements.

Downtime across this redundant pair of modules is driven by the following four system characteristics:

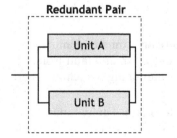

Figure 7.3   Reliability Block Diagram of Redundant Pair

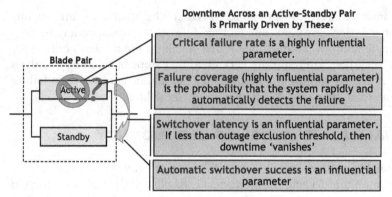

Figure 7.4   Robustness of Active-Standby Redundancy Pair

1. **Critical failure rate** is the rate of service-impacting failure events. As described in Section 1.3, "Error Severity," failure events are commonly classified as minor, major, and critical. Availability modeling is concerned with critical failures that impact the system's primary service.

2. **Failure coverage** is the probability that the system will rapidly detect and correctly isolate a critical failure to the appropriate recoverable module.

3. **Switchover latency** is the time it takes for the system to recover service onto the redundant "standby" unit.

4. **Automatic switchover success** is the probability that the automatic switchover operation is successful.

Note that while some reliability engineers define *coverage* to be the probability of automatically detecting, isolating, and recovering a failure successfully, it is often more useful to decompose this broad notion of coverage into separate failure coverage and automatic switchover success probabilities. Mathematically, *traditional coverage* is the product of failure coverage and automatic switchover success probability. This decomposing of these parameters is more useful than traditional coverage for several reasons:

1. **Values are estimated independently.** Failure coverage is estimated by analyzing results of fault insertion test campaigns and switchover success is estimated from analyzing results of switchover test campaigns.

2. **Parameters are improved by different feature investments.** Failure coverage is improved by adding more failure detection and fault isolation logic; switchover success is improved by hardening switchover and recovery logic.

3. **Outage events appear very different to enterprises.** Faulty failure coverage results either in undetected (*silent*) failures or in diagnostic fail-

ures; unsuccessful switchover events are generally recognized as unsuccessful automatic recoveries or *failed failovers*.

4. **Decomposed parameters are easier for decision makers and staff to understand.** While the implications of inadequate traditional coverage are unclear to many, the realities of silent and diagnostic failures, failed failovers, and failed automatic recoveries are clear to experienced decision makers and staff who have familiarity with real-world outages. The ability to point to actual field outages and identify which events became outages because of inadequate failure coverage and which escalated to outages due to unsuccessful switchover is very useful, and enables one to concretely illustrate the customer impact of inadequate failure coverage or poor automatic switchover success probability.

A continuous-time Markov model can be constructed to quantitatively model the interrelationship between service downtime, the four parameters enumerated above, and other parameters; Markov modeling is discussed in Section 7.4.1.

7.3 FAILURE MODE AND EFFECTS ANALYSIS

Failure mode and effects analysis (FMEA) is a method for considering the service impact of failures. FMEA is generally organized in tables with a row for each module being considered and a column for each service functionality or scenario being considered. Each cell in the table indicates what, if any, effect a particular failure will have on the service offered by the system. The effects generally fall into three broad categories:

1. **No impact.** A particular failure has no impact on a particular aspect of service.

2. **Transient impact.** A particular failure has a brief impact on service while the system automatically detects, isolates, and recovers service. Ideally, the duration of transient impact will be explicitly characterized, such as *"less than 2 second disruption."*

3. **Impact.** A particular failure impacts service until failure is manually repaired.

The value of FMEA is best understood with an example. Consider a session-oriented service delivered by the hypothetical system made up of a simplex module A, a pair of active-active modules B and a pair of active-standby modules C. The redundancy arrangement of this hypothetical system is illustrated in Figure 7.5.

When considering a session-oriented service, one is primarily concerned with two effects:

1. Impact on existing user sessions

2. Impact on requests to establish new user sessions

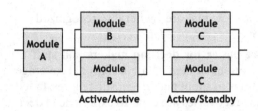

Figure 7.5 Hypothetical System for FMEA Example

Table 7.1 Failure Mode and Effects Analysis (FMEA) Example

Module	Impact on existing user sessions	Impact on requests for new user sessions
Module A (simplex)	**Impact**—existing user sessions are lost.	**Impact**—new user sessions cannot be established until A is repaired.
Module B (active-active redundancy)—**failure of either active module**	**Transient impact**—service will be impacted for less than 2 seconds for the half of active users served by the module that failed.	**No impact**—module that is up will respond to new session request before module that is unavailable, and hence will promptly accept new session request.
Module C (active-standby redundancy)—**failure of active module**	**Transient impact**—service is impacted for 15 seconds as standby system is promoted to active status.	**Transient impact**—service impacted for 15 seconds as standby system is promoted to active status.
Module C (active-standby redundancy)—**failure of standby module**	**No impact**—failure of standby has no impact on service provided by active module.	**No impact**—failure of standby has no impact on service provided by active module.

One might also be concerned with the following effects for session-oriented services:

- Impact on pending requests to establish new user sessions when failure occurs
- Impact on pending user commands, transactions, or requests
- Impact on pending session termination requests

The specific service effects to consider will vary based on the primary functionality of the system. Table 7.1 gives a sample failure mode and effects analysis for the hypothetical system illustrated in Figure 7.5.

The service impact of each failure should be compared to the maximum acceptable service disruption latency expectation and identify which, if any, failures are likely to produce unacceptable service impacts. FMEA tables can be very effective tools for explaining reliability risks to decision makers and project team members. To make it easier to quickly recognize the failure modes that do not meet the system requirements, one might fill FMEA cells with little or no service impact with green, cells with unacceptably slow automatic recovery with yellow, and cells showing profound loss of service with red; one can then focus on driving red and yellow cells to green. Changes to the redundancy arrangement, service switchover/recovery time, and other design attributes can be considered to make the system's architecture and design more compliant with the system's reliability expectations and requirements.

In addition to considering module failures, one can complete a similar analysis for planned activities like software patch, software upgrade, and different system hardware growth scenarios. Each procedure of interest is shown on a separate row, and the nature and duration of service impact caused by successful execution of the procedure is captured in respective cells. Acceptability of each procedure's service impact can then be assessed against the system's requirements and expectations. Note that brief service impacts associated with planned activities may be more acceptable for some systems because planned activities can be scheduled into convenient (e.g., off-peak, low-usage) times.

7.4   AVAILABILITY MODELING

A simple mathematical definition of availability is:

$$Availability = \frac{Uptime}{Uptime + Downtime}$$

Downtime for modules arranged in series can generally be combined to roughly estimate system availability as:

$$Availability_{System} = \frac{525,960 - \sum_{Modules} Annualized Module Downtime}{525,960}$$

525,960 is the number of minutes in an average year (365.25 days per year times 24 hours a day times 60 minutes per hour). Per-module downtime can be crudely estimated as

$$Downtime_{Annualized} = CriticalFailureRate_{Annualized} * TypicalOutageDuration$$

For example, if a software module fails about twice a year and it typically takes 15 minutes of outage time to restore service, then the annualized module downtime is 30 minutes (2 fails per year times 15 outage minutes per failure).

If the module being considered is redundant or highly available, then the typical outage duration should be the short time required for the system to automatically detect the failure, isolate it to the appropriate recoverable unit, and execute the proper recovery mechanism. Outages that are not successfully recovered automatically will be recovered more slowly, often via manual actions of maintenance engineers. The downtime for a highly available module can be roughly estimated as:

$$Downtime_{HAModule} = DowntimeOfAutomaticallyRecovered$$
$$CriticalFailures_{Annualized} + DowntimeOfManual$$
$$RecoveredCriticalFailures_{Annualized}$$

Since traditional coverage is the percentage of critical failures that are automatically detected, isolated, and recovered successfully in the required time (and is estimated as the product of failure coverage and automatic switchover success probability), one can estimate downtime per module as follows:

$$Downtime_{HAModule} = CriticalFailureRate * Coverage *$$
$$AutomaticallyRecoveredOutageDuration +$$
$$CriticalFailureRate * (1 - Coverage) *$$
$$ManuallyRecoveredOutageDuration$$

If *AutomaticallyRecoveredOutageDuration* can be driven below the maximum acceptable service disruption latency, then the successfully recovered critical failures will not be considered outages and thus can be excluded from downtime and availability calculations. Thus, module downtime for systems with rapid automatic failure detection, isolation, and recovery can roughly estimate downtime as:

$$Downtime_{HAModule} = CriticalFailureRate * (1 - Coverage) *$$
$$ManuallyRecoveredOutageDuration$$

This simple algebraic availability modeling is sufficient for rough estimates, but is inadequate for accurately estimating downtime of common redundancy arrangements like active-standby, active-active, or N + K load-sharing because duplex failures and factors like partial capacity loss of failures in load-share redundancy arrangements are not considered. Markov modeling is a best practice for redundant and highly available modules and systems.

7.4.1   Overview of Architecture-Based Markov Availability Modeling

Architecture-based availability models capture the relationships between hardware and software failure rates and other availability-related parameters to understand the likely unplanned service downtime of the system. A best practice for mathematically modeling of system availability is architecture-based continuous-time Markov modeling. This modeling tracks the real-world behavior of a system via a simple conceptual model, such as Figure 7.6. The system begins in the **normal operation** state. At some point a failure occurs, and the system is forced either into an **impaired state** in which service remains available or into a **service-impacted** down state in which service is unavailable.

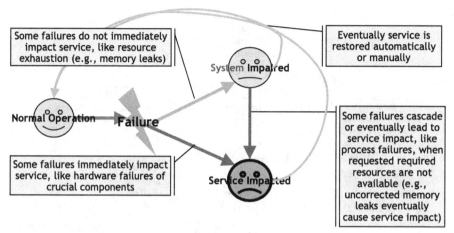

Some failures do not immediately impact service, like resource exhaustion (e.g., memory leaks)

System Impaired

Eventually service is restored automatically or manually

Normal Operation   Failure

Some failures immediately impact service, like hardware failures of crucial components

Service Impacted

Some failures cascade or eventually lead to service impact, like process failures, when requested required resources are not available (e.g., uncorrected memory leaks eventually cause service impact)

Figure 7.6   Highest-Level-Availability Model

If the impaired state is not repaired or recovered, then the system may transition from the impaired state to the service-impacted state. Eventually the failure(s) are repaired or recovered, and the system moves back to the normal operation state.

Conceptually, service availability is the percentage of time the system is in the normal operation state; depending on the definition of *system-impaired* state, time in that state may be fully available, partially available, or unavailable. The percentage of time spent in the service-impacted state (perhaps plus some or all of the system-impaired time) is unavailablity. Continuous-time Markov modeling provides a mathematical technique to quantify the portion of time spent in each of these states, and thus predict service availability.

To better understand Markov availability modeling, consider the example of a simple active-standby system. It doesn't matter if one considers hardware failures or software failures because the modeling is essentially the same, although the various input parameters will be different. Figure 7.7 shows a Markov state transition diagram for an active-standby pair of modules. Architecture-based system-availability models often consider the system availability of each critical simplex or redundant module in the reliability block diagram and sum the module downtimes to estimate the overall system downtime. For example, the downtime for the hypothetical system in Figure 7.5 would be the sum of downtime for simplex module A plus downtime across the pair of active-active modules B, plus downtime across the pair of active-standby modules C.

The generic active-standby Markov state diagram in Figure 7.7 consists of the following system states:

- **State 1—Duplex Operation.** Both active and standby units are functioning properly; system is UP.

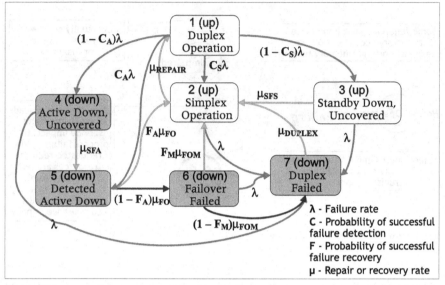

Figure 7.7   General Active-Standby Markov Transition Diagram

- **State 2—Simplex Operation.** One unit is active and functioning properly, and one unit is known to be down (presumably repair of the down unit is planned or in progress); system is UP.

- **State 3—Standby Down, Uncovered.** Active unit is functioning properly but the standby unit has failed silently so neither the system nor human operators are aware that the standby is unavailable to recover service if the active unit fails; system is UP.

- **State 4—Active Down, Uncovered.** Active unit has failed but that failure has not yet been detected, and hence service recovery has not yet been initiated; system is DOWN.

- **State 5—Detected, Active Down.** Active unit has failed, failure has been detected and service recovery has been initiated, but service recovery to standby has not yet completed; system is DOWN.

- **State 6—Failover Failed.** Automatic failover from failed active unit onto standby unit has failed to complete successfully; system is DOWN. Manual recovery is typically required to restore service after failed automatic failover.

- **State 7—Duplex Failed.** Both active and standby units have failed and/ or failed to recover service; system is DOWN. Manual repair is typically required to restore service following duplex failure.

The transitions between the states in Figure 7.7 are mathematically modeled with the following parameters:

- λ—**Failure Rate** gives the rate of service-impacting failures on the active side; this model assumes that the rate of failures that render standby unavailable to recover service is the same as the failure rate of active side. Hardware failure rates are typically expressed as either hours of *mean time between failures (MTBF)* or as *failures per billion hours of operation (FIT)*. Software failure rates are often expressed as critical failures (e.g., crashes or failovers) per system per year.

- C_A—**Failure Coverage Factor on Active Side** gives the probability that a failure on the active side is automatically detected and isolated within a specified time (typically the nominal detection time in the system's robustness budget). Note that *isolated* means that the system correctly diagnoses the failure to the active side, rather than reporting that the failure is on another element or on the standby side.

- C_S—**Failure Coverage Factor on Standby Side** gives the probability that a failure on the standby side is automatically detected and isolated within the specified time. Failure coverage factor on standby side is often lower than active-side failure coverage factor because standby side is often not routinely executing as much functionality of the hardware and software as frequently as on the active side, and thus is less likely to promptly detect a failure.

- μ_{FO}—**Automatic Failover Rate.** Characterizes how fast the system automatically fails over from active unit to standby unit. This time is assumed to include failure detection and isolation latency, as well as failover latency, in this example. As a rate is the mathematical reciprocal of the duration, μ_{FO} = 1/typical_automatic_failover_duration.

- μ_{FOM}—**Manual Failover Rate.** If automatic failover does not complete successfully, then manual intervention by a human operator is required; this parameter estimates the rate of a typical manual recovery. As a rate is the mathematical reciprocal of the duration, μ_{FOM} = 1/typical_manual_failover_duration. The human operator will generally wait significantly longer than the typical automatic failover time to give the system sufficient opportunity to recover automatically. If the system doesn't automatically recover in a reasonable length of time, then the human operator will manually debug the problem, identify an appropriate recovery action, and manually initiate recovery action. Occasionally, the human operator will misdiagnose the problem or other factors will complicate the manual recovery, so manual recoveries will sometimes take longer. Note that availability models deliberately use "typical" or "median" value estimates rather than worst-case values; assuming median values are used, half of the manual failovers will be faster (better) and half will be slower (worse).

- μ_{REPAIR}—**(simplex) Repair Rate.** This parameter estimates the mathematical reciprocal of the typical time required to complete a repair of a failed active or standby unit (i.e., μ_{REPAIR} = **1/repair_time**). For hardware failures, repair rate typically captures the time to deliver spare hardware to failed system, replace the failed FRU, restart software, and return the module to service. For software failures, the repair rate typically captures troubleshooting and restarting application plus platform software.

- μ_{DUPLEX}—**Duplex Failure Repair Rate.** This parameter estimates the mathematical reciprocal of the typical time to recover from so-called *duplex failure*, in which both active and standby units have failed (i.e., μ_{DUPLEX} = **1/duplex_failure_repair_time**). While the time to repair a single FRU is likely to be the same if one FRU or two FRUs have failed, the time to repair a duplex software failure or to repair the software portion of a hybrid hardware plus software failure is likely to be longer than the simplex repair rate for software.

- μ_{SFA}—**Uncovered Error Detection Rate ACTIVE SIDE.** This parameter estimates the mathematical reciprocal of the typical time to detect an uncovered failure on the active side. Operationally, if the system fails to automatically detect a failure, then eventually the failure will be manually detected by a human operator, alarmed by adjacent systems, or reported by end users.

- μ_{SFS}—**Uncovered Error Detection Rate STANDBY SIDE.** This parameter estimates the mathematical reciprocal of the typical time to detect an uncovered failure on the standby side. Since the standby unit is not providing service to end users or continuously interacting with adjacent systems, uncovered failures on standby side elements are often detected via explicit manual tests, such as routine execution of the standby unit via routine manual switchover. In a manual switchover, the human operator will command the system to switch service to the standby side to verify proper operation of the standby unit. If the standby unit is not operational, then service will not be successfully recovered onto the standby unit, so the human operator will switch service back to the previously active unit and schedule repair of the failed standby unit.

- F_A—**AUTOMATIC Failover Success Probability.** Automatic failover is a complex operation, and occasionally service will not failover successfully; this parameter estimates the probability that automatic switchover will succeed.

- F_M—**MANUAL Failover Success Probability.** Troubleshooting failures that were not properly recovered automatically by the system will take diligent effort by a maintenance engineer and will typically take the time estimated as the mathematical reciprocal of μ_{FOM} (Manual Failover Rate). This parameter (F_M) estimates the probability that manual recovery actions will successfully restore service in approximately the typical manual recovery time ($1/\mu_{FOM}$). "Hard" problems may take significantly longer than this typical time. One minus manual failover success probability ($1 - F_M$) events will be hard and take substantially longer than the typical manual failover latency. For simplicity, the additional latency for hard problems is assumed to be the same as the duplex failure recovery time ($1/\mu_{\text{DUPLEX}}$).

To vastly simplify modeling calculations, all time-related input parameters are converted to hourly rates. Thus, a duration (e.g., **typical_manual_failover_ duration**) of 15 minutes translates to an hourly rate of 4 (60 minutes per hour divided by 15 minutes per event equals 4 events per hour). Likewise, failure rates expressed as hours of mean time between failures or failures per year or FITs are translated to failures per hour.

Although hardware-specific and software-specific failure rates, recovery latencies, and other modeling parameters are often quite different, Table 7.2 gives plausible system-level parameters that cover both hardware and software failures that are used in this example.

Table 7.2 Nominal Input Parameter Values for Example Generic Active-Standby Model

Assumed input parameters			
Parameter		Value	Comment
HOURLY Failure Rate	λ	0.00045631	Assume 4 fails per year
Coverage Factor on Active Side	C_A	95.0%	Assume good coverage factor on active side
Coverage Factor on Standby Side	C_S	90.0%	Assume slightly worse coverage factor on standby side
HOURLY Automatic Hardware Failover Rate	μ_{FO}	240	Assume 15-second automatic failover
HOURLY MANUAL Hardware Failover Rate	μ_{FOM}	4	Assume 15-minute manual failover
HOURLY (Simplex) Repair Rate	μ_{REPAIR}	1	Assume 60-minute simplex repair time
HOURLY Duplex Failure Repair Rate	μ_{DUPLEX}	0.25	Assume 4-hour duplex repair time
HOURLY Uncovered Fault Detection Rate ACTIVE SIDE	μ_{SFA}	2	Assume 30 minutes to detect silent failure on active side
HOURLY Uncovered Fault Detection Rate STANDBY SIDE	μ_{SFS}	0.04166667	Assume 24 hours to detect silent failure on standby side
AUTOMATIC Failover Success Probability	F_A	99.0%	Assume automatic failover is very reliable
MANUAL Failover Success Probability	F_M	99.5%	… and manual failover is even more reliable

A continuous-time Markov model can be created for the state transition diagram in Figure 7.7 to produce the results in Table 7.3. One can solve simple Markov models with a spreadsheet or with more powerful mathematical programs that support construction and solution of Markov models. Construction and solution of continuous-time Markov models is beyond the scope of this book; interested readers should consult appropriate references like [Trivendi02].

Table 7.3 shows that the system is predicted to be available (up) 99.9982% of the time. The system is predicted to be unavailable 0.0018% of the time, or 9.55 down-minutes per system per year. The bulk of this predicted downtime is from uncovered downtime of active unit, meaning that the active unit has failed but the system did not promptly and accurately detect the failure. The distribution of service downtime is visualized in Figure 7.8.

Conveniently, each of these downtime categories represents easy-to-understand error states, and the time spent in each of these error states can be reduced by appropriate investment in features and testing. Consider each down state separately.

- **Covered downtime.** This state captures the time spent in successful automatic failure detection, isolation, and recovery. Time in this state is reduced by reducing critical failure rate or reducing automatic failover latency (which is logically the sum of automatic failure detection and isolation time plus automatic failover time). Note that the time spent in the covered downtime state can often be excluded from availability calculations if latency of successful failure detection, isolation, and recovery is shorter than the maximum acceptable service disruption latency.

- **Uncovered downtime.** This state captures the time spent in uncovered or silent failure. Time in this state is reduced primarily by improving failure coverage and reducing critical failure rate.

- **Failed failover downtime.** This state captures the time spent when automatic recoveries have failed and manual recovery is required. Time in this state is reduced by improving automatic switchover success probability and by improving manual recovery procedures following unsuccessful automatic recovery.

- **Duplex downtime.** This state captures the time spent in the rare situation of a dual or duplex failure. Typically, a duplex failure occurs because there was an uncovered or silent failure on one of the redundant elements and this was not discovered until the other unit failed. Duplex downtime also accrues if a failure occurs on the redundant unit before the failed active unit can be repaired. Duplex downtime is reduced by improving failure coverage, such as via routine switchovers that verify that standby elements are fully operational, and through good sparing and maintenance policies to assure that failures are promptly repaired to minimize time in simplex operation.

Table 7.3 Downtime Prediction for Example Generic Active-Standby Model

Availability of generic active-standby model	Uptime				Downtime				
	Duplex uptime	(Covered) simplex uptime	Uncovered (silent) simplex	**Overall uptime**	Uncovered downtime	Covered downtime	Failed Failover downtime	Duplex downtime	**Overall downtime**
State number	1	2	3		4	5	6	7	
State name	Duplex operation	Simplex operation	Standby down, uncovered		Active down, uncovered	Detected active down	Failover failed	Duplex failed	
Annualized minutes	524902.80	479.04	568.62	525950.45	5.99	1.00	0.60	1.97	9.55
Percentage	**99.7990%**	**0.0911%**	**0.1081%**	**99.9982%**	**0.0011%**	**0.0002%**	**0.0001%**	**0.0004%**	**0.0018%**

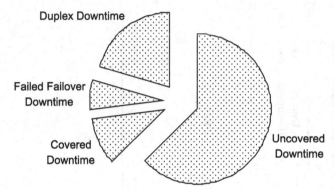

Figure 7.8   Classification of Predicted Downtime

As stated in the beginning of this chapter, the four most influential product-attributable modeling parameters are often:

1. Critical failure rate
2. Failure coverage factor
3. Switchover latency
4. Switchover success probability

Each of these parameters is considered in a separate section.

7.4.1.1   Critical Failure Rate

Critical failures, by definition, impact the ability of a module to provide the module's primary functionality. The rate of critical failures is the frequency of these events, and thus determines how often the robustness mechanisms protecting a particular module should be activated to automatically detect, isolate, and recover from failure.

Critical failure events are often factored to:

- **Hardware failures.** Hardware fails for well-understood physical reasons (detailed in Section 3.5, "Error Category: Field-Replaceable Unit (FRU) Hardware"). Hardware failure rates are minimized by well-known hardware design-for-reliability practices (e.g., electrical and thermal derating, environmental stress testing) and high-quality manufacturing processes. Hardware failure rates are well characterized by hardware failure rate predictions and from field return data, and are generally smaller than the overall software failure rate.

- **Platform software failures.** Modern systems typically leverage third-party operating system, middleware, database, and other platform software. This platform software has often been widely deployed and accrued millions of hours of service, and thus is often very reliable and has a very low failure rate. Operationally, a system's platform software failure rate is primarily improved by installing software maintenance releases from suppliers of platform software modules that should fix residual software defects. Size and complexity of platform software will vary between modules and between systems, yet platform software failure rate is often lower than the failure rate of the hardware hosting the platform software and far lower than the application software failure rate.

- **Application software failures.** Application software changes with each major and minor release, and unlike platform software it is less likely to have the benefit of millions of hours of service to drive software maturity. Thus, more high-severity software defects are likely to remain in application software than in platform software. These residual software defects (detailed in Section 3.6, "Error Category: Programming Errors," Section 3.7, "Error Category: Data Error," and elsewhere in Chapter 3) can cause failures when activated in field operation. Application software failures often significantly outnumber both platform software failures and hardware failures.

Figure 7.9 illustrates the sensitivity of critical failure rate on downtime of the sample active-standby pair. Note that doubling the critical failure rate more than doubles system downtime because of the increased risk that the standby unit will have failed and be down when the active unit fails, called a *duplex failure*.

Application software failure rates are reduced via eliminating residual software defects using the following techniques:

- **Good development processes and practices.** Comprehensive, consistent, and controlled requirements, architecture, interface, and design documentation is the foundation for high-quality software. Qualified

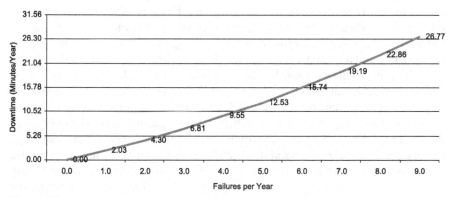

Figure 7.9 Failure Rate Sensitivity Analysis

and trained staff, good development processes and management, and other factors contribute to the creation of high-quality software with few residual defects.

- **Static and dynamic analysis tools.** A variety of software tools are available to detect errors in software source code, from compilers and linkers, to sophisticated static and dynamic analysis tools. It is cheap and fast to find defects via software tools, and thus development teams should take full advantage of available tools to identify (and then fix) as many errors as possible in the coding phase.
- **Code reviews and inspections.** Code reviews and inspections are a common technique for identifying software defects.
- **Testing.** Unit testing, integration testing, feature testing, robustness testing, stability testing, and other testing strategies are a best practice for identifying software defects.
- **Root-cause analysis and corrective actions.** Inevitably some defects will escape to the field. After these defects are exposed in the field, they should be promptly debugged and corrected. Root-cause analysis should be completed for critical failures to identify how each defect was able to escape to the field and what corrective actions can be taken to prevent similar defects from escaping.
- **Other quality improvement activities.** Quality assurance activities will identify quality improvement programs that address specific product development weaknesses or improve development efficiency. Many of these activities directly or indirectly reduce failure rates by eliminating residual defects earlier in the development process so fewer defects escape to the field, and thus customers experience a lower critical failure rate.

7.4.1.2 Failure Coverage Factor

Failure coverage factor is the probability that a system with automatically detect and correctly isolate a failure rapidly. Failures that are not properly covered are called *uncovered*, or sometimes *silent, sleeping* or similar euphemisms. Failure coverage factor is critical for a high-availability system because redundancy and automatic recovery mechanisms are of less value if the system doesn't activate them promptly after a failure occurs. Failure coverage factors will vary with the nature of the failure, and are generally estimated separately for hardware failures and software failures. Failure coverage factors may vary across modules, depending on the nature of the modules and effectiveness of audits and other robustness-improving mechanisms. Since failure coverage factors generally improve as systems mature and robustness mechanisms are improved, expanded, and fine-tuned, one generally observes that the failure coverage factor for mature software is higher than for new or substantially reworked modules.

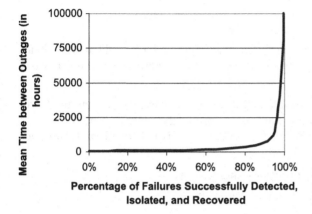

Figure 7.10   Mean Time between Outages as a Function of Coverage Factor

Uncovered (silent) failures are the events that are not automatically detected and isolated successfully by the system, and hence must be recovered manually. These uncovered events often contribute the bulk of the service downtime. A critical failure event will escalate into a service outage if it isn't detected, isolated, and recovered within the maximum acceptable service disruption time. The relationship between traditional coverage factor (product of failure coverage and automatic switchover success) and the mean time between outages is highly nonlinear. Figure 7.10 illustrates the nonlinear impact of coverage on mean time between outages for a system that experiences one critical failure, such as the crash of a required software process, every month. The striking feature of this graph is the nonlinear response of mean time between outages to increasing robustness effectiveness (coverage); as the coverage approaches perfect (100%), outages become much rarer. Obviously, if coverage were perfect, meaning that all failures were automatically detected, isolated, and recovered with negligible service impact, then there would be no service outages, and hence mean time between outages would be infinite, as shown in Figure 7.10.

Hardware failure coverage (probability of automatic detection of hardware failures) is primarily a function of hardware design and platform software. Hardware failure coverage is improved by:

- Well-designed hardware that provides driver software with visibility to all circuits and devices
- Well-designed software drivers that carefully monitor interactions with hardware devices, including carefully checking status codes, parity, checksums, and other indications for signs of failure or improper behavior
- Guard timers on hardware-related operations to assure that nonresponsive hardware devices are promptly detected

- Hardware audits that periodically verify that hardware components and modules are functioning properly
- Hardware fault insertion testing (see Section 11.5.1, "Hardware Fault Insertion") to verify that hardware failure coverage mechanisms work rapidly and reliably

Software failure coverage—the probability of successful automatic detection and isolation of software failures—is primarily a function of application and platform software. Software failure coverage is improved via techniques like:

- Heartbeating of key processes and systems
- Process, thread, and resource monitoring
- Data integrity monitoring
- Software fault insertion testing (see Section 11.5.2, "Software Fault Insertion")

7.4.1.3   Switchover Latency

Systems with redundancy must include mechanisms to switch traffic between the redundant modules. This switch can generally be activated either via manual command or via an automatic mechanism. This book uses *switchover* to refer to switching explicitly activated by command. Switchovers are routinely executed on production systems to verify that standby elements are fully operational, during software upgrades to minimize service disruption, and during manual recovery. *Failover* is used to refer to redundancy switches activated automatically by a system's robustness mechanisms. Fundamentally, the same redundancy switching mechanisms are used; the difference is whether the switch was explicitly requested by an external user or automatically initiated by the system itself. Since it is much easier to measure the latency of a redundancy switch that is activated by an external user (e.g., a human tester or test automation script), this book generally refers to *switchover latency* as the value that is measured in the lab. This book assumes that latency for redundancy switching is essentially the same for both externally triggered (switchover) versus internally triggered (failover) switches. If this assumption is not valid, then system architects should have clear understanding of why not, and appropriate corrections can be applied when budgeting and managing service disruption latencies.

Switchover latency is a function of two characteristics:

1. **Platform switchover latency.** Platform software is responsible for promoting the standby unit to *active* and for redirecting traffic to the promoted unit. This latency may vary by blade type and is likely to be the same for all applications running on that blade type.
2. **Application switchover latency.** Application architecture determines how fast a promoted application instance will be made ready to deliver

service to end users; this will vary by blade type, and may vary by application configuration, such as the number of active or provisioned users.

Switchover/recovery latency is optimized by carefully selecting appropriate units of recovery (see Chapter 4, "Failure Containment and Redundancy"), and testing those mechanisms (see Chapter 11, "Robustness and Stability Testing") to optimize performance and reliability. In some cases, the failure effect may be so profound or switchover latency so long that previously active client sessions are lost or terminated, and thus additional latency (and perhaps user intervention) is necessary to restore user service, but this should be rare.

7.4.1.4 Switchover Success Probability

Successfully switching service from a failed module to a redundant module is crucial to rapidly recovering service after failure. Since the failed module is likely to be in a degraded and abnormal state, the switching mechanism and recovery logic must be very robust, and operate successfully across the range of possible module failure scenarios. Since critical software failures may be more likely when the system is operating under heavy load, redundancy mechanisms must reliably operate under full engineered load.

Automatic switchover success is generally a function of two characteristics:

1. **Platform switchover success.** Platform software must robustly switch application service to redundant unit for any conceivable application or platform software failure or hardware failure.

2. **Application switchover success.** Standby application instance must robustly be promoted to active regardless of the purported or actual state of the previously active instance or other system characteristics.

Automatic switchover success is less than perfect (100%) because switchover is typically triggered after a system has experienced a critical failure, and thus the system is in a compromised and unexpected (and perhaps even unknown) state. Automatic switchover success is statistically verified by attempting large numbers of switchovers in a wide variety of system states with heavy traffic load.

7.5 PLANNED DOWNTIME

Downtime for successful and unsuccessful planned and procedural activities is generally estimated with a simple algebraic model. Throughout a system's useful service life, numerous software patches, updates, and upgrades will be applied, some hardware growth may occur, and other significant planned actions will occur. Unlike random failure events that are unpredictable, planned events often occur regularly and are scheduled weeks or even months in advance. Most planned events will complete successfully and experience the expected service impact (which may be no service impact). A small portion of these events may fail, and could thus accrue unexpected service downtime. Planned downtime can thus be estimated by enumerating all planned events that may impact service with successful or unsuccessful execution, and then completing the following for each identified procedure:

1. Estimate the number of times this procedure will be executed during the system's useful service life. System's designed useful service life will vary from application to application; 3-, 5-, or 10-year service-life expectations are common for many computer-based systems.

2. Estimate the normal duration of service impact for successfully executed procedure, often 0 seconds of impact per event.

3. Estimate the percentage of executions that will successfully complete with normal service impact. Success probabilities often vary inversely with complexity and magnitude of system change; for example, success probability for applying patches or hot-fixes is generally higher than for installing major system upgrades.

4. Estimate the median or nominal service disruption latency for exceptional procedural execution events that do not complete with the expected service disruption time.

One can easily construct a simple spreadsheet to estimate the accumulated service downtime for successful and unsuccessful planned events over the system's designed service life; the accumulated result can then be divided by the system's designed service life to normalize the result into annualized downtime. An example prediction is shown in Table 7.4.

Service downtime per successful event is a function of system's architecture and design. Success probability is influenced by factors including:

- **Automation of procedures.** Less direct human involvement means lower risk of human error.

- **Simplicity of procedures.** Simpler procedures are more likely to succeed. For example, a software upgrade that does not require a database schema change and data migration is more likely to succeed than an upgrade that has major database changes.

- **Quality of scripts.** Scripts that carefully verify initial conditions and check all status conditions are more likely to be executed without failure.

- **Fault tolerance of scripts.** Support of rollback, safe stopping points, and other failure tolerance and containment techniques reduces risk of service-disrupting failures.

- **Quality of generic and customer-specific MOP documentation.** Clear, complete, and correct documentation that has been thoroughly tested reduces risk of human error when executing procedures.

Table 7.4 Example Planned Downtime Model

Nominal downtime for standalone (Nongeoredundant) network element					
Event	Events in 5 years	Success probability	Down minutes per SUCCESSFUL event	Down minutes per UNSUCCESSFUL event	5 Year down minutes
Nominally product-attributable planned and procedural events					
Software update (includes security and reliability patches)	10	99.5%	0.2	15	2.74
Operating system update (includes security and reliability patches)	5	99.5%	0.2	30	1.75
Software upgrade (major release)	5	99.0%	0.2	30	1.50
Hardware growth	2	99.0%	0	20	0.40
Operating system upgrade (major release)	1	99.5%	1	60	0.30
Total 5-year maintenance events:	**7**		**Total 5-year downtime:**		**1.90**
Annualized maintenance events:	**1.4**	**Annualized planned maintenance downtime:**			**0.38**

- **Robustness testing of procedure.** Has quality and fault tolerance of scripts been thoroughly tested? Thorough testing of likely failure scenarios assures robustness and completeness of scripts and written procedures.

See Section 5.11, "Procedural Considerations," for further information on reducing downtime associated with planned and procedural activities.

7.6 PROBLEMS

The following problems consider a "target system" identified by the instructor:

1. Construct a reliability block diagram of the target system.
2. Construct failure mode effects analysis table for the target system.
3. Explain how failure coverage factor impacts service availability.
4. Explain how a Markov transition diagram for an active-active redundancy arrangement would differ from Figure 7.7—General Active-Standby Markov Transition Diagram.

7.7 FOR FURTHER STUDY

For further information, readers should consider [Trivedi02], [Pukite98], [Bauer09], or one of the other references available on reliability modeling.

Part Three

Design for Reliability

Chapter 8

Reliability Requirements

The high-level qualitative reliability expectations of high-availability systems typically cover two characteristics:

1. **Service availability**, such as *no single failure shall cause an unacceptable service disruption and the system will rarely be unavailable for service*, and *it shall be possible to execute all routine maintenance activities without causing unacceptable service disruption.*

2. **Service reliability**, such as *the probability that user service will be delivered with specified quality shall be acceptably high.*

As these expectations are not precise enough to be verifiable, more detailed reliability requirements must be crafted to drive detailed design and formal verification; this chapter covers how to formulate such requirements.

8.1 BACKGROUND

High-level reliability requirements primarily focus on two key points:

1. **Characterize "acceptable" service impacts** within which the system's robustness mechanisms automatically recover from inevitable failures. Note that acceptable service impacts may be different for unplanned failures and planned activities like software upgrades; thus different service impact requirements may be defined for planned activities. Formal definitions of *acceptable* service impact are used to set pass criteria for robustness testing and verification of planned activities, and hence are formally verified when executing those test campaigns.

2. **Quantitative service availability and reliability expectations.** Service availability is often quantified as 99.9% (three 9's), 99.99% (four 9's), 99.999% (five 9's), and so on, and service reliability is often quantified as defects per million (DPM) operations. While service reliability can be measured as DPM during stability testing, service availability is

Design for Reliability: Information and Computer-Based Systems, by Eric Bauer
Copyright © 2010 Institute of Electrical and Electronics Engineers

impractical to directly verify through formal testing. Thus, service availability is generally verified through modeling, and reliability requirements often specify quantitative minimum performance metrics of various key reliability-impacting parameters that can be easily measured during robustness testing, like minimum probability of switchover success.

Reliability requirements are directly driven by a rigorous definition of service outage because outage downtime directly contributes to service unavailability and the maximum acceptable service impact implicitly defines the minimum chargeable service outage.

8.2 DEFINING SERVICE OUTAGES

Important systems delivering key services will be carefully managed and measured. A primary measure of the system is whether it is fully operational (up) or in a partially degraded or totally unavailable state. In some cases, this metric will be formally defined in contractual service-level agreements and financial penalties may be invoked if the system doesn't deliver a minimum level of service. Thus, the starting point for availability requirements is to clearly characterize exactly how customers will define and measure outages and compute service downtime. Observed service availability is driven by several factors:

- Primary service offered by the system
- Formal definition of outage or downtime, including minimum chargeable capacity or functionality loss and how partial outages will be prorated
- Understanding how unavailability events will be measured and how service unavailability will be calculated

Each of these factors is discussed individually.

8.2.1 Defining Primary Services

Chapter 2, "System Basics," explained that systems deliver at least one primary service to end users or client systems, and are likely to expose functionality to add or configure users, to manage inevitable faults and failures, to monitor system usage and performance, and so on. As different services offered to different users and entities may feature different grades of service, it is essential to clearly articulate the primary service interface that will be addressed by reliability and availability requirements. Service expectations of non–primary service interfaces are likely to be somewhat lower, and thus it is often not necessary to invest expense and diligence to drive non–primary service interfaces to the same reliability requirements as the primary service interface(s).

All highly available systems will focus on the primary service interface used by target customers; some system suppliers will also consider primary interfaces used by enterprise OAM&P staff to assure that the system can be robustly operated 24/7/365. For some systems, service availability must be carefully considered for other interfaces as well, such as support for regulatory or compliance mechanisms.

As an example, consider the interfaces offered by a hypothetical voice-mail system. The obvious primary service interfaces of a voice-mail system are:

- Caller's interface to hear recorded announcement and prompts to record voice messages
- Subscriber's interface to retrieve messages and record announcements

The following four service interfaces are likely to be exposed to OAM&P staff:

1. **Provisioning interface,** to add new subscribers, reset passwords, and so on. Note that the inability to add new subscribers in real time (e.g., activate a new mobile device or a web-based service account) may prompt a customer to abandon the purchase and go to a competitor. Thus, it may be as important to reliably add new customers as it is to reliably deliver service to existing customers.

2. **Management visibility and control interface** offers OAM&P staff accurate real-time status of the operational behavior of the target system. If the management visibility and controllability is compromised, then the enterprise might be forced to rely on customer support calls to detect service impairments or outages, and risk longer service outages.

3. **Interfaces for routine maintenance, network planning, and operations items** are also exposed to OAM&P staff and other systems, but they generally do not require exceptional service availability.

4. **Interfaces to legal or regulatory compliance systems** must be considered on an application-by-application and customer-by-customer basis, but are not likely to require exceptional service availability unless they relate directly to public safety.

Clearly, the quality of service offered by the subscriber's interface both to retrieve their messages and for self-care is crucial to their perception of overall service quality, but they are certainly concerned about the ability of callers to successfully deposit messages for them as well. Less obvious is the importance of service availability of the provisioning interface exposed to enterprise OAM&P staff. If the provisioning interface is unavailable, then new subscribers cannot be added in real time, and hence the potential customers may not be able to activate service instantly, so they might simply go to a competitor whose systems are operational so that they can complete their purchase or subscription in real time and start consuming the application/service of interest.

A common pattern is that when services are new, novel, or free, then service availability expectations often start lower, but as the service becomes more common, mature, or expensive, then customers often expect it to be virtually flawless. Increasingly, customers expect the end user service to be highly available, but also the provisioning interface to add new users must be highly available. For example, if a customer is in a retail store buying a wireless device, then she expects the new device to be activated as she completes the purchase so she can use it as she leaves the store.

8.2.2 Formally Defining Outages and Maximum Acceptable Service Disruptions

Best practice is to formally define service outages so that system architects, developers, system testers, quality and support engineers, and enterprise customers agree on precisely what events should and should not be classified as outages. This formal definition should directly drive test pass criteria for robustness testing and classification of field failure events, and indirectly drives reliability analysis activities like failure mode and effect analysis (FMEA) and reliability modeling. This formal outage definition should also be aligned with the outage definition used in contractual service-level agreements for service availability.

In some cases, industry standards offer detailed service outage definitions, such as TL 9000 in the telecommunications industry [TL9000]. TL 9000 gives formal service outage definitions for a wide range of product categories; as an example, consider product category 1.2.7, application servers for "Equipment that provides IP based multimedia services" such as instant messaging. Total outage for application servers is defined by TL 9000 as:

Total loss of ability to provide IP based multimedia services

Partial outage for application servers is defined as:

- *Loss of more than 5% of the IP based multimedia services*
- *Loss of stable service sessions*
- *Total loss of one or more but not all services*
- *System congestion which impacts greater than 5% of all session set-up attempts*
- *85% or more of the service subscribers experience a session delay of 3 seconds or greater for a period longer than 30 seconds*
- *Interface switchovers lasting longer than 60 milliseconds*
- *Total loss of one or more OA&M functions (default weight is 5%)*
- *Total loss of visibility from Element Management System (default weight is 10%)*

Application server and *outage* definitions for all other product categories are also covered by the following two stipulations:

- *Unless otherwise stated [above], an **unscheduled** event must be longer than 15 seconds to be considered [a Network Element] Impact outage*

- *Unless otherwise stated [above], a **scheduled** event must be longer than 15 seconds to be considered [a Network Element] Impact outage*

One can easily see how the concrete outage definition above can directly drive pass criteria for robustness testing of an application like an instant messaging system. Likewise, formal outage definitions for other system types can drive pass criteria for robustness testing of other systems.

An outage definition should be translated into a formal requirement to drive design and testing, such as:

No single hardware or software failure shall cause a service disruption of greater than 15 seconds for more than 10% of active system users.

Note that this requirement was narrowed to hardware or software failures because a single network or power failure can render service unavailable to users, but those events are outside the scope of product requirements.

8.2.3   Measuring and Calculating Availability

Good outage definitions should be well aligned with the tools and processes that will be eventually used to measure unavailability. Section 12.1.1, "Measuring Service Availability," describes specific techniques that can be used to measure service availability. While the outage definition will not generally specify the specific service assurance product or method to use for gathering and analyzing field data, it is useful for system testers, especially robustness and stability testers, to use the same service assurance product(s) and methods to determine whether a chargeable outage occurs when executing each robustness test case and during stability test runs.

8.3   SERVICE AVAILABILITY REQUIREMENTS

Service availability requirements are generally structured as both of the following:

1. High-level requirement that ultimately drives service-level agreements for service availability
2. Detailed requirements that drive design and testing of the target system

Each of these is considered separately.

8.3.1   High-Level Service Availability Requirements

Having defined events accrue downtime, one can then set a service availability requirement by addressing three questions:

1. **What types of downtime events are covered?** Outage events are typically triggered by one of two broad categories of events.

- **Unplanned events** cover hardware, software, procedural, and other failures.
- **Planned events** cover successful scheduled OAM&P activities like software upgrades and system growth.

Availability requirements often implicitly cover only unplanned events, but requirements should explicitly define whether requirements cover only unplanned events or unplanned plus planned events. Unsuccessful planned events, such as unsuccessful upgrades, can cause service downtime, and they could plausibly be covered in either category.

2. **The scope of system outage attributability** generally falls into one of three general categories:

   (a) **Software** considers only service downtime attributed to failures of application software, rather than those triggered by underlying hardware or operating system (often furnished by enterprise or system integrator), errors by enterprise staff operating the system, or external causes like power failures. This is may be used for software applications that run on system hardware furnished by the enterprise customer.

   (b) **Product attributable** considers only service downtime attributed to the system's software, hardware, documentation, integration, or support, rather than errors attributed to enterprise staff operating the system or external causes. This scope is common for integrated systems that include application software integrated with target hardware.

   (c) **All causes** considers downtime caused by software, hardware, human, or other factors broadly under the control of the enterprise operating the system; force majeur causes like fires, floods, earthquakes, terrorist acts, and so on are generally excluded from consideration.

3. **Are prorated partial outage events counted, or are only total service outage events considered?** For large systems, partial capacity loss and partial functionality loss events are more common than total outage events because relatively few failure scenarios in a well-designed large system can impact all users or all functionality. If partial outages are counted, then the formal outage definition should clearly define both the minimum impact of a chargeable partial outage and how it will be prorated.

4. **What is the maximum annualized per-system downtime requirement?** Downtime is often prorated to include partial outages and is generally normalized on a per-system basis. Note that many systems support different configuration options with different system availability expectations. Best practice is to explicitly specify availability requirements for

each configuration with different redundancy arrangements, such as standalone, active–cold standby, active–hot standby or active-active. Although it is often easier to measure downtime events, maximum downtime requirements are traditionally framed as service availability percentage rather than unavailability. Since most readers cannot easily map a number of nines service availability rating to a maximum number of annualized, prorated minutes of downtime, it is best to include both a service availability percentage and the equivalent annualized downtime value.

Thus, a service availability requirement can be framed as:

1. **The high availability (active/standby) configuration of the system shall achieve product-attributable, prorated service availability for both planned and unplanned events of at least 99.999% service availability (<5.3 annualized down-minutes) using TL 9000 product-attributable service outage definition.**

2. **The normal (standalone) configuration of the system shall achieve product-attributable, prorated service availability for both planned and unplanned events of at least 99.95% service availability (<263 annualized down-minutes) using TL 9000 product-attributable service outage definition.**

If an industry standard or technical reference cannot be used to specify outage counting rules, then the requirements should explicitly define the outage/downtime counting rules.

8.4 DETAILED SERVICE AVAILABILITY REQUIREMENTS

It is impractical to directly verify high-level service availability requirements via lab testing, and thus one typically relies on mathematical modeling to establish detailed service availability requirements to assure the feasibility and likelihood of achieving the requirement. Detailed and directly verifiable service availability requirements fall into the following broad categories:

- Behavioral requirements
- Failure rate requirements
- Latency requirements
- Probabilistic requirements

8.4.1 Behavioral Requirements

Behavioral requirements capture system behaviors or characteristics that are expected in highly available systems and assumed by mathematical modeling. As many of these assumed behaviors and characteristics should be verified as is practical. Sample behavioral requirements include:

- **All recovery actions are automatic.** Automatic actions can generally be triggered faster than human maintenance engineers can troubleshoot a problem and manually initiate recovery actions. Thus, to assure the shortest possible service disruption, recovery actions should be automatic whenever possible. In addition, manual actions add expense for enterprise OAM&P staff and inconvenience for end users. For example, no one wants to have to manually reset clocks on appliances and other electronics throughout their house after a power disruption. Manual action by enterprise staff should not be required for recovery service following failure of system software or hardware. This maps to a behavioral requirement such as this:

  System shall recover automatically from any single hardware, software, power, network, or procedural error.

- **No persistent impact from failure event.** There should be no persistent secondary failures, either within the failed system or in adjacent systems. Hardware and system data are typically vulnerable to persistent failures, and thus one should assure that a primary event other than a hardware failure does not cause system data to be lost or cascade to a hardware failure. For example, a power surge, undervoltage, or power outage should not cause data stored on disks to be lost, damaged, or destroyed and thus require restoration from backup; or disk heads to crash on hard disks or other hardware components to fail permanently and thus require FRU replacement. Testable requirements can be written explicitly stipulating that key persistent data is not compromised during failure, such as:

  No failure shall result in users' personal data (e.g., address book, call log) or configuration settings (e.g., call forwarding programming) being changed or lost.

Software patches, updates, upgrades, and retrofits, as well as hardware growth, are part of normal system maintenance and operations. Many enterprises schedule these activities for off-hours maintenance windows and notify users in advance that service may be limited or unavailable during that period due to planned maintenance activity. Although it is unquestionably simpler, cheaper, and less risky to perform maintenance activities on a system that is offline, 24/7/365 systems and services must be continually available, and thus cannot generally schedule their service to be offline. To meet these continuous availability expectations, 24/7/365 systems add further behavioral requirements:

- **It shall be possible to replace any FRU without unacceptable service disruption.**
- **Applying and activating patches, updates, and upgrades shall not impact service.**
- **It shall be possible to grow the system without unacceptable service disruption.**

- **It shall be possible to degrow the system without unacceptable service disruption.**

8.4.2 Failure Rate Requirements

Critical failure rates are highly influential parameters, and should be considered separately for hardware and software. Hardware failure rates can be predicted via well-known methodologies like MIL-HDBK-217F [MIL217F] or Telcordia SR-332 [SR332], and thus requirements can be created for hardware failure rates to be less than a particular value as predicted using a specified methodology. Software failure rate prediction is inherently a softer subject, and it is harder to accurately apply software reliability prediction methodologies to software development teams than it is to apply hardware reliability prediction methodologies to hardware development teams. Nevertheless, acceptable software quality and/or maximum critical software failure rates should be addressed either via software reliability requirements or the quality plan, and those should directly and quantitatively drive the release criteria covered in Section 11.9.

High-level maximum critical failure rate requirements may be specified for a system such as:

- **No hardware FRU shall have a predicted failure rate yielding a predicted annual return rate of greater than 5%.**
- **Rate of service-impacting critical software failures (both covered and uncovered) shall not exceed one event per system per month.**

8.4.3 Latency Requirements

Latency requirements should specify the maximum latency for influential reliability-related parameters, such as:

- Switchover latency for service-critical modules/FRUs
- Restart latency for restartable modules/FRUs
- System restart latency

Ideally, all system latencies included in availability models should be covered by latency requirements; the specified latency value should be used in the models; and system testing should formally verify each value.

8.4.4 Probabilistic Availability-Related Requirements

Just as it is unrealistic to expect that any complex software system is completely free of residual defects, it is unrealistic to believe that 100% of all possible failures will be detected, isolated, and recovered automatically within the maximum acceptable service disruption latency. A more realistic expectation is that the probability of successfully detecting, isolating, and recovering will be very high, and that system testers can analyze their robustness test results to determine if a minimum quantified probability of success has been achieved. Best practice is to establish requirements for all probabilistic system parameters used in availability models, such as:

- **At least [Value]% of likely critical software failures shall be detected, isolated, and recovered automatically.** [Value] may be 80% to 90% for early product releases, and should grow to 98% to 99% as the system matures.

- **At least [Value]% of likely critical hardware failures shall be detected, isolated, and recovered automatically.** [Value] may be 80% to 90% for early hardware deployments that benefited from hardware fault insertion testing, and should grow to 99% as hardware benefits from ongoing improvements and maturity.

- **At least [Value]% of switchover/failover recovery actions shall succeed.** [Value] may be 95% to 98% for initial product release and should grow to 99% as the system matures.

A plan for improvement in probabilistic requirements can be captured via a simple table such as the one shown here.

Parameter	R1.0	R1.1	R1.2	R2.0
Software failure coverage	85%	90%	93%	95%
Hardware failure coverage	90%	94%	96%	98%
Switchover success probability	90%	95%	98%	99%

Failure coverage requirements are met by investing in error detection features (see Chapter 6, "Error Detection") and thorough robustness testing (see Chapter 11, "Robustness and Stability Testing"). Switchover success probability is improved through careful design of failure recovery mechanisms (see Chapter 4, "Failure Containment and Redundancy") and extensive robustness testing of recovery mechanisms (see Chapter 11, "Robustness and Stability Testing"). These requirements are validated by running a statistically significant number of robustness test cases or failover activations to verify that these probabilities are achieved.

8.5   SERVICE RELIABILITY REQUIREMENTS

Service availability requirements cover only failures large enough to accrue service downtime, but end users are vulnerable to all impairment events, including transient conditions, degraded service, and failures otherwise too small to be classified as formal service outages or downtime. To address this gap, one can frame service reliability requirements that consider service from the perspective of an individual user, rather than homogenizing the experience of all users. Service reliability requirements are easiest to consider by focusing on failures of individual service requests, such as failed transactions or sessions. A convenient metric for service reliability is *defects per million operations (DPM)*. The notion is to set a maximum rate of properly formed and authorized transactions that will fail to complete successfully in the maximum specified time when the system is operating at or below engineered capacity. Note that maximum service response times should be explicitly specified in quality-of-service or performance requirements and are not considered here. Since overload control mechanisms will often discard packets when traffic exceeds engineered capacity, it is often reasonable to exclude overload conditions from service reliability requirements.

Most systems support a variety of service or transaction types, and often these services have very different complexities and thus different expected reliabilities. For example, a database query (read) operation is inherently simpler than a database update (read-modify-write) operation, and thus query operations are likely to be somewhat more reliable than update operations. Thus, separate service reliability requirements may be defined for different classes of operations, such as:

- **No more than 5 properly formed and authorized user query operations per million (< 5 DPM) shall fail to complete in the maximum specified time when the system is operating at or below its engineered capacity.**

- **No more than 10 properly formed and authorized user update operations per million (< 10 DPM) shall fail to complete in the maximum specified time when the system is operating at or below its engineered capacity.**

- **No more than 50 properly formed and authorized OAM&P transactions per million (< 50 DPM) shall fail to complete in the maximum specified time when the system is operating at or below its engineered capacity.**

Service reliability requirements should be directly verified in stability testing (see Section 11.8, "Stability Testing").

8.6 TRIANGULATING RELIABILITY REQUIREMENTS

It is best to triangulate system reliability requirements by considering all the factors that drive service availability and reliability expectations, including the following concrete items:

- **Historic performance** of similar systems or previous generations of systems from the supplier or competitors represents a de facto performance baseline.

- **Industry standards.** Some industries have detailed standards for measuring service quality, reliability, performance, and availability, and these references can be excellent starting points for developing reliability requirements.
- **RFIs and RFPs.** Sophisticated customers for some systems will write detailed and verifiable requests for proposal (RFPs), requests for information (RFIs), or other written specifications, and these documents can also serve as excellent input to reliability requirements.
- **Written service-level agreements** offered by the enterprise or customer to their end users often precisely define the base service reliability and availability metrics, measurement methodology, and quantitative expectations; these service-level requirements can be generally extrapolated to the system-level requirements that apply to any individual system supporting service delivery to end users.
- **Contractual performance requirements** offered or committed by the supplier to customers should be used as essential input when developing system reliability requirements.

One should also recognize that reliability and availability expectations are influenced by other, softer factors, including:

- **Target end-user market**, because users in different markets may have different expectations. For example, users in North America or Western Europe may have different expectations than users in Sub-Saharan Africa.
- **Market position of the enterprise**, because end users may have different reliability and availability expectations for smaller enterprises than for tier-1 enterprises.
- **Commercial terms of service**, because end users may tolerate lower reliability and availability from free services than from services that they directly pay for.
- **Quality, reliability, and availability claims of competitors.**

Suppliers must carefully consider all of these factors to decide what service reliability and service availability expectations will be acceptable to their target customers and when.

8.7 PROBLEMS

The following problems consider a "target system" identified by the instructor:

1. Define *total service outage* for the target system.
2. Quantitatively define *partial service outage* for the target system.
3. Give high-level service availability requirements for the target system.

4. Give three verifiable behavioral requirements that support the high-level service availability requirements for the target system.

5. Give three verifiable latency requirements that support the high-level service availability requirements for the target system.

6. Give three verifiable probabilistic requirements that support the high-level service availability requirements for the target system.

7. Give two verifiable service reliability requirements covering planned activities for the target system.

Chapter 9

Reliability Analysis

Having established reliability requirements and constructed a system design that automatically detects and recovers failures, one can perform reliability analysis to assure that the architecture meets the reliability requirements. Flaws and weaknesses in the system's design for automatic failure detection, isolation, and recovery that are identified and addressed in the design stage are much cheaper and less impactful on overall project schedule and resources than flaws that are discovered in system testing, and far better than flaws that escape to the field and lead to customer-impacting outage events.

Effective reliability analysis can be performed via the following steps:

1. Enumerate recoverable modules.
2. Construct reliability block diagram(s).
3. Characterize impact of failure and recovery actions.
4. Characterize impact of procedures.
5. Verify adequacy of automatic detection and recovery from applicable errors.
6. Consider failures of robustness mechanisms.
7. Prioritize reliability gaps to address.

Each of these steps is discussed in this chapter.

We will consider a simplified, generic application server as a sample for analysis in this chapter, comprised of:

- *Frontend* blades hosting network server processes that communicate with users
- *Backend* blades hosting database server processes
- *Management* blades hosting OAM&P and control processes
- *Chassis* elements providing power, cooling, IP connectivity, and so on.

Design for Reliability: Information and Computer-Based Systems, by Eric Bauer
Copyright © 2010 Institute of Electrical and Electronics Engineers

9.1 STEP 1: ENUMERATE RECOVERABLE MODULES

It is most convenient to use the system's recoverable modules as the focus of a reliability analysis because there are a finite number of supported recovery options mitigating an infinite number of potential failures. Redundant or field-replaceable hardware modules are the foundation of robust system designs. Systems often support recovery of processes or other software modules that run on FRUs rather than requiring all software recoveries to occur at the FRU level. Good system design will use sufficiently fine-grained recoverable modules so that failures can be contained and recovered with the shortest practical service disruption to the smallest possible portion of system users. Any failure that cannot be mitigated via activating a recoverable hardware or software module must likely be recovered at the system level, and thus risks disrupting all of the system's users.

9.1.1 Recoverable Hardware Modules

One begins an enumeration of recoverable modules by considering all of the *field-replaceable units* (FRUs) of the system. For this sample system these are assumed to be:

- **Processor blades.** The three blade types (frontend, backend, and management) may be hosted on identically configured blades, or they might be hosted on blades configured with different storage, memory, processor, or other hardware capabilities. Each distinctly configured blade type should be considered separately.

- **Disks.** Hard disks contain high-performance rotating mechanical platters that wear out sooner than electronics. Since hard disks are likely to fail before the processor electronics that they support, hard disks are often deployed as field-replaceable units. Note that since disks on production systems are often filled with service-related data, it may be necessary to copy data onto a replacement disk from backup before the system is fully operational. If field-replaceable disks are supported, then they should be explicitly included in the list of field-replaceable units. For simplicity, assume our sample system has disks mounted on processor blades so disks are not separate FRUs.

- **Chassis or backplane.** All blades must be installed in a chassis or backplane to obtain power and communicate with each other.

- **Chassis-related FRUs.** Many systems support field-replaceable fans, power modules, alarm cards, Ethernet switches, and so on. Each of these chassis-related FRUs should be enumerated.

The list of FRUs can then be organized into a table showing the hardware redundancy configuration for each blade as well as whether failure or repair

Table 9.1 Sample Hardware Failure Analysis Study

Module	Hardware redundancy	Single point of failure	Single point of repair
Diskful processor FRU hosting management blade	Active-standby	No	No
Diskless processor FRU hosting frontend blade	Load shared across N+1 blades; N is the number of blades required to serve the system's engineered capacity; 1 additional blade is deployed for redundancy	No	No
Diskful processor FRU hosting backend blade	Active-standby	No	No
Backplane	Redundant electrical connections on backplane	No	**Yes, in single backplane configuration**
Power module	Active-active	No	No
Ethernet switch	Active-active	No	No
Fan assembly	Active-active	No	No
Chassis management module	Active-standby—failure of chassis management is not service impacting	No	No

of each module will impact service, as in Table 9.1. Note that *single point of failure* and *single point of repair* are subtly different concepts that must be considered separately. *No single point of failure* (see Section 5.1, "Robust Design Principles") means that redundant hardware components mitigate any single hardware failure. *No single point of repair* means that it is possible to replace any individual FRU without impacting service. Removing or repairing an FRU takes all hardware components on that FRU out of service, so unless the system is designed to carry service across another FRU, the FRU will be a service-impacting single point of repair (see Section 5.1, "Robust Design Principles").

Our sample system has sufficient hardware redundancy to assure that no single hardware failure need cause a service outage; however, in the single backplane configuration, if the backplane fails, then service will be impacted to repair or replace the backplane assembly. Ideally, all active components should be on FRUs rather than directly attached to backplane or chassis, and thus the risk of hardware failure of the backplane is very low. However, it is possible that the mechanical and electrical connections between FRUs and the backplane or chassis will be bent or damaged. While a bent connector pin in one slot should not impact service on other slots or the overall system, the bent pin will eventually need to be repaired when all other slots are filled. At that point electrical power must be disconnected from the backplane to enable a technician to safely repair the damage or replace the backplane. Disconnecting electrical power from the backplane obviously impacts service provided by all FRUs installed on that backplane. Note that many high-availability systems explicitly use multiple chassis and distribute redundant hardware FRUs across several chasses to assure that backplanes are neither single points of failure nor single points of repair.

9.1.2 Recoverable Software Modules

It is common to implement finer-grained software recoverability than the FRU level to minimize impact of software failure recovery. For our sample system, let us assume the following software architecture:

- **Frontend blade** hosts a multithreaded *network server* process controlled by one *control daemon* process. Assume user traffic is distributed across frontend blades via virtual IP address, DNS round robin, or an external load balancer. If architecturally feasible, multiple instances of frontend processes could be used to minimize the impact or *footprint* of a critical software failure in one instance of the frontend process. The control daemon process on the frontend blade does the following:
  - Starts automatically when the frontend blade boots up
  - Loads and configures required middleware
  - Starts network server process
  - Actively monitors health of network server process

  If a network server process fails or is deemed insane, then the control daemon will clear the failed or insane network server instance and start a new process instance of network server.

- **Backend blade** hosts multiple instances of one or more *backend server* processes, all controlled by one control daemon process. To both simplify software development and better contain critical software failures, let us assume that different backend functions were distributed across several different process types. For instance, one process type might handle queries and searches, another process type might handle updates, and other process types might handle administrative operations like database backups. All process types and middleware are configured so that critical software failure of any process instance will not impact any other process instances, and each process type can be restarted independently without impacting any running processes. The control daemon process on the backend actively monitors and recovers any backend processes that fail or are deemed insane.

- **Management blade** hosts one *master control daemon* process and one operations, administration maintenance and provisioning process 'OAM&P.' The master control daemon process on the management blade both boots and monitors the local OAM&P process, and actively monitors the daemon process instances running on all frontend and backend blades. If the master control daemon deems one of the frontend or backend blades to be unavailable or insane, then it will activate appropriate FRU-level recovery. FRU-level recovery will direct middleware and application mechanisms to shift traffic away from the failed FRU to a redundant FRU. On failure, the master control daemon will push alarm status to element management systems to keep human maintenance engineers fully informed of the system's operational status and the autonomous actions the system is taking to restore service. Note that the management blade FRUs are arranged in an *active-standby* configuration, thus enabling the master control daemon process on the standby to actively monitor the master control daemon process on the active blade, and vice versa. If the master control daemon process on the standby deems the active blade to be insane or unavailable, then it can promote itself to *active*, seize control of the system, and raise appropriate alarms without impacting user service.

Software redundancy can be conveniently summarized in Table 9.2.

Note that communications, high-availability, database, and other middleware and platform mechanisms must be appropriately configured to enable these recovery mechanisms to operate properly, but those are application- and platform-specific details that must be addressed for specific systems.

9.1.3 Recoverable Software Platform Modules

Operating systems, communications middleware, databases, and other software platform components can occasionally fail or degrade to the point that software restart of the affected processor becomes necessary. At minimum, all platform software should be configured so that each FRU can be restarted without impacting service on any other FRU. Ideally, all platform software can be restarted independently on each processor on each FRU with multiple independent microprocessors, network processors, digital signal processors, or field-programmable gate arrays. Our sample system will assume a single microprocessor on each processor FRU with platform software configured so that each blade can be independently rebooted without impacting service on other blades.

Table 9.2   Sample System's Software Processes

FRU	Process	Multiple process instances on FRU?
Frontend blade	**Network server** communicates directly with networked users. Manages user sessions including identification, authentication, authorization, accounting, and application protocol processing. Note that the network server process is also responsible for detecting and controlling overload of the application protocol interface to the system.	No
Frontend blade	**Control daemon** monitors health of network server process and application-related middleware on frontend blade.	No
Backend blade	**Query server** implements application and business logic for user queries that were proxied by network server process on frontend blade. Traffic is distributed uniformly in a load-sharing arrangement across N+1 process instances; N process instances carry engineered load and 1 additional process instance is deployed for redundancy.	Yes
Backend blade	**Update server** implements application and business logic for user updates that were proxied by network server process on frontend blade. Traffic is distributed uniformly in a load-sharing arrangement across N+1 process instances; N process instances carry engineered load and 1 additional process instance is deployed for redundancy.	Yes
Backend blade	**Admin server** implements administration and operations commands that were proxied by OAM&P process on management blade. Traffic is distributed uniformly in a load-sharing arrangement across N+1 process instances; N process instances carry engineered load and 1 additional process instance is deployed for redundancy.	Yes
Backend blade	**Control daemon** monitors health of query server, update server, admin server, and application-related middleware on backend blade.	No

Table 9.2 Continued

FRU	Process	Multiple process instances on FRU?
Management blade	**Master control daemon** has overall control of application, including startup, proactive monitoring of control daemons, processes, and throughput, and managing FRU-level redundancy. Monitors health of local OAM&P server, application-related middleware, and master control daemon on mated management blade. Master control daemon manages overload control across the entire system, such as activating overload controls on frontend blades if backend blades get overloaded.	No
Management blade	**OAM&P server** communicates with element management and operations support systems. Note that OAM&P server process is also responsible for detecting and controlling overload of the OAM&P interface to the system.	No

9.2 STEP 2: CONSTRUCT RELIABILITY BLOCK DIAGRAMS

As explained in Section 7.1, reliability block diagrams visualize the redundancy arrangement of recoverable modules. The order in which modules are arranged in the diagram is arbitrary, so one can arrange them in a way that is meaningful or appropriate for the target system. Figure 9.1 shows a high-level RBD of the sample system. Since failure of the chassis management module has no direct service impact, it has been omitted from the diagram.

Note that Figure 9.1 does not detail the structure of platform or application software on each of the blades. As explained in Section 7.1, each block in an RBD can be exploded into a more detailed diagram. Figure 9.2 shows the RBD of the frontend blade; Figure 9.3 shows the RBD of the backend blade; Figure 9.4 shows the RBD of the management blade.

While one can theoretically keep expanding RBD blocks down to discrete hardware components or small software modules, once all of the redundancy in a module has been visualized there is seldom much point in further diagramming the nonredundant modules.

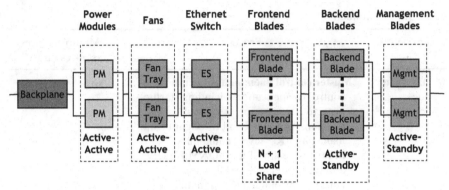

Figure 9.1   High-Level Reliability Block Diagram for Sample System

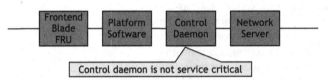

Figure 9.2   Reliability Block Diagram of Frontend Blade

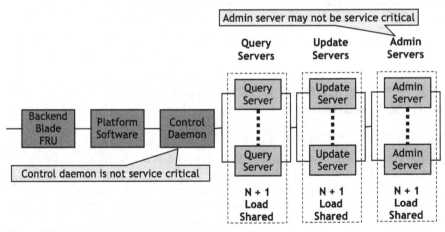

Figure 9.3   Reliability Block Diagram of Backend Blade

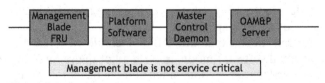

Figure 9.4   Reliability Block Diagram of Management Blade

9.3 STEP 3: CHARACTERIZE IMPACT OF RECOVERY

The formal definitions of total and partial service outage for the target system that were defined or referenced in the system's reliability requirements should determine exactly which system functionality is service critical. The minimum to consider in reliability analysis is the impact of recovery actions on each service or functionality that is covered by total outage definition; when possible, reliability analysis should consider the service impact of the services included in the system's definition of partial outage. For our sample application we will assume four simple service impacts:

1. Impact on existing user sessions
2. Impact on pending user transactions
3. Impact on new user sessions
4. Impact on new user transactions

Different applications are likely to have somewhat different impact metrics to consider, but the principle is the same. This exercise considers the nominal impact of failure and automatic recovery of each recoverable module. Service impacts generally fall into three categories:

1. **No impact.** No user-visible impact of failure and recovery of this module.
2. **Service temporarily impacted.** Service is briefly unavailable while automatic failure detection, isolation, and recovery mechanisms operate; service is fully restored when automatic actions complete.
3. **Service impacted or lost.** User service is significantly impacted. Explicit recovery actions are likely to be required by user or client software, such as restarting a session, redialing a call, reloading a webpage, or by retrying a user operation.

Impact of hardware failures for our sample system is shown in Table 9.3. Table 9.3 reveals:

1. Failure of the frontend blade FRU will briefly impact existing sessions and pending transactions. Client software should detect loss of pending and new transactions (including session setup requests) via expiration of a client's transaction timer. The networking mechanism used to distribute client traffic across frontend servers (e.g., virtual IP address, external load balancer, DNS) should route traffic away from the failed frontend blade to an operational frontend blade. Depending on client software, the particular transaction, and other factors, the transaction may be automatically retried by the client software or the transaction failure may be reported to the user. Different system architectures could reduce impact of frontend blade failure, such as by replicating pending transaction data across redundant frontend blade and having backend blades return results to both active and standby frontend blades.

Table 9.3 Hardware Failure Mode Impacts

Module	Impact on existing user sessions	Impact on pending user transactions	Impact on new user sessions	Impact on new user transactions
Diskful processor FRU hosting management blade	No impact	No impact	No impact	No impact
Diskless processor FRU hosting frontend blade	Existing sessions are lost	**Pending transactions are lost;** client will detect lost request via expiration of transaction request timer	No impact because new user sessions will be served by an operational frontend blade.	New user transactions will fail and prompt client to reconnect to an operational frontend blade
Diskful processor FRU hosting backend blade	No impact	**Pending transactions lost;** frontend blade will timeout and return error to user	No impact	No impact
Chassis, including backplane	No impact on noncatastrophic failure; **service impact on backplane/chassis repair**	No impact on noncatastrophic failure; **service impact on backplane/chassis repair**	No impact on noncatastrophic failure; service impact on backplane/chassis repair	No impact on noncatastrophic failure; **service impact on backplane/chassis repair**
Power module	No impact	No impact	No impact	No impact
Ethernet switch	No impact	No impact	No impact	No impact
Fan assembly	No impact	No impact	No impact	No impact
Chassis management module	No impact	No impact	No impact	No impact

2. Failure of backend blade FRU will impact user transactions that were pending on that blade. The simplest option is for the frontend blade to return a retry-type error status to clients for pending transactions that were lost so clients know to promptly retry their requests. Different system architectures could reduce (or increase) the impact of backend blade failures. For example, interblade timeouts could be engineered so that if backend blade failure causes pending transactions to be lost, then there is sufficient real-time for the frontend blade to retry all pending transactions to other backend blades and return those results before application protocol timeouts expire. For some transactions the frontend might be able to send the same request to two different backend blade instances, use the first response, and discard the second response.

3. In the highly unlikely event that the backplane is damaged, then the system must be taken offline at some point to repair or replace the backplane as a planned, nonemergency maintenance activity. In the even more remote possibility of catastrophic failure of the backplane, the system is unavailable until the backplane can be replaced on an emergency basis. Distributing redundant FRUs across multiple chasses can reduce the service impact of chassis failures.

Similarly, the impact of software recoveries of our sample system is shown in Table 9.4.

Table 9.4 reveals:

1. Failure of the frontend server will cause active sessions to be disrupted until service can be switched to redundant frontend server process instance. User requests pending with failed frontend process will be lost, and should be retried by client after expiration of an application transaction timer to the then-promoted standby frontend server.

2. Failure of query or update processes will impact user transactions that were pending against the process instance that failed. If application protocol timing requirements are sufficiently generous, then the network server frontend may be able to cancel and retry lost transactions against query or update process instances that are still available. Different software, system, and database architectures can reduce (or increase) the impact of query or update process failures.

3. While failures of control daemon or master control daemon are not service impacting, recovering the control daemon requires the blade to be restarted and recovering the master control daemon requires the system to be restarted. More sophisticated designs can enable control and master control daemons to be recovered without restarting application processes, blades, or the entire system.

Other software failures should not directly impact user experience.

Table 9.4   Software Failure Mode Impacts

Module	Impact on existing user sessions	Impact on pending user transactions	Impact on new user sessions	Impact on new user transactions
Network server on frontend blade	Existing sessions are lost	**Pending transactions are lost**; client will detect lost request via expiration of transaction request timer	No impact because new user sessions will be served by an operational frontend blade	New user transactions will fail and prompt client to reconnect to an operational frontend blade
Control daemon on frontend blade	No impact on user service due to failure; frontend blade must eventually be restarted to regain management visibility and controllability	No impact on user service due to failure; frontend blade must eventually be restarted to regain management visibility and controllability	No impact on user service due to failure; frontend blade must eventually be restarted to regain management visibility and controllability	No impact on user service due to failure; frontend blade must eventually be restarted to regain management visibility and controllability
Query server on backend blade	No impact on stable sessions	**Lost**	No impact because requests to failed query server to validate and initialize a user session will time out and be automatically retired to another (presumably operational) query server	No impact because new transactions are routed to an operational query server
Update server on backend blade	No impact on stable sessions	**Lost**	No impact because update server not used to establish new sessions	No impact because new transactions are routed to an operational update server

Table 9.4 Continued

Module	Impact on existing user sessions	Impact on pending user transactions	Impact on new user sessions	Impact on new user transactions
Admin server on backend blade	No impact on user service	No impact on user service	No impact on user service	No impact on user service
Control daemon on backend blade.	No impact on user service due to failure; backend blade must eventually be restarted to regain management visibility and controllability	No impact on user service due to failure; backend blade must eventually be restarted to regain management visibility and controllability	No impact on user service due to failure; backend blade must eventually be restarted to regain management visibility and controllability	No impact on user service due to failure; backend blade must eventually be restarted to regain management visibility and controllability
Master control daemon on management blade	No impact on user service due to failure; system must eventually be restarted to regain management visibility and controllability of system	No impact on user service due to failure; system must eventually be restarted to regain management visibility and controllability of system	No impact on user service due to failure; system must eventually be restarted to regain management visibility and controllability of system	No impact on user service due to failure; system must eventually be restarted to regain management visibility and controllability of system
OAM&P server on management blade	No impact on user service	No impact on user service	No impact on user service	No impact on user service

If additional levels of software failure recovery besides process recovery are supported, such as processor or virtual machine-level recovery, then failure impact analysis studies of those levels of recovery can be completed. Similar analyses can be repeated either for failure impact of specific user operations, activities, or transactions, and/or for failure impacts on provisioning activities or any other entity that, interacts with the system.

Failure impacts and durations are estimated in the architecture and design stage and are checked during unit testing. System testing should verify that the service impacts on hardware and software failures are no worse than specified in impact tables such as Tables 9.3 and 9.4.

9.4   STEP 4: CHARACTERIZE IMPACT OF PROCEDURES

It is important to assure that the service impact of maintenance activities is acceptable. Table 9.5 reviews the service impact of FRU replacement and growth for the sample system, and Table 9.6 reviews the service impact of various maintenance activities. *Note*: We assume that the system supports maintenance commands to gracefully migrate traffic away from frontend and backend blades so user traffic can be drained from those FRUs before they are physically removed from the system, thereby minimizing user impact.

Table 9.5   FRU Replacement or Growth Impacts

FRU replacement or growth	Impact on existing user sessions	Impact on pending user transactions	Impact on new user sessions	Impact on new user transactions
Adding more frontend FRU to grow capacity	No impact	No impact	No impact	No impact
Frontend FRU replacement	No impact	No impact	No impact	No impact
Adding more backend FRU to grow capacity	No impact	No impact	No impact	No impact
Backend FRU replacement	No impact	No impact	No impact	No impact
Management FRU replacement	No impact	No impact	No impact	No impact
Chassis, including backplane	Impact on chassis repair	Impact on chassis repair	Impact on chassis repair	Impact on chassis repair
Power module replacement	No impact	No impact	No impact	No impact
Ethernet switch replacement	No impact	No impact	No impact	No impact
Fan assembly replacement	No impact	No impact	No impact	No impact
Chassis management module replacement	No impact	No impact	No impact	No impact

Table 9.6 Service Impact of Maintenance Procedures

Module	Impact on existing user sessions	Impact on pending user transactions	Impact on new user sessions	Impact on new user transactions
Install application software patch without database schema change	**Lost; service is unavailable when software is installed and activated**	**Lost; service is unavailable when software is installed and activated**	**Lost; service is unavailable when software is installed and activated**	**Lost; service is unavailable when software is installed and activated**
Install application software upgrade with database schema change	**Lost; service is unavailable when new software is installed, database is upgraded, and new software is activated**	**Lost; service is unavailable when new software is installed, database is upgraded, and new software is activated**	**Lost; service is unavailable when new software is installed, database is upgraded, and new software is activated**	**Lost; service is unavailable when new software is installed, database is upgraded, and new software is activated**
Upgrade firmware on processor blades	No impact because blades are upgraded one at a time	No impact because blades are upgraded one at a time	No impact because blades are upgraded one at a time	No impact because blades are upgraded one at a time
Upgrade firmware on Ethernet switch	No impact	No impact	No impact	No impact
Upgrade firmware on chassis management module	No impact	No impact	No impact	No impact
Apply (security or stability) patch to operating system	No impact because blades are upgraded one at a time	No impact because blades are upgraded one at a time	No impact because blades are upgraded one at a time	No impact because blades are upgraded one at a time
Apply (security or stability) patch communications, high-availability or database middleware	No impact because blades are upgraded one at a time	No impact because blades are upgraded one at a time	No impact because blades are upgraded one at a time	No impact because blades are upgraded one at a time
Database backup	No impact	No impact	No impact	No impact

Table 9.5   quickly reveals:

- In the highly unlikely event that the backplane is noncatastrophi-cally damaged, the system must be taken offline at some point to repair or replace the backplane as a planned, nonemergency maintenance activity. In the even more remote possibility of catastrophic failure of the backplane, the system is unavailable until the backplane can be replaced on an emergency basis. Distributing redundant FRUs across multiple chasses can reduce the impact of chassis repair/replacement.

Note that more sophisticated upgrade strategies could minimize service impact of software upgrade, update, and patch, such as permitting new soft-ware to be installed while previous software version continues to operate, and supporting rolling upgrades in which blades are upgraded one at a time while live traffic is served by other blades. One should also consider service impact of eventually upgrading the version of operating system, database, or other middleware elements. It may be possible to arrange for rare planned activities including major software retrofits such as upgrading operating systems to be scheduled into special maintenance periods during which service can be unavailable.

9.5   STEP 5: AUDIT ADEQUACY OF AUTOMATIC FAILURE DETECTION AND RECOVERY

Chapter 3, "What Can Go Wrong," enumerated the categories and types of common errors that systems are susceptible to. We now methodically consider how the system will detect and mitigate each applicable category and type of error. Ideally, system hardware, platform software, and application software implement and deploy common mechanisms to detect, isolate, and recover from most classes of failures across some or all applicable modules so that error detection, isolation, and recovery need not be considered module-by-module for every type of error. For instance, platform software and high-availability middleware can be configured so that any critical hardware failure will automatically trigger a switchover to redundant FRU. Thus, one should verify that circuit design and software drivers will detect all error types in the FRU hardware error category and that hardware audit software proactively monitors hardware that might fail silently so that failures can be detected as quickly as possible.

For each error type in each error category from Chapter 3, "What Can Go Wrong," one should consider how the following five points will be addressed by each service-critical module:

1. How will the failure be detected?
2. What entity will isolate the failure and initiate recovery action?
3. What recovery action will be triggered?

4. If failure isn't promptly detected, isolated, and recovered, will this failure trigger a cascade of secondary failures?

5. If failure isn't detected by the primary mechanism, then what secondary mechanisms will automatically detect the failure(s)?

If any of these points is not acceptably covered by the proposed architecture and design, then additional failure detection or recovery mechanisms can be added. Operationally, one can build a table for each applicable error category for the platform software or for each recoverable module.

9.6 STEP 6: CONSIDER FAILURES OF ROBUSTNESS MECHANISMS

By definition, failure isolation and recovery software operates when the system is in a degraded state, and thus there is a higher risk of software failure during activation of robustness software, including failure to isolate the failure to the correct recoverable module and/or failure of the recovery action itself. Thus, robust systems should include several layers of failure detection, isolation, and recovery so that if one layer of detection, isolation, and recovery is unsuccessful, then another layer can address the fundamental failure. Note that robustness latency budgets typically apply to primary robustness mechanisms. If those primary mechanisms fail, then the system should make a best effort to promptly and automatically recover rather than simply requiring manual recovery.

The two failure modes to consider are:

1. **Silent failure.** Failures that the system does not promptly detect are said to be *silent failures* or *sleeping failures*. For example, the worker thread that supports user service might be stuck but the process's health check mechanism might continue to report that the process is alive and well because of limitations or defects in the process's health-check logic. In this case, process, queue, or system throughput monitoring might reveal that the process is not performing as expected, and could raise an alarm to facilitate manual debugging or perhaps even trigger a suitable automatic recovery action.

2. **Failed recovery.** Switchover actions are often complicated and a module's state is often unpredictable following failure, so automatic recovery actions may occasionally fail to complete successfully. In addition, the system may isolate the failure to the wrong recoverable module and thus trigger the wrong recovery action. Ideally, robust systems will monitor progress of recovery actions, and if they do not promptly clear the failure, then appropriate escalated recovery actions will be executed.

While it is impractical to attempt to automatically detect and recover from every conceivable double-failure scenario, many silent failures and failed recoveries can be detected and raised as appropriate alarms to human maintenance engineers even if automatic recovery is not attempted in these cases.

9.7 STEP 7: PRIORITIZING GAPS

Inevitably, reliability analyses will identify various scenarios in which failures will cause the system to be noncompliant with reliability requirements. Conveniently, the magnitude of noncompliance can be estimated quantitatively using the system's partial and total outage definition. By applying reasonable expected outage duration to each type of noncompliant failure event, one can estimate the prorated downtime per noncompliant failure event. Multiplying that per-event downtime by the estimated annual rate of each particular failure event, one can estimate the annualized downtime expected for each noncompliant failure event type. The estimated annualized downtimes can then be sorted in descending order to construct a crude initial prioritization of gaps to consider.

As individual failures are likely to be very rare, it is generally sufficient to use very rough failure rate parameters, such as one failure per month/year/ decade/century of system service. Alternatively, one can use a quantitative risk index or proxy for the failure rate with 1 lowest risk of failure and 10 highest risk. Multiplying per-event impact by the risk of failure produces a product that can also be used to prioritize gaps to consider. Quantifying the risk, rate, severity, or other characteristics of failure into normalized values (often 1 to 10) that can be multiplied or summed to create an overall per-scenario risk factor is called *failure mode effects and criticality analysis*; this well-known technique is used in military (MIL-STD-1629A) and other industries [McDermott08][Stamatis03].

As a further step, one can then hypothesize alternative architectures, designs, and system behaviors that might reduce the downtime for a specific failure event and/or reduce the rate of occurrence of a specific failure event, and thus produce a hypothetical *what-if* downtime estimate for a hypothesized alternative architecture, design, or behavior. By comparing the baseline downtime estimate to the what-if downtime estimate, one can estimate the incremental benefit of a hypothesized alternative architecture, design, or behavior. The incremental downtime benefits of proposed what-if designs can also be ranked in descending order of downtime improvement. Each alternative architecture, design, or behavior has a development cost that can be estimated. Dividing the estimated downtime saved by the estimated cost gives a crude metric of *saved annualized, prorated down-minute per unit of cost* which is easy for project team members to understand and convenient to use.

9.8 RELIABILITY OF SOURCED MODULES AND COMPONENTS

A rich ecosystem of independent hardware and software suppliers as well as free and open-source software are available to system architects and designers today. In addition, many system suppliers have existing hardware and software assets that can be reused to shorten time to market and reduce development expense. In general, software and hardware modules and components that have been deployed in commercial service should be more mature and reliable than new modules because residual software defects and hardware design and manufacture problems have already been exposed by customers and corrected by the supplier. Unfortunately, sourced modules and components are not always highly reliable when deployed in particular systems, and thus some reliability diligence is appropriate when selecting sourced modules and components to integrate into a system.

9.8.1　Module Reliability Risk

In theory, a module or component operated in the same or similar operational profiles should exhibit fairly consistent failure rates. For example, if a software module, say a protocol stack, has demonstrated reliability when deployed on a particular operating system using a particular protocol configuration option with a particular traffic mix and traffic load, then, assuming these particulars are the same, the protocol stack is likely to be capable of reliable operation when integrated into the target system. Any operational profile characteristics that differ between the target system and the volume deployment configuration of the module or component under consideration increases the risk that undiscovered residual defects might be exposed in development, testing, and deployment of the target system.

Thus, the initial reliability-related topics to consider when evaluating reuse of an existing module or component are:

- **How similar is the target system's operational profile to operational profiles that the module has previously supported?** Each facet of operational profile that differs increases the risk that residual defects exist in the module, documentation, or procedures. Ideally, components will be used in the target system in exactly the way that the component's supplier intended the component to be used; architecting and deploying a component in a nonstandard way that the supplier never intended or tested obviously increases the risk that previously unknown residual defects will be exposed. The key operational profile items for software modules or components include:
  - Target operating system and middleware
  - Traffic (or input command) mix to component
  - Traffic load through component
- **What is the actual field failure rate of this module?** Good suppliers should accurately know how well their products perform in the field based on product returns, support/complaint calls, warranty expense, product reviews, formal quality reports from customers, and softer items like reputation for quality. There is always risk that some, many, or most

critical failures are not reported back to the supplier, and thus one should apply good judgment when evaluating field failure data offered by the supplier.

Given the risk that not all failures may have been reported back to the component supplier, it is best to validate the plausibility of the failure rate suggested by the supplier against other data when possible. Other checks one can make to validate the plausibility of purported failure rates of sourced software components include:

- **Number and nature of critical defects described in release notes.** Release notes often describe workarounds, recommendations, or limitations to mitigate the risk of known residual defects. In addition, release notes for maintenance releases, service packs, and hot fixes/emergency patches typically enumerate the critical defects that are corrected. By definition, each of these critical defects escaped from the supplier's major release development and test process. Estimating the number, severity, and risk of defects that escaped the supplier's development and test process in previous releases is useful in estimating the likely risk of current and future releases.

- **Frequency of regular maintenance releases/service packs, and hot fixes/ emergency patches.** Hot fixes or emergency patches offered by software suppliers indicate that critical defects escaped into the field and then presented a clear and present risk to at least some customers. While rapidly responding to customer needs by promptly issuing hot fixes or emergency patches is desirable, the number of hot fixes required between maintenance releases should be small. Likewise, the frequency of maintenance releases should be reasonable. Not only do excessively frequent maintenance releases indicate that a large number of residual defects escaped and continue to be rapidly discovered by customers, but installing each maintenance release increases the operating expense of enterprises. Even if enterprises elect not to install the emergency patch or maintenance release, then they are likely to spend time and effort to review the release notes and assess the likely incremental reliability improvement afforded by the patch, and then make a business decision on whether to install it or wait for a future maintenance or regular release.

- **Frequency of prophylactic system restarts.** A common workaround for systems that are not completely stable is to periodically schedule prophylactic system restarts to rejuvenate the software. While many PC users will routinely reboot their laptops every day or so to assure stable operation of application software, highly available systems should not require any prophylactic system restarts. If possible, learn whether end customers of the module or component being considered routinely restart their systems such as every week or month or quarter. If some of them do (perhaps because their system documentation or release notes recommend it), then carefully consider if any of the underlying instability that prompts periodic restart is attributable to the module being considered.

It is common for product teams to execute formal testing to evaluate sourced modules to assure that they meet the overall functional requirements in the operational context of the system's software and hardware environment. In addition to assessing functional (e.g., performance) requirements, this testing should include stability testing. If the module supports any high-availability functionality, then some robustness tests (see Chapter 11) should be executed to assure that these mechanisms work properly in the context of the system.

9.8.2   Assessing Supplier's Reliability Diligence

If credible field data and evaluation test results are not sufficient for off-the-shelf products, or if any custom development is being considered, then it is appropriate to evaluate the supplier's design for reliability processes that are used for the specific product. Design for reliability diligence can be assessed via the assessment presented in Chapter 15, "Appendix: Assessing Design for Reliability Diligence."

In addition, one can audit the process and execution quality of the supplier. Higher-quality development processes generally deliver software that is more compliant with system requirements and contain fewer residual defects than less mature development processes.

9.8.3   Integration Considerations

Sourced modules, like modules developed by the product team, must be integrated into the system's architecture so that failures are contained to recoverable modules, inevitable failures can be rapidly detected, and service can be rapidly and reliably recovered. System requirements and reliability budgets are likely to cascade failure detection and recovery latency requirements to the sourced module, which must be met by the overall system design. Robustness testing should include test cases verifying acceptable behavior for likely failure modes of the sourced component. Stability testing should be structured to include significant load on sourced modules to assure that the system integration is good.

Suppliers of sourced components and modules often have formal mechanisms to inform customers of product change notices, security alerts, maintenance releases, changes to support arrangements, and so on. System suppliers should arrange for this information to flow to an appropriate product team member who can carefully evaluate security alerts, maintenance patches and releases, product change notices, and upgrades to decide which of these updates are applicable to the system, the risk to the system of not changing to mitigate the risk, and what the most appropriate mitigation action is for the system.

9.8.4 Discussion

Industry standards often exist to make it easier to swap one module or component with another. For instance, if AA batteries from one supplier prove to be unreliable, then one can select an alternative battery supplier and easily replace the batteries with no impact on system software, hardware, system configuration, procedures, or documentation. Components and modules that are not thoroughly defined by industry standards will be more complicated and more expensive to replace if the selected module or component proves unreliable. For example, if a sourced middleware component like a database or protocol stack proves unreliable, then significant changes to software, system configuration, procedures, and documentation may be necessary, as well as significant retesting. Thus, it is prudent to carefully consider the cost of changing a particular component or module when deciding how much diligence to perform when selecting the supplier. The harder (i.e., more expensive) it is to reverse a poor supplier selection decision, the more thorough the selection diligence should be.

9.9 PROBLEMS

The following problems consider a "target system" identified by the instructor:

1. Enumerate recoverable modules of the target system.
2. Identify and give redundancy strategy for redundant modules of target system.
3. What service impact criteria are most appropriate to consider for a failure mode effect analysis of target system and why?
4. Complete a failure mode impact analysis table for three FRUs of the target system.
5. Complete a failure mode impact analysis table for three software modules of the target system.
6. What maintenance procedures of the target system are at risk of disrupting service?
7. Identify or hypothesize three failure scenarios that are noncompliant with reliability requirements; rank and justify the priority for addressing each of these hypothetical noncompliances.

Chapter 10

Reliability Budgeting and Modeling

Service availability requirements are impractical to verify via system testing, and thus mathematical modeling is the best practice for verifying feasibility and likelihood of meeting high-level service availability requirements. Availability modeling is typically used in conjunction with budgeting of service downtime and latencies, and targeting of input parameters.

Operationally, the budgeting and modeling process includes the following steps:

1. **Factor the chargeable downtime contributors into manageable categories.** Typically unplanned hardware-attributed downtime, unplanned software-attributed downtime, successful planned and procedural activities, and unsuccessful planned and procedural activities are used.

2. **Budget overall system downtime across different downtime categories.** Both the overall total budget and budget allocation may change through the product's lifecycle and from release to release.

3. **Develop models to estimate the downtime for each category.** Architecture-based Markov models are the best practice for unplanned hardware and software modeling; simpler algebraic models can be used for systems with simpler architectures, planned and procedural activities, and systems with less stringent reliability requirements.

4. **Estimate input parameters to create best estimate of downtime by category.** Likely values of modeling input parameters at system release can be estimated and plugged into models to create a best estimate of system downtime at system release.

5. **Adjust input parameters and/or downtime budgets to establish feasible and acceptable performance targets for software and hardware to**

---

achieve within the system's development plan and schedule. Modeling and budgeting should make it easier to manage reliability-improving features and testing just as ordinary features are managed. The risk of failing to meet the customers' expectations for a particular product attribute must be balanced against the overall business case and project plan, and feature content, time-to-market, development cost, and quality must be balanced by decision makers.

6. **Create and manage appropriate latency budgets.** Achieving service availability requirements generally requires the system to automatically detect, isolate, and recover from failures very rapidly. The best practice to assure that this complex process occurs fast enough is to construct and manage robustness latency budgets.

Development teams often have somewhat different development practices, experience, knowledge, and approaches, so these steps may be executed in different order, and repeated and refined at different points in the system development process. Each of these activities is discussed separately.

10.1   DOWNTIME CATEGORIES

System downtime accrues for three general product-attributable reasons:

1. **Successfully executed planned procedures.** Systems may be designed to have brief service disruptions when activating software upgrades or when performing other planned procedures. Customers often have qualitative—and perhaps quantitative—expectations for maximum acceptable service disruptions for successfully executed planned procedures such as "non–service affecting" or "hitless." Many enterprises will tolerate brief service disruptions during executions of planned procedures like software upgrade and schedule those events into maintenance periods in off-hours to minimize user disruption.

2. **Unsuccessful or botched planned procedures.** Software upgrade/retrofit and other planned procedures are inherently complex and carry a nonnegligible risk of failure. The target for successful upgrade execution is often 99% and other procedures should be even more reliable. If a 99% upgrade success target is met, then 1% of upgrades may fail and some of those failures will temporarily impact the system's ability to deliver service. While systems are designed to automatically detect, isolate, and recover from all or most typical software and hardware failures, an unsuccessful upgrade or other planned procedure often leaves the system in a vulnerable state in which automatic mechanisms may not function normally (e.g., because system was running in simplex while one side was being upgraded). Thus, downtime from unsuccessful

planned procedures may be somewhat longer than for unplanned events. Fortunately, software upgrades generally occur infrequently; however, when failures do occur, the downtime may be significant. Note that many enterprises track planned events separately from unplanned events (e.g., may use a trouble tracking system to track unplanned events and some separate work management system to track planned events). In addition, planned events are often performed in off-hours when traffic volume is lower so that any outage would affect fewer users.

3. **Unplanned events such as hardware or software failures may cause service to become unavailable.** Note that outage duration may be extended due to mistakes by maintenance engineers when executing emergency recovery procedures, but that downtime is generally attributed to unplanned events rather than to either successful or unsuccessful procedures category. Downtime associated with unplanned events is often the majority of recorded product-attributed service downtime.

Downtime can also be caused for other reasons like loss of power or failure of supporting system (e.g., authentication, authorization, or accounting servers) or facility (e.g., IP connectivity), but those other causes are outside of the scope of the system itself, and hence are excluded from product-attributable downtime calculations and thus are not considered in this book.

10.2 SERVICE DOWNTIME BUDGET

The marquee requirement of high-availability systems is often 99.999% availability—*five 9's*—meaning no more than 5.26 prorated minutes of product-attributable service downtime per system per year. Note that non-product-attributable outages, such as downtime due to unavailability of power, communications facilities, or other factors that are beyond the scope of the system supplier are not generally charged against a system's 99.999% service availability expectations. To methodically manage achieving this very challenging downtime target, the best practice is to construct a budget that allocates the service downtime into categories that can be managed separately. One generally begins with broad categories for hardware-attributed downtime, software-attributed downtime, downtime for successful planned and scheduled activities, and downtime for unsuccessful planned or procedural activities. These broad categories can be tailored to better map to the specific architecture and maturity of the particular system. Table 10.1 gives a sample allocation of the 315 seconds of annualized downtime that are permitted for a 99.999% availability system.

Each of these categories is considered separately.

Table 10.1   Sample 99.999% Downtime Budget

	Product-attributable downtime category	Annualized target for 99.999%		Percent
		Seconds	minutes	
Basic 99.999% expectations includes:	**Hardware attributable—target: 30 seconds = 0m30s**			
	Hardware Failures—service downtime triggered by hardware failures.	30	0.5	10%
	Software attributable—target: 225 seconds = 3m45s			
	Platform software failures— service downtime due to software failures of platform software.	120	2	38%
	Application software failures— service downtime due to software failures of application software.	105	1.75	33%
Product- attributable 99.999% expectations also includes:	**Planned and procedural attributable—target: 60 seconds = 1m0s**			
	Successful scheduled activities—service downtime by design for successful upgrade, update, retrofit, hardware growth, and other scheduled or planned maintenance activities.	0	0	0%
	Unsuccessful procedural activities—service downtime attributed to unsuccessful or botched maintenance activities such as upgrade, update, retrofit, hardware growth, and provisioning.	60	1	19%
	Total	**315**	**5.25**	
	Availability	**99.999%**		

10.2.1   Hardware-Attributed Downtime

Hardware-attributed downtime covers service downtime triggered by hardware failure, specifically the time when service is unavailable while a failure is being detected, isolated, and recovered to a redundant unit. Market expectations and the system's reliability requirements should set the maximum acceptable service disruption latency so that the system can be explicitly designed to recover faster than that. Hardware failures that trigger service disruptions of less than the maximum acceptable service disruption latency can thus be excluded from the hardware downtime budget. Assuming the system is designed with hardware redundancy to assure that no single hardware failure should disrupt service (commonly called *no single point of failure*), hardware downtime should only be caused by one or more secondary failures, such as:

- **Detection failure.** System does not automatically detect the hardware failure in seconds or less.

- **Isolation failure.** System does not correctly isolate the failure to the correct FRU, and thus executed the wrong recovery action.

- **Silent failure of standby.** Standby unit had previously failed but the system was unaware of the failure, and thus the system was unknowingly operating in simplex (nonredundant) configuration when failure of primary unit occurred.

- **Recovery failure.** Switchover to redundant FRU fails to complete successfully.

- **Duplex failure.** Redundant hardware unit fails before the first unit can be replaced or repaired.

- **Slow successful automatic detection, isolation, and recovery.** Automatic recovery took longer than maximum acceptable service disruption latency and thus attributable downtime accrued for the event.

A human maintenance engineer will intervene in all of these cases (except for slow, successful automatic recovery) to manually diagnose the failure and recovery service.

10.2.2 Software-Attributed Downtime

Software-attributed downtime covers service downtime triggered by software failure, including from programming errors, resource leaks, data inconsistency/ corruption, core dumps, application protocol failures, and so on. Software faults that are automatically detected, isolated, and recovered within the maximum acceptable service disruption latency do not accrue chargeable service downtime and hence can be excluded from consideration. Thus, software-attributed service downtime will come from the following software problems:

- **Failure not automatically detected**, thus automatic recovery is not initiated promptly.

- **Failure not properly isolated**, thus wrong recovery actions are initiated.

- **Failure not properly contained**, thus the fault cascades before automatic recovery can complete successfully.

- **Automatic recovery action fails**, thus slower manual recovery actions or secondary automatic recovery mechanisms are required to restore service.

- **Unacceptably slow automatic failure detection, isolation, and recovery** that exceed maximum acceptable latency.
- **Architecture or design limitation does not permit automatic recovery from the particular failure mode.** For example, profound data corruption may require data to be manually restored from backup.

Failed or unacceptably slow automatic recoveries will be manually recovered by maintenance engineers. Typically, the outage latency for the small number of faults that are not successfully automatically detected and recovered contributes the vast majority of software-attributed service downtime.

10.2.3   Successful Planned Activities

System architecture and design determines whether it is feasible for various planned, nonemergency activities like software upgrade and hardware growth to be performed in-service (while the system is actively serving users). The term *24/7/365* refers to a system that is continuously available, not a system that has scheduled downtime semiannually, quarterly, monthly, or weekly. Thus, service downtime allocated to successful scheduled activities for highly available systems is often less than one minute per system per year, and high-availability systems with non-service-impacting software patch and upgrade often budget 0 minutes to successful planned activities.

10.2.4   Unsuccessful Planned Activities

Inevitably, some complex scheduled activities like upgrade or update will fail and some of these failures will impact service. These failures can occur for reasons such as:

- A failure occurred on the active side while system was in simplex state executing a procedure, and thus the system was unable to recover service on the redundant unit.
- The system encountered an unexpected state during the procedure.
- Human error occurred in execution of the procedure.

As with hardware and software failure categories, quality activities strive to minimize the rate of unsuccessful procedural activities. In addition, the enterprise operating the system must also assure that its maintenance engineers are fully trained and have complete and correct operational policies and appropriate tools to enable reliable execution of manual procedures.

10.3   AVAILABILITY MODELING

Mathematical modeling is used to assure that it is technically feasible for the system to meet its availability and reliability requirements. Best practice is to separately manage unplanned hardware and software downtime using an architecture-based Markov availability model and using a simple algebraic model for successful and unsuccessful planned activities. The reason separate models are used is that these two sets of fault triggers and recovery behaviors are fundamentally different. Unplanned hardware and software failures are best modeled considering the rate of random fault or failure events and modeling the expected behavior of robustness mechanisms via failure coverage factors, recovery latencies, and escalation strategies. Planned activities, by their very nature, are executed on regular schedules, and thus this downtime is fundamentally driven by execution rate and success probability of each planned activity, rather than in-service time. Each of these is considered separately. Typically, unplanned hardware plus software downtime is modeled via an architecture-based Markov model (see Section 7.4, "Availability Modeling") and planned plus procedural downtime is addressed with a simple algebraic model (see Section 7.5, "Planned Downtime").

10.4 UPDATE DOWNTIME BUDGET

Once the model or models have been constructed, one inputs feasible parameter values that reflect how the system should perform after initial feature gaps and potential quality issues are addressed. The downtime prediction based on favorable but feasible input parameters should meet the system's availability requirement; if favorable but feasible inputs are not likely to achieve system's availability requirements, then the system architecture or quality, reliability, and robustness expectations need to be reconsidered to lower the requirements or plan to eventually improve the system. If the feasible but flattering inputs are predicted to achieve the system's availability requirement, then the system's downtime budget should be aligned to be consistent with that prediction. Since this feasible but flattering prediction is likely to be better than requirement, it will consume less downtime than is budgeted. It is typical to adjust the budget to be roughly consistent with the allocation (by percentage) of predicted downtime, although the revised downtime budget will often include a bit of margin beyond the favorable but feasible prediction.

One then estimates the likely values of model input parameters at system release date and inputs those values into the model to predict the likely system downtime at system release. For early system releases, the likely system downtime will often be greater than the feasible but flattering inputs used to create the revised downtime budget. By comparing the likely downtime prediction with the feasible but flattering downtime prediction one can estimate the magnitude of the gap in predicted downtime. This gap highlights both where availability-improving feature and test investments should be made, and the likely magnitude of risk of achieving the system's availability expectations.

Figure 10.1 summarizes the results of availability modeling and budgeting for the sample system discussed in Chapter 10. Downtime predictions and budgets are made for all elements in the service delivery path; the management blades are excluded because failure of one or both management blades does not impact user service.

Component	Annualized, prorated, unplanned hardware plus software downtime (in minutes)			
	Feasible	Budget	Likely in release X.y	Gap in release X.y
Frontend blades	1.70	2.25	3.73	65.8%
Backend blades	1.80	2.50	4.21	68.4%
Management blades	Management blade is not in service delivery path, and hence not included in service availability predictions			
Chassis, etc.	0.20	0.50	0.48	-
Total	3.70	5.25	8.42	60.4%
Availability	99.9993%	99.9990%	99.9984%	

Figure 10.1   Sample Downtime Predictions and Budget

- The "Feasible" column gives the downtime predicted for the failure rates, failure coverage factors, switchover success probabilities, and so on, that the development team believes the element will achieve when planned and proposed features are implemented, the system has matured, and initial deployment issues have been addressed. Note that the feasible availability predicted by the model is significantly better than the 99.999% requirement assumed for the sample system.

- The "Budget" column sets downtime targets that meet the system's 99.999% service availability requirement. The budget is set based on engineering judgment and the feasible predictions. The budgeted downtime percentages should be similar to the feasible downtime percentages, meaning the module with the highest feasible prediction should have the highest budgeted downtime, and so on.

- The "Likely in release X.y" column gives the predicted downtime based on current best estimates of input parameters at time of customer deployment of system release X.y. Modeling input parameters are initially estimated by subject matter experts based on historic performance of previous releases, system architecture and design, and engineering judgment. As the system is integrated, it is possible to measure many timing parameters, such as switchover times. After the first pass of robustness testing completes, it is possible to revise estimates of failure coverage factors and switchover success probabilities, and when final pass of robustness testing completes, those parameters can be updated. Failure rates are estimated by carefully analyzing field performance of previous releases to establish a baseline, and considering design and test results of current hardware and software to make a best estimate of field failure rates. The value of "Likely in release X.y" should be reassessed at key points throughout the development program.

For instance, one typically estimates availability based on a proposed development plan early in the program, and updates the prediction when development completes based on which reliability/availability-related features actually made it into the system and performance observed in unit testing, and makes a final prediction when system verification has thoroughly tested the system in general and the robustness mechanisms in particular.

- The "Gap in release X.y" column shows the gap between likely downtime in release X.y and budget.

Unplanned hardware and software downtime is managed by reducing the rate of critical failures through diligent quality activities, assuring that inevitable failures are contained, detected, and automatically recovered, as detailed in Chapter 4, "Failure Containment and Redundancy," Chapter 5, "Robust Design Principles," Chapter 6, "Error Detection," Chapter 9, "Reliability Analysis," Chapter 11, "Robustness and Stability Testing," and Section 12.1, "Analyzing Field Outage Events."

10.5 ROBUSTNESS LATENCY BUDGETS

Once a maximum service disruption latency requirement is established, one can budget that requirement into specific latencies for automatic failure detection, isolation, and recovery. As failures in different error categories will be detected, isolated, and recovered using different mechanisms, different robustness latency budgets may be appropriate for different error scenarios. Figure 10.2 shows a sample robustness latency budget to meet a 5-second service disruption requirement.

A generic robustness latency budget includes the following major buckets:

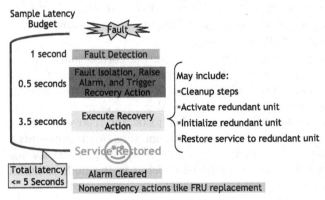

Figure 10.2 Sample Failure Latency Budget

- **Error detection** estimates time to detect an error. The time allocated is used to establish timeout values and frequency of status checks, scans, or other scheduled checks. Some faults (e.g., checksum errors on messages or serial buses or Ethernet packets) will be detected instantaneously. Some faults (e.g., dropped IP packets) will be detected indirectly, such as via expiration of timers. Other faults (e.g., memory or resource leaks) will be detected by periodic scans. For example, corrupted messages should be detected in microseconds, lost messages should be detected in milliseconds to seconds, and resource leaks that create resource exhaustion hazards should be detected in tens of seconds or minutes. As a practical matter, set the budgeted error detection latency to the expected or typical latency of the primary error detection mechanism.

- **Fault isolation.** A single activated fault may cascade to numerous detected errors and failures. For example, a particular hardware failure may cause messages received by one FRU to report checksum errors; three obvious fault hypotheses could explain this detected behavior:
  1. Hardware fault on FRU sending the message
  2. Hardware fault on the communications switch FRU, or network facility between sending and receiving modules
  3. Hardware fault on the FRU receiving message that detected the checksum error

  As the hardware recovery actions for sending FRU, switch FRU, receiving FRU, and networking cables/facilities are likely to be different—and activating the wrong recovery action will delay service restoration and potentially impact users not affected by the primary fault—one wants to select the right recovery action the first time. One should budget sufficient time for the system to accurately isolate the fault and activate the appropriate recovery mechanisms. Note that fault isolation may include deliberately waiting to confirm the fault diagnosis via repeated fault indications or other strategies before activating a potentially disruptive fault recovery mechanism. Engineering the latency budget for fault isolation is an optimization problem of balancing the risk of false positive (thus triggering unnecessary, disruptive recovery action) against a longer service disruption or outage.

- **Raise alarm.** Systems should promptly raise the correct alarm to the element management system so that the maintenance engineer responsible for the system is promptly informed. The maintenance engineer will carefully monitor the alarm, and if it does not clear fast enough, then the engineer will initiate manual diagnostic and recovery actions. Raising an alarm is usually a quick activity, and thus often represents a negligible portion of the recovery latency budget. Thus latency for raising the appropriate alarm could be covered in the fault isolation category if desired, and omitted.

- **Execute recovery actions.** The specific recovery actions will vary with the nature of the fault, the system's architecture, and perhaps the

context and scope of the original fault and subsequent failure cascade. Often recovery actions will include some or all of the following items:
- **Promote redundant unit to "active."** In active-standby arrangements, explicit system operations may be required to promote cold, warm, or hot standby units to active operational status.
- **Direct new activities away from failed unit to an operational unit.** For instance, load-balancing mechanisms like Internet Domain Name Server (DNS) should stop providing the IP address of the failed unit.
- **Initialize/synchronize redundant unit.** Redundant unit must acquire and synchronize status of sessions and operations that will be retained.
- **Cleanup/abort failed, stuck, or pending work.** Depending on the system context when the recovery action occurs and the nature of the recovered module, it may be necessary to abort pending database transactions, release allocated resources, force clients and adjacent systems to reinitialize sessions, or take other actions.
- **Service restored.** After executing recovery actions, the system should return to operational status. If the executed recovery actions did not restore the system to operational status, then secondary error detection, isolation, and recovery mechanisms should execute more appropriate recovery actions to automatically restore the system to service. For purposes of latency budgeting, one considers service restoration to be the stopping point.
- **Alarm cleared.** Although latency budget does not extend after service is restored, it is essential that any alarm(s) raised when the failure was detected be promptly cleared. If the alarm is not promptly cleared, then the human operator may be misled to believe that manual failure diagnostic and recovery actions are required that might unnecessarily impact service. Also, as some enterprises will measure outage durations as the elapsed time between raising and clearing critical alarms, delayed clearance of critical alarms can suggest that the system's service availability is poorer than it actually is. Alarm clearance latency is not typically included in the robustness latency budget because service is already restored.
- **Nonemergency maintenance actions.** Non-service-critical recovery actions such as replacing failed hardware modules or rebooting blades may also be required, but the latency for those non-service-critical steps is not included in the robustness latency budget because service has already been restored and hence these actions do not prolong the service outage.

There are often several different failure latency budgets depending on the nature of the fault or failure detected. A decision to use multiple budgets is often driven by:
- **Nature of the fault detected.** Some faults like resource or memory leaks can be detected before they escalate to critical failures, and thus the system need not meet stringent detection, isolation, and recovery

latencies for subcritical faults. This leniency enables one to scan for subcritical faults every few minutes (or even hours), rather than having to scan every second.

- **Latency of appropriate recovery action.** As the recovery action for some critical errors may take longer than for others, it may be necessary to shorten detection and isolation budgets to compensate and meet the system's maximum acceptable service disruption latency requirement.
- **Latency of error detection and isolation mechanisms.** Indirectly detected failures (e.g., via expiration of timeouts) inherently takes longer than directly detected failures (e.g., processor exceptions). In addition, many indirectly detected failures (and some directly detected failures) cannot be immediately isolated to the appropriate recoverable unit, and hence sufficient time must be budgeted to confidently isolate the failure to the appropriate recoverable module.

One now carefully considers whether likely service-impacting failures will be detected, isolated, and recovered within the budgeted service disruption latency to assure that the proposed allocations for failure detection, isolation, and recovery are all feasible and optimal. For instance, it is infeasible for a 5-second failure detection budget to be achieved with a 2-second guard timer and 2 retries (for a total of 3 requests) before declaring failure; either the guard timer can be shortened (e.g., to 1.5 seconds) or the retry count can be reduced (e.g., to 2), or the latency budget can be increased, or a different failure detection mechanism can be used. "Optimal" means that the product is able to achieve the required robustness with the lowest overall development expense. For instance, if it is easier to shorten failure detection than to shorten failure recovery, then the project should arrange the latency budget with shorter failure detection allocations to lower overall development expense.

Robustness latency budgets are generally easy for engineers to verify during system integration. If latency budgets are not met, then engineers can analyze system behavior to determine where time is spent during failure detection, isolation, and recovery activities, and shorten it. Formal robustness testing generally verifies only the overall latency, rather than measuring the individual failure detection, isolation, and recovery phases.

10.6 PROBLEMS

The following problems consider a "target system" identified by the instructor:

1. Define a robustness latency budget for an aspect of the target system.
2. Define service downtime budgets for unplanned failures for the target system both by downtime category (e.g., hardware-attributed, software-attributed) and by system module (e.g., FRU). Justify downtime allocations.

Chapter 11

Robustness and Stability Testing

Robustness testing assures that the complex mechanisms that automatically detect, isolate, and recover failures work properly to assure that a system will achieve high service availability; stability testing assures that a system functions properly under a sustained load of heavy and mixed traffic to assure that a system will deliver high service reliability. This chapter covers how to plan, execute, and evaluate results of robustness and stability testing.

11.1 ROBUSTNESS TESTING

Robustness testing verifies the robustness design and mechanisms of a system by confronting it with likely failure scenarios to verify that the system automatically detects, isolates, and recovers from failures within a specified time. The goals of robustness testing are:

- **Verify system meets reliability requirements** for rapid automatic failure detection, isolation, and recovery. This implies very broad testing of numerous different failure scenarios.
- **Verify that the recovery mechanisms are highly reliable** and thus able to recover from the broadest range of failure types in the broadest range of system states. This implies exercising each of the major recovery scenarios many times to assure reliable operation.
- **Estimate reliability-related modeling parameters from lab measurements** and data to better estimate system availability, thus assuring system availability requirements are likely to be met. This implies careful measurement and analysis of test results.

This section begins by framing the context of robustness testing and factoring the infinite space of possible failures using the ingredient and error framework

Design for Reliability: Information and Computer-Based Systems, by Eric Bauer
Copyright © 2010 Institute of Electrical and Electronics Engineers

defined in Chapter 3, "What Can Go Wrong," into useful categories of robustness testing. Practical considerations for selecting robustness test approaches are reviewed, followed by a discussion of robustness test techniques. The section ends with a brief discussion of selecting robustness test cases and analyzing robustness test results.

11.2 CONTEXT OF ROBUSTNESS TESTING

Robustness testing is the practical validation of the reliability analysis described in Chapter 9, "Reliability Analysis." The robustness testing campaign should:

- Characterize service impact of hardware failure modes.
- Characterize service impact of software failure modes.
- Characterize service impact of planned and procedural activities—note that this is often covered in test plans for the procedures themselves, such as in the software upgrade test plan.
- Characterize service impact of likely power, network, and application protocol (payload) impairments.
- Verify that critical failures are likely to be automatically detected, isolated, and recovered.
- Verify reliability of automatic recovery actions.

Test results can be evaluated against test pass criteria derived from the system's reliability requirements.

Most of the robustness requirements described in Chapter 8, "Reliability Requirements," are directly verifiable, via:

- **Explicit test case(s).** Either simulate a fault situation or execute a specific maintenance activity.
- **Explicit pass criteria.** Reliability requirements should explicitly characterize the key features of successful recovery, such as not producing a chargeable partial or total service outage per the system's formal outage definitions.
- **Statistical analysis of test results.** Because there is an infinite set of possible failures to detect and it is unrealistic to assume that robustness software functions perfectly in every possible failure scenario, it is more practical to focus on probability of success. Assuring higher success probabilities requires more test cases to be executed successfully; statistical confidence limits can be used to determine the exact number of test cases that must be attempted and the number that must pass to demonstrate a quantified level of statistical certainty (e.g., 60%, 90%, etc.). These techniques can be used both when selecting the number of test cases and iterations to be used, and when reporting actual results.

11.3 FACTORING ROBUSTNESS TESTING

Chapter 3, "What Can Go Wrong," used eight product-attributable error categories to characterize the errors that will confront a system in the real world. A practical purpose of robustness testing is to verify that the system reacts properly to any of these errors. Figure 11.1 illustrates the conceptual model of a typical system within the context of a network solution. Lightning bolts are shown to highlight primary robustness test points. From left to right:

- Requests received from the client system on behalf of the end user can be malformed, flawed, malicious, or otherwise unexpected.
- Supporting systems that the target system interacts with can fail, like authentication, authorization, and accounting servers, database servers, license management servers, element management systems, and so on.
- IP networking to some or all of the adjacent systems and end users can be disrupted.
- Processes and threads can fail.
- FRUs can fail.
- Power can be disrupted.
- High-availability infrastructure and redundancy features can fail.
- Both persistent and volatile storage can be compromised.
- Interaction with a human maintenance engineer can be incorrect due to human error, flaws in documented procedures, insufficient training, and so on.

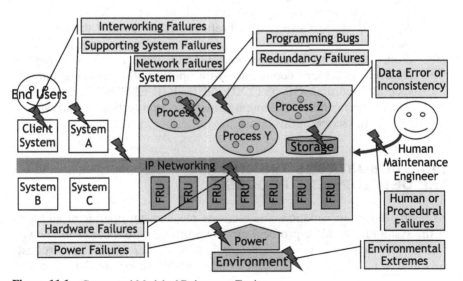

Figure 11.1   Conceptual Model of Robustness Testing

- The system's hardware can experience environmental extremes like high ambient temperature or relative humidity, or corrosive gases.

Robustness testing of each of these error categories is performed using various techniques that are covered in this chapter:

- **FRU Hardware** is tested via *hardware fault insertion* testing, which is described in Section 11.5.1.
- **Programming errors** can be tested via several techniques, including:
  - *software fault insertion* testing, which is described in Section 11.5.2.
  - *Concurrency* testing, which simultaneously executes multiple operations to stress concurrency control mechanisms that synchronize sharing of resources. Stability testing in Section 11.8 can be structured to provide some coverage of concurrency testing.
- **Data inconsistencies or errors** are tested via direct manipulation of persistent or volatile storage. This is often included in the broader category of software fault insertion testing, which is described in Section 11.5.2.
- **Redundancy** testing is often called *resiliency testing* or *failover testing*, and is described in Section 11.5.3.
- **System power testing** is described in Section 11.5.4.
- **Network error testing** is described in Section 11.5.5.
- **Application protocol failure testing** is described in Section 11.5.6.
- **Procedural testing** verifies that likely errors that occur when executing nonemergency and emergency procedures are properly addressed; this is described in Section 11.5.7.
- **Environmental testing.** System hardware and physical design must be designed to withstand the extremes of heat and cold, moisture and dryness, dust, corrosive gases, vibrations and mechanical shocks, and so on that the system is likely to encounter over its operating life. This is often referred to as *design environmental stress testing* and may be required to achieve compliance with appropriate industry standards, such as Telcordia's GR-63-CORE NEBS [GR-63-CORE] standard for telecommunications equipment. Environmental testing of hardware is outside the scope of this book.

11.4 ROBUSTNESS TESTING IN THE DEVELOPMENT PROCESS

As failure detection, isolation, and recovery mechanisms operate at all levels of the system from subtle protocol errors up through gross hardware, power, and network failures, it is often appropriate to test different aspects of robustness at different points in the development cycle. All failure detection and isolation code should be verified at the unit testing level, and as much recovery functionality should be tested as is possible. Integration testing should verify that detected faults are properly isolated, that the correct recovery mechanism is activated, and that the recovery mechanism executes successfully. System-level testing should verify that broad classes of errors are properly detected, isolated, and recovered as stipulated in the system's requirements, and that robustness mechanisms are highly reliable by successfully completing many switchovers/failovers and recoveries. Network-level testing verifies that the system properly recovers from failures of supporting systems and gross network failures. Particular development organizations may have different phases of testing and/or map robustness testing into their development process somewhat differently, but the point is that aspects of robustness testing occur at several phases across unit-, integration-, system-, and network-level testing.

11.5 ROBUSTNESS TESTING TECHNIQUES

This section reviews generally applicable techniques for simulating likely faults and errors to verify proper operation of robustness mechanisms. When selecting a robustness testing technique or mechanism, one should consider the following factors:

- **Reproducibility.** It is essential that any test be easily reproducible so that any failure can be methodically debugged and the fix carefully verified.
- **Fault insertion is uncorrelated with host software.** Ideally, one should be able to inject a fault at any time, independent of the precise state of the software.
- **Minimal incremental development expense.** Ideally, robustness test tools, techniques, and plans can be reused by similar applications to minimize overall development expense. In addition, test execution should not result in permanent damage to any hardware.
- **Use of unmodified hardware.** Hardware is typically not cheap (especially prototype models and preproduction units), and thus one does not want to compromise or sacrifice any FRUs for fault insertion testing if not essential.
- **Failure fidelity.** Inserted failures should mimic likely field failure accurately enough to realistically exercise failure detection mechanisms.

11.5.1 Hardware Fault Insertion

FRU failures should be simulated via hardware fault insertion (HFI) mechanisms rather than by physically removing FRUs from a running system. While physically "pulling" an FRU from a running system requires minimal planning and preparation, it is a poor simulation of hardware failure because modern systems are often explicitly designed to detect and manage *hot-swap* events. Thus FRU removal is likely to appear to the system primarily as a configuration or equipage change, rather than a hardware failure. Hence, FRU removal forces equipage-related mechanisms to be executed, rather than testing hardware failure detection mechanisms. Mechanisms that simulate specific hardware failures are thus vastly superior to simply "pulling packs" for assuring robustness for hardware failures. Note that HFI mechanisms should be used to verify correctness of every hardware alarm supported by the system, as well as to verify the accuracy and correctness of every online, offline, and power-on diagnostic self-test. Thus, HFI testing is likely to be used in functional testing of hardware alarms and hardware diagnostic software.

The following well-known hardware fault insertion techniques are reviewed:

- Fly-wires and modified hardware
- JTAG-based hardware fault insertion
- Driver manipulation, reconfiguration, or reprogramming
- Simulated hardware fault insertion

A discussion of the relative benefits and drawbacks of each hardware fault insertion technique is then given.

11.5.1.1   Fly-wires and Modified Hardware

Traditionally, hardware faults in digital circuits were inserted by manually pulling key signals to logic "low" or logic "high" via a *fly-wire* tied to ground or power with appropriate electrical resistance in series to avoid permanently damaging the FRU. As components have evolved to surface-mount attachment and multilayer boards became typical (meaning some signals do not appear on either exposed surface of the board), it is now often infeasible to use fly-wires to access many signals of interest. To address this, designers should consider the need for hardware fault insertion in circuit layout so that signals of interest are accessible via physically convenient mechanisms on the outer layer of circuit boards. Some teams even modify FRUs to create so-called *failable packs* on which electrical traces have been cut and replaced with manual switches that can be used to conveniently activate and deactivate failures. Unfortunately, failable packs tend to be fragile and are thus less reliable than unmodified boards. Therefore, these failable packs are often dedicated to robustness testing because after physical modifications have been made they are no longer reliable enough for other deployment, test, or development purposes. Budget constraints prevent many failable packs from being constructed, so they are often shared by the various teams that require them.

If hardware fault insertion is considered during the schematic capture and layout phase of hardware design, then signals of interest might be explicitly exposed on outer layers to facilitate hardware fault insertion via manual jumpers or fly-wires. Some teams even include transistors on key electrical connections to reversibly break connectivity between different circuits to facilitate manufacturing test, and these mechanisms can be reused to simulate hardware failures in system robustness testing.

11.5.1.2 JTAG-based Hardware Fault Insertion

JTAG is an abbreviation for *Joint Test Action Group*, which created the IEEE 1149 [IEEE1149] standard for *boundary scan* testing. Boundary scan testing was developed to efficiently test integrated circuit devices and manufacture quality of circuit boards and FRUs. JTAG is also used as the interface to program devices like *field-programmable gate arrays (FPGAs)*, and *complex programmable logic devices (CPLDs)*, and for processor emulators and debuggers.

The IEEE 1149 standard defines controllable cells that buffer each input or output lead on an integrated circuit, as shown in Figure 11.2. These buffer cells are arranged in a logical daisy chain to create a huge shift register. In normal operation, these cells pass electrical signals unimpeded; during test execution, these cells can be configured to drive a programmed signal (logic "0", logic "1", or high impedance) or to sample the electrical signal driven into that cell from the device itself or from external circuitry. This ability to drive and read pin-level signals enables hardware test engineers to verify electrical connectivity for virtually all electrical connections on an FRU and to perform more sophisticated tests. Note that JTAG functionality is typically controlled via a five-wire cable that connects an external PC or test fixture to

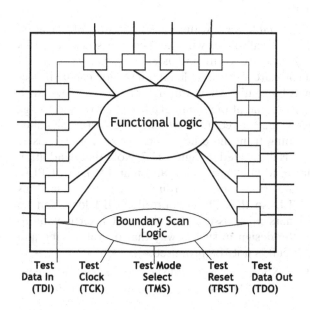

Test	Test	Test Mode	Test	Test
Data In	Clock	Select	Reset	Data Out
(TDI)	(TCK)	(TMS)	(TRST)	(TDO)

Figure 11.2 Simplified Boundary Scan Reference Architecture

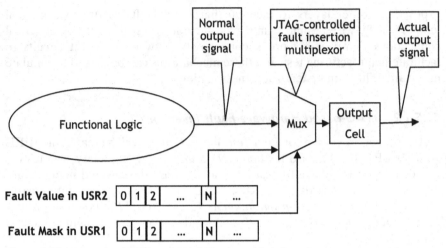

Figure 11.3   Example of Pin-Level JTAG Hardware Fault Insertion

a five-wire header on the FRU under test. The PC or test fixture is separate from the system under test and JTAG commands (often called "tests") can be applied at any time the board is powered on.

JTAG can be used to simulate hardware faults via the following scenarios:

- **Gross device failure.** Switching all of a device's boundary scan cells to high impedance (called "HIGHZ") state will electrically isolate the target component from the rest of the circuit, thereby simulating a profound device failure.

- **Pin-level failure.** Controllable logic within an FPGA or CPLD can be used to selectively fail critical signals with stuck-at-0 or stuck-at-1. This logic can be activated via JTAG control registers, and thus be operated independent of host software. Controllable fault insertion can be implemented on key signals by routing them through multiplexer logic with a fault value coming from one of the boundary scan user registers (e.g., USR2) and the mask value that controls whether the correct signal or fault value is used coming from the other boundary scan user register (e.g., USR1); this logic is illustrated in Figure 11.3. Note that in addition to using this mechanism to fail "native" signals on an FPGA or CPLD, one may be able to route critical circuits through otherwise-unused pins on the FPGA or CPLD so that JTAG-controlled HFI logic can be applied. Circuit designers must assure that the fault insertion multiplexer is added into the design in such a way that overall timing and performance of the circuit is not compromised.

- **Device reconfiguration.** Some power module controllers and clock controllers are configured via JTAG, so one can simulate some failures/

impairments by simply reconfiguring the device, such as disabling one of the device's outputs.

Since the JTAG control mechanism is completely separate from the software executing on processors on the FRU, JTAG-driven failures can be injected any time that the FRU is powered on. The failures can be both inserted and cleared via JTAG commands driven by an outboard PC running commercial JTAG test software.

A hardware project's JTAG/boundary scan engineer can explain what JTAG-based hardware fault insertion is feasible for a particular design and can create appropriate tests. Faults inserted via programmable logic on FPGAs or CPLDs will require support from the logic designer to include JTAG-controlled multiplexors, and so on, for key signals.

11.5.1.3   Driver Manipulation, Reconfiguration, or Reprogramming

Device drivers can sometimes be manipulated via host software to disable a device, alter device input or output, or change processing logic and hence behavior of the device. These manipulations can often be done via software debugger commands, via operating system commands or mechanisms, or via custom software. Note that the process of executing the software that reconfigures the device puts the system software into a particular state that may cause failure detection and recovery to be different from when the system is operating normally.

As driver software is often complex and subject to strict real-time performance requirements, manipulation of this code creates the risk that driver software failures will be introduced. Thus, one must be exceptionally careful to assure that any driver reconfiguration or reprogramming is benign and does not introduce unintended defects into test or production code.

11.5.1.4   Simulated Hardware Fault Insertion

Some hardware simulation tools are powerful enough to emulate software executing on simulated hardware. If one is fortunate enough to have such a rich simulation environment, then one can simulate faults in the simulated hardware and verify that the emulated software behaves appropriately.

11.5.1.5   Discussion

System architects and testers should work with circuit designers, JTAG engineers, and infrastructure/device driver software developers to determine the most cost-effective way to simulate likely hardware failures. Note that the optimal suite of HFI capability may be achieved by designing support for multiple techniques onto each FRU. For example:

- JTAG-controlled gross device failure (HIGHZ) for all JTAG devices supporting HIGHZ

- Routing key signals through FPGAs to enable JTAG pin-level HFI
- Using JTAG-configured clock controllers that can be reconfigured to simulate clock skew and failure
- Using JTAG-configured power module controllers that can be reconfigured to simulate power module failures
- Exposing key electrical connection to circuitry on outer layers of FRU to enable those signals to be pulled to logic low or logic high via fly-wires
- Including transistors onto critical signals to facilitate disabling signals to simulate hardware failure
- Manipulating software drivers to simulate critical hardware failures that are not otherwise accessible

11.5.2   Software Fault Insertion

Software faults can be inserted or injected by manipulating either program text or program data, including system state. These manipulations can be performed at compile time or runtime. Compile time fault insertion, often called *software mutation*, offers tremendous flexibility and precision in the range of faults that can be inserted but requires additional configuration management, compilation, linking, storage, and tracking of the various mutant software versions. In contrast, runtime fault insertion is generally simpler because a single binary image can be used for most or all software fault insertion (SFI) testing. Note that the SFI binary, like a verbose debugging binary, may be slightly different from the final production binary because it includes additional logic that may not be included in the standard commercial version of the product, but there are likely to be few SFI binaries, rather than a menagerie of mutant binaries. There can also be blended software fault insertion techniques in which specially written software can be selectively activated to insert faults or errors at runtime. Common techniques to simulate programming errors, data errors, or redundancy failures include:

- **Software platform commands.** Operating systems and software platform components like database management systems include numerous commands to directly manipulate processes, resources, database records, and so on. These commands (e.g., kill) can be used to directly manipulate processes, files, and numerous system and platform resources to simulate a variety of fault and error conditions.
- **Software debugger.** A software debugger generally enables a wide variety of fine-grained manipulations of running processes and threads, and program data. For example, threads can often be suspended or breakpoints established to simulate nonresponsive or aberrant software behavior, and debuggers allow one to directly alter the contents of variables or data structures.

- **Fault triggering subroutines or commands.** Application- or platform-specific routines or commands can be written to simulate some faults or errors, such as routines that gradually consume specific resources (e.g., eat heap memory, or spin in an infinite loop), alter checksums, and so on.
- **Modified software libraries.** Operating system or platform libraries can be modified or wrapped with a preprocessing layer that enables some calls to return failure based on a counter, state variable, or other configuration mechanism. Such modified libraries may be convenient ways to simulate faults that may otherwise be difficult to create.
- **Modified source code (software mutation).** Some faults are easiest to simulate by actually changing application or platform source code to coerce faults. This generally requires more effort than any of the previous techniques because each fault must be coded, compiled, linked, and loaded onto the target system, and retesting inherently requires the fault to be separately rebuilt with proper build options. Thus, this technique is generally used only for software faults and errors that cannot be simulated any other way.

An additional mechanism to consider is logically accelerating the system's clock to detect problems in background or monitoring mechanisms. If the system can be fooled to believe that, perhaps, one hour of actual real time is a couple of days of system time, then one can simulate a year or more of in-service system time in about a week of actual real time. This enables one to assure that hourly, daily, weekly, or other occasionally executed mechanisms function properly (e.g., without slow resource leaks). The implementation specifics of clock acceleration will vary based on the operating system and hardware architecture, but the fundamental notion is reconfiguring the operating system to expect fewer ticks of the system's real-time clock interrupt per second. For example, if the operating system normally expects 100 clock interrupts per second, then one might reconfigure the operating system on the system-under-test to expect far fewer clock interrupts, such as 3 clock interrupts per second. While this change will impact some aspects of normal system operation, it should enable one to simulate a long operational period without system reboot. Since changing the clock may impact overload control and other core application logic, it may be appropriate to run a lighter traffic load against the system for the duration of the clock acceleration test.

11.5.3 Redundancy Testing

Best practice is to provide commands to manually trigger all switchover and recovery mechanisms so that maintenance engineers can manually recover from failures that are not properly detected, isolated, or recovered automatically by the system. These manual commands can be used to methodically verify the reliability of each recovery mechanism when the system is operating in a wide variety of states. Each recovery mechanism should be executed many, many times to assure it is highly reliable.

If the system supports active-standby redundancy, then both hardware and software faults should be individually inserted onto the standby unit to assure that the system promptly detects and alarms failures on the standby unit. Recovery onto a failed redundant element is also a scenario to consider. While one can't successfully recover service onto a failed element, the primary risk is that a routine switchover to verify that standby unit is operational will eventually detect a failed standby unit. In this case, the system should support graceful restoration of service back to the previously active unit, rather than leaving the system in the awkward state of being stuck on a failed standby unit when the previously active unit is fully operational and available for service. HFI mechanisms can be used to simulate hardware failures on standby modules, and programming error mechanisms can be used to simulate software failures on standby modules.

11.5.4   System Power Robustness Testing

System power can be easily disrupted by manipulating power entry and/or power distribution mechanisms. Best practice is to test a large number of power failure and recovery cycles to assure that the system is highly likely to successfully recover from a power failure when power is reapplied, regardless of the system's state or activities when the power failed. In particular, one needs to assure that regardless of the state of any update operations against persistent storage, the system automatically restarts, checks, and repairs persistent storage when power is reapplied. This verification can be done via a software-controlled relay on the system's power feed. The test fixture closes the relay to apply power to the element, waits a predefined period to let the system correctly start up, and then verifies correct system operation. If the system is not operating properly, then the test stops to permit the system to be debugged. Otherwise, traffic load is applied to the system—ideally a load that frequently writes and reads from persistent storage—and at a random time the relay is opened to cut power to the system. The relay is left open for ten or more seconds to assure that the hardware completely powers down. The fixture then closes the relay to apply power, and the test cycle repeats. After hundreds of cycles with no failures, one can be confident that the system will automatically recover from power failures.

In addition to complete power failures, systems should gracefully recovery from brief power impairments, such as events that cause lights to flicker and home electronics to reset. A risk is that power is restored—possibly triggering a system restart—while the system is in the midst of flushing data to persistent storage and stabilizing the system following power failure indication. For example, switching a circuit breaker off and then on again causes a brief power impairment.

11.5.5   Network Fault Testing

Profound network failures can be simulated by manually disconnecting network connections to adjacent systems. Failures of supporting systems should also be simulated by failing individual instances of each type of supporting system to assure that the target system promptly detects unavailability of the supporting system and reconnects to an alternative system instance. Supporting systems should also be restarted to simulate failures or planned activities like software upgrades to verify graceful reconnection and service continuity by target system. Corrupted, lost, or out-of-sequence packets are simulated via test equipment that manipulates the flow of packets.

11.5.6   Application Protocol Fault Testing

Application protocol testing is accomplished through a combination of mechanisms:

- **Protocol test suites** verify that the system operates properly with a wide variety of valid and invalid protocol syntaxes and semantics
- **Interoperability testing.** Test with legacy/earlier versions of elements that the target system interworks with as well as systems from other suppliers to assure that the system correctly handles older protocol versions and different interpretations of protocol specifications.
- **Client simulators** can generate deliberately wrong messages to assure acceptable handling of incorrect or malicious messages.
- **Overload testing** stresses the system by generating input traffic levels above engineered capacity to assure that congestion control mechanisms work properly. Overload testing should explicitly simulate likely traffic surges, as well as recovery from regional power failure or network failure events. One should verify overload controls on all interfaces that are accessible to users outside the enterprises' intranet.
- **Protocol "fuzz" testing** that provides random inputs to various protocol interfaces and within messages.
- **Boundary testing** that verifies proper handling of boundary values of various protocol fields. For example, if a field supports a range of data values from "M" to "N," then also verify proper handling of "M − 1" and "N + 1" input values.

11.5.7   Procedural Robustness Testing

Robustness testing of procedures assures:

   1. Maintenance procedures have a low probability of execution failure.

2. Impact of likely human failures is minimized.

3. Failures (both related to and independent of the procedure being executed) can be recovered with minimal service impact.

To verify that documented maintenance procedures are reliable, one should execute key procedures several times, including:

- "Hot" FRU removal and FRU insertion
- Software upgrade, update, patch, and retrofit
- Software rollback from undesirable or unsuccessful upgrades, updates, or patches
- Hardware growth

To verify that likely impact of human errors is minimized, one should:

- Verify that all written procedures are complete, clear, and correct.
- Verify that clear confirmation questions are presented before executing service-impacting commands.

To verify that likely failures encountered during execution of procedures can be recovered with minimal service impact, one should:

- Verify that the system checks preconditions and general requirements prior to initiating execution, such as verifying that sufficient free disk space is available.
- Verify that the system can be recovered if failures occur while upgrading a database, operating system, or other third-party elements.
- Verify that if an upgrade script encounters unexpected data values in databases or configuration files, then the data migration or upgrade behaves gracefully so the upgrade can be cleanly stopped and the system rolled back to the previous system state.
- Verify that if application software fails during the upgrade, then the system can be restored.
- Verify that if hardware fails during the upgrade, then the system can be restored.
- Verify that if the network or adjacent systems (e.g., license management server) fail during upgrade, then the system can be restored.

11.6 SELECTING ROBUSTNESS TEST CASES

Given an infinite space of possible failures and an infinite set of states that a system can be in when a fault occurs, yet finite resources for testing, one must select robustness test cases wisely. The primary objectives when constructing the suite of robustness test cases to execute are:

1. **Verify proper detection of all categories of potentially service-impacting failures.** One must balance depth of testing in specific error categories against breadth of testing across all applicable test categories. In addition, one must balance the investment in testing against the customers' tolerance of less-than-perfectly robust behavior and the business's willingness to risk failing to meet customers' robustness expectations.

2. **Verify reliability of all recovery mechanisms.** One must execute all recovery mechanisms sufficiently under a variety of operational circumstances to assure that these mechanisms will perform reliably when activated, even when the system is in a degraded state.

One should carefully analyze root causes of field outages to identify which failure containment, detection, isolation, and recovery mechanisms failed to operate properly in recent releases, and explicitly add robustness tests to assure reliable operation of those mechanisms; this is detailed in Section 12.1, "Analyzing Field Outage Events."

A portion of robustness tests that have consistently passed in previous releases should be automated or retired in each new release to free resources to execute new robustness tests. As tests that consistently pass are automated or retired and new ones are selected, testers should be careful to assure that investment in robustness testing is appropriately balanced across robustness test categories. Beyond assuring that no robustness category is inadvertently neglected, one should consciously align robustness testing resources based on:

- **Predicted failure rates.** Critical failure rates are not uniform across software modules, FRUs, and procedures. Since higher critical failure rates mean robustness mechanisms will be executed more often, it is prudent to invest more in robustness testing of modules that are more likely to fail.

- **Historic outages.** Failures of automatic robustness mechanisms that led to service outages of deployed systems are obviously areas for increased robustness test coverage.

- **Catastrophic risk.** Some mechanisms, like geographic redundancy disaster recovery procedures, may be rarely executed but are so crucial that they should be methodically verified for all major releases.

11.7 ANALYZING ROBUSTNESS TEST RESULTS

Pass rates for categories of robustness tests are natural metrics, and results are easy to compare against statistical reliability requirements like switchover success probability and failure coverage factors. Mature test organizations may use statistical confidence limits to characterize the number of test cases or iterations required to deem a requirement met. For example, demonstrating a 95% switchover success probability metric with 60% statistical confidence implies 23 iterations with 0 failures, or 40 iterations with 1 failure, or

62 iterations with 2 failures. As not all scenarios present the same risk, one might invest more test effort to increase confidence of meeting statistical robustness requirements associated with more likely failure scenarios.

The probability that a system will automatically detect, isolate, and recover a failure in the specified time (called *coverage factor*) is the crucial robustness metric to estimate and manage to maximize system availability. Conceptually, the actual coverage factor observed in the field should be somewhere between the robustness test pass rate of first pass testing and the robustness test pass rate of final pass testing. The logic of this is that first pass testing is a proxy for the success probability the first time system is exposed to a new failure, while final test pass results should represent the best-case overall probability. Since testers should carefully select robustness test cases to assure that most likely failure scenarios are addressed via robustness test cases first, one can assume that robustness tests that were not executed in current or previous releases are less likely to occur than the probability of the failures that have been simulated in robustness testing. Therefore, the weighted probability of the system successfully detecting, isolating, and recovering from expected failures should be somewhere between first and final test pass rates. For example, assume 100 fault insertion scenarios are tested against a particular hardware or software module and the initial test pass rate was 90% and the final test pass rate was 100%. The simplest estimate of failure coverage factor (probability of that module successfully detecting, isolating, and recovering an arbitrary failure) is the average of these two values: 95%. Arithmetic average is not necessarily the best estimate, but it certainly is defensible; more sophisticated estimates can also be made. For example, if the 100 fault insertion scenarios are likely to cover the most likely failure scenarios, then the probability that a typical failure will be successfully detected, isolated, and recovered in less than the maximum acceptable service disruption latency may be closer to the final pass rate than to the arithmetic average of first and final pass rates of robustness testing. Estimates should be calibrated and validated via analysis of field data when it becomes available.

11.8 STABILITY TESTING

Stability testing, sometimes called *endurance* testing, applies several days of heavy and mixed user and operational traffic to the system to simulate production operation. While operating reliably over a finite period does not enable one to directly estimate the critical software failure rate, it can expose a wide variety of critical and subcritical failures, indicating that a system is not yet ready for commercial service. In addition, service reliability can be directly measured by analyzing results of the millions or thousands of transactions or requests that will be processed during several days of a single stability test run. While outages are caused by activation of residual critical software faults, individual transactional failures on systems operating at or below engineered capacity are generally caused by activation of subcritical residual software (including design and architectural) faults. Since the same development process creates and removes both critical and subcritical defects, defect insertion and removal characteristics of critical faults is likely to be correlated with defect insertion and removal characteristics of subcritical software faults. Thus, service or transactional reliability (e.g., defects per million transactions—DPM) can serve as a crude proxy for number of residual subcritical defects, and this metric is likely to be roughly correlated with the number of residual critical software defects. Although transactional reliability may be weakly correlated with critical software failure rate, it is highly correlated with quality of service or quality of experience. After all, every failed transaction is likely to impact an individual user or OAM&P engineer. The higher the rate of defective transactions, the lower the customer's perception of service quality and reliability is likely to be.

11.8.1 Stability Test Approach

The objective of stability testing is to simulate three or more days of heavy, mixed service to assure that the system is completely stable. As stability testing should include both heavy user traffic and OAM&P activities, it is convenient to simulate the daily traffic patterns expected on a system with peak user traffic through a long (perhaps 16-hour) busy period, and a heavy period of maintenance activity (perhaps 4 hours) with a lower level of user traffic; the additional 4 hours in a 24-hour cycle can be used to transition between busy and maintenance periods. The complete stability test should be at least 72 hours (3 days) of uninterrupted operation (i.e., no reboots or restarts). The normal phase of stability testing should expose the system to a heavy traffic load that never exceeds the rated load of the system configuration under test. Thus overload control mechanisms should not be activated, and hence any failed transaction or request represents activation of a software, design, or architectural defect.

Stability testing should explicitly exercise all supported user and OAM&P interfaces of the system to their full engineered capacities. OAM&P traffic should cover fault and alarm management, user provisioning, performance management, service management, backups, routine diagnostics, and so on. Since systems are not generally designed to serve maximum user and OAM&P loads simultaneously, one should stagger the maximum user traffic and maximum OAM&P loads to avoid overloading the system. Simulating a daily cycle of heavy user traffic for approximately 16 hours, heavy OAM&P traffic for 4 to 6 hours, and a couple of hours to transition traffic between maximum user load and maximum OAM&P load is typical. Note that during maximum user traffic load there is a modest OAM&P load running, and a modest user traffic load is served during maximum OAM&P load period. This is graphically illustrated in Figure 11.4.

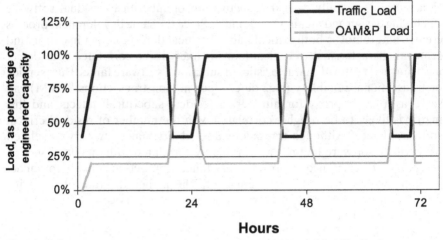

Figure 11.4   Example of System Loading During Normal Phase of Stability Testing

User traffic load should include the broadest practical range of user operational scenarios to assure stability of the broadest portion of user-related
software. OAM&P traffic should include:

- Adding, modifying, and deleting user accounts
- Adding, modifying, and deleting system resources or objects
- Data backup
- Retrieving and reporting usage and performance data
- Routine system diagnostics and audits

The specific user traffic and OAM&P operations chosen should be
designed to force operations that exercise concurrency controls, such as having
valid users authenticated while simultaneously adding, modifying, and deleting other user accounts. Normal stability testing can be complemented with
an adversarial phase of stability testing that pushes traffic levels to overload,
and simulates switchovers, failures, and other adversarial scenarios to verify
that the system returns to stability and normal operation after the overload
or adversarial scenario is automatically addressed.

11.8.2   Measures and Metrics

Stability test runs often generate reams of log, performance, audit, and other
data because a system is run at full engineered load for days and should successfully process millions of operations or transactions. Distilling all of this
data into meaningful metrics can be challenging. Applicable stability test
metrics can be broadly classified into the following categories:

1. **Throughput metrics.** Summarize successful operations and transactions. The primary data for throughput metrics is often results recorded by test tools or clients that drive test traffic into the system, or by the system's own performance metrics. The simplest metrics to consider during stability testing are number of operations attempted and number that failed. Note that counting the handful of transactions per million that fail is easier for most people to grasp than 990,000-plus transactions per million that are likely to succeed. As the system will be running mostly at engineered capacity for hours during stability testing, it is likely that millions of user operations or transactions will have been attempted and thousands of OAM&P operations. Results can be easily converted into defects per million (DPM) as follows:

$$DPM = \frac{NumberOfFailures}{NumberOfAttempts} * 1,000,000$$

Transactional latency, such as 95th percentile latency, is interesting but often much harder to measure when the system is running at full engineered capacity. Throughput results can be summarized by class of transactions or operations, such as:

22.7 million user query transactions processed with 8.3 DPM (requirement < 10) and 95% completing in less than 135 milliseconds (requirement < 150 milliseconds).

2. **Error counts.** Faults or errors can occur during the stability run, and these can cause alarms to be raised, processes to fail, and so on. Some of these errors may be minor and expected, such as perhaps dropping an occasional transaction because a fixed-size buffer is full at the instant that a new message arrives; some of these errors may be major, such as a process crashing and being automatically restarted; some of these errors may even be critical and prevent the stability run from completing without manual recovery. The number and nature of alarms and errors should be measured. Both severity and duration of alarms should be considered when assessing a stability run. Error count results can be summarized simply as follows:

No critical, major, or minor alarms during stability test run.

3. **Resource usage.** As a stability test run drives a system to full engineered capacity, there will be heavy usage of system resources like CPU, heap memory, and file systems. The stability run should be long enough that most resource leaks can be detected by comparing several snapshots of resource usage during the run. While one would expect some growth in resource usage as the stability test starts and the traffic load is increased from 0% to 100% of engineered load, after the first full cycle of 100% user and 100% OAM&P traffic the system's resource usage should stabilize, and resource usage should not continue to grow

for the rest of the run. One should measure resource usage at one or more points in the middle of the stability run and at the end of the run to see if any growth in resource usage is detectable. Any growth in resource usage is likely to indicate a leak (e.g., a memory leak) that can eventually cause a critical failure in the field. Resource usage results can be summarized with statements like:

Memory and other resource usage stopped increasing after the first 24 hours of the stability test run.

Typically, organizations will summarize the results of a stability run with a variety of quantitative values, and text explaining any anomalies. For example, stability test results might be summarized with the following 8 pieces of data:

1. Planned and actual duration of stability run
2. Whether the run completed as planned without manual intervention (or explanation of any manual intervention)
3. DPM and total count of logon, query, update, and other simulated end-user operations
4. DPM and total count of operations, administration, maintenance, and provisioning operations by simulated OAM&P users
5. Count, duration, and explanation of any critical alarms or errors
6. Count, duration, and explanation of major alarms or errors
7. Count, duration, and explanation of minor alarms or errors
8. Confirmation that no resource usage growth was observed (or explanation of resource growth)

Stability runs can also be used to verify some system performance and capacity requirements because the system will be operated at full engineered capacity for hours. Sophisticated organizations will instrument stability test runs so that capacity and performance requirements can also be validated. Thus, stability test results may also include results of performance and capacity measurements that were captured during the stability test run.

Establishing explicit "pass" or "fail" criteria for each of these parameters may require some experience both to debug the stability test scripts and to characterize typical system behavior. After analysis of several stability test runs one should understand what system behavior is expected. Unacceptable field performance in previous releases might indicate that stability criteria for any unacceptable releases were too lax and thus that stability criteria should be raised for future releases.

11.8.3 Stability Requirements

Best practice is for stability testing to be driven by one or more stability requirements that are established early in the development stage. As explained in the previous section, it may be hard to set quantitative pass criteria for stability test measures and metrics before one has completed and analyzed several stability test iterations, and thus one may wish to approach stability requirements in two steps. The first step is to define the general parameters of stability testing, and the second step is to define quantitative and qualitative pass criteria. General parameters of stability testing should include:

- Minimum duration of testing, such as 72 or 96 hours.
- Specify rated engineering load on system for both user and OAM&P activities. During stability testing the load will be pushed to rated engineering load, and performance will be evaluated against transactional reliability and latency requirements.
- Specify the traffic load mix and volume to be used, such as which user and OAM&P commands shall be included in the stability run, and in what ratios. Maximum supported user transaction rates for various system configurations are usually specified in configuration requirements. If maximum OAM&P rates (e.g., maximum rate at which subscriber accounts can be provisioned per hour) are not specified in configuration requirements, then the stability requirements should define these values.

Quantitative pass criteria can include:

- Specify transactional reliability and latency requirements, such as less than 10 defects per million (DPM) on all operations and median latency of 10 milliseconds for query operations, 30 milliseconds for update operations, and so on.
- Specify maximum number of acceptable system alarms during stability run, such as:
  - 0 critical alarms raised
  - 0 major alarms raised
  - No more than 5 minor alarms raised, all of which shall be automatically cleared in less than 60 seconds
- Characterize *completely stable* to set test pass criteria. While there are an infinite number of possible failures that can occur during a stability run, it is useful to generally define what "completely stable" or "acceptably stable" means for the system under test, and testers will explicitly verify each of these criteria. These criteria generally include:
  - No crashed, failed, stuck, or hung processes or threads
  - No core dumps
  - No hardware failures
  - No ongoing growth in resource usage or consumption (i.e., no memory leaks)
  - No performance or throughput degradation

11.9 RELEASE CRITERIA

Before deciding to release a system to customers, development teams should consider three fundamental questions regarding system quality and reliability:

1. **Have requirements been adequately verified?** Development processes should have sufficient traceability to assure that plans exist to verify each requirement prior to system release. Because schedule or other challenges often arise that block and delay test case execution, projects often have formal criteria for the percentage of test cases that must be attempted prior to release; minimum of 95% of test cases attempted is common. Of course, an acceptable percentage of test cases must pass for the final software release; a minimum final test pass rate of at least 95% is common.

2. **Have all known critical and major defects been appropriately addressed?** The vast majority of critical and major defects discovered in system verification should be fixed prior to release. However, the risk of not fixing some defects may be acceptably low and thus fixing may be deferred to a maintenance release, or even accepted as a *known defect*. In these cases, the defects will often be documented in the customer documentation so customers are aware of the risk, and perhaps are given a workaround. The key is to assure that there are no known defects that are likely to present an unacceptable risk to customers in field deployment and operation.

3. **Is the number of unknown residual critical software defects likely to be low enough to achieve acceptably reliable operation in field deployment?** Critical software failures that escalate to service outages are largely caused by activating residual, previously unknown software defects. Unfortunately, this unknown parameter must be estimated because techniques do not exist to directly measure the number of remaining (unknown) residual software defects in a module or system.

The first two questions are relatively straightforward because they deal with known facts and data: Requirements, test plans, test results, and discovered defects are all well understood, so business and engineering judgment can be applied to the data. Estimating the number of residual defects remaining in a system and assessing the risk of achieving the system's reliability requirements with that number of residual defects is a profoundly different problem. In adition to these general software quality questions, decision makers should also consider robustness test results, stability test results, and best estimate of service availability.

11.9.1   Robustness Testing Results

Robustness tests are generally more challenging to pass than sunny-day functional tests, and so it is often harder for development teams to drive the pass rate for robustness tests to 100% than it is for other test plans. Thus, one should always consider if the attempted and passed rates for only robustness tests achieved the system's overall test attempt and test pass criteria, or if poor results of robustness testing were washed out when averaged with sunny-day test results. If the test attempt or test pass rate for robustness tests is below the system's overall criteria, then this presents a risk that inevitable critical failures will not be automatically detected, isolated, and recovered, thus requiring manual action by customers' staff to resolve a service outage.

Low robustness test execution or pass results can be clearly presented to decision makers as a risk with a statement like:

17 of the 67 robustness tests did not pass on the system, and thus there is elevated risk that critical failures will escalate to service outages and require manual actions to recover, rather than being automatically detected and recovered by the system.

This leads to mitigation plans such as:

100% of the 67 robustness tests will be executed and passed in Maintenance Release 1.

11.9.2   Stability Testing Results

Stability testing demonstrates how well the system performs under heavy and varying loads of user and OAM&P traffic. Any failures or anomalies in results of final stability test results are cause of concern, and should be disclosed to decision makers before making a release readiness decision. Ordinary, successful stability test results can be disclosed to decision makers with a simple statement like:

System demonstrated complete stability during 72.6 hour stability run, mostly performed at full system capacity, and achieved:

- **7.3 defective user transactions per million (target < 10) in 36.5 M user transactions**
  - **Previous release (R2.1) demonstrated 8.2 DPM in 32.7 M user transactions**
- **63.2 defective OAM&P transactions per million (target < 100) in 2.1 M OAM&P operations**
  - **Previous release (R2.1) demonstrated 71.1 DPM in 1.9 M OAM&P transactions**

11.9.3 Estimating System Availability at System Release

Project teams should analyze available data prior to system release to make a best estimate of likely system availability and frankly present that best estimate to decision makers. Best practice is to consider at least the following:

- Does the number of estimated high-severity residual defects appear acceptably low, especially compared to acceptability of previous releases?

- Do robustness test results demonstrate that the system is likely to automatically detect, isolate, and recover from inevitable failures without producing unacceptable service disruptions?

- Do stability test results demonstrate that the system is completely stable under a prolonged heavy and varying load of user and OAM&P traffic?

- When actual measured latencies and final best estimates of failure coverage factors, switchover success rates, critical failure rates, and so on are input to availability model, what is the best estimate of service availability (which may be expressed as a range), and how does this estimate compare to the availability requirement for the release?

Availability is inherently a difficult parameter to estimate because it is driven by rare critical failure events that are not properly detected, isolated, and recovered automatically by the system. A single outage often impacts a monthly measurement of a small population, and a couple of outages can significantly impact a quarterly result of a small or medium population size. Despite these inherent field performance and measurement risks, it is best for the reliability prime or a system architect or a system tester to offer a quantitative best estimate or best estimate range of service availability for decision makers to consider when making a release decision. This estimate may be framed simply for decision makers with a statement like:

Best estimate of annualized unplanned hardware plus software downtime is 10 to 30 minutes (99.994% to 99.998%) against a 5.3 down-minute (99.999%) requirement.

Decision makers will recognize that the reliability of the specific software release is close to the target, but it is not likely to achieve the target over a large population of elements across a long period. Decision makers can use this information to reset customers' expectations, accelerate plans for reliability-improving features and testing in future releases, and take other appropriate mitigating and corrective actions.

11.10   PROBLEMS

The following problems consider a "target system" identified by the instructor:

1. Define pass criteria for robustness tests for the target system.
2. Identify the network interfaces to the system that should be considered for robustness testing.
3. What software fault insertion techniques are most appropriate for the target system, and why?
4. Propose test cases to verify two redundancy mechanisms of the target system.
5. Propose test cases to verify the robustness of one of the target system's supported application protocols.
6. What is the purpose of stability testing?
7. Propose a mix of user traffic for stability testing of the target system.
8. Propose a mix of OAM&P traffic for stability testing of the target system.
9. What metrics should be recorded during stability testing of the target system?
10. Propose pass criteria for stability testing of the target system.

Chapter 12

Closing the Loop

After the system is released to the field, one should carefully monitor field performance to determine if it is meeting customers' expectations for service availability and service reliability. If service reliability or service availability is not meeting expectations, then a roadmap of reliability and availability improvements can be constructed and executed to efficiently drive the system to meet expectations. This chapter details both analyzing field outage data and reliability roadmapping.

12.1 ANALYZING FIELD OUTAGE EVENTS

Enterprises deploy systems to address concrete business needs like delivering some commercially important service to end users or to support some aspect of product or service delivery or some business process, or to monitor, manage, provision, or operate one or more of those systems. Service availability of some systems directly impacts an enterprise's ability to serve its customers, while other systems impact the enterprise's ability to operate efficiently. Sophisticated enterprises will measure and carefully monitor service availability and quality of crucial systems; bonus payments of enterprise staff may be tied directly to achieving high service availability or determined indirectly via customer satisfaction metrics. Thus, sophisticated enterprises will often know how reliably critical systems are able to deliver service in their network.

The strategic challenge for system suppliers is to assure that the deployed system meets the service availability and reliability expectations of their customers. Beyond careful design, development, and testing, and promptly supporting emergency recoveries, the tactical challenge for the system supplier is:

1. Acquire details of product-attributable outage events.
2. Analyze outage events to determine root causes.

Design for Reliability: Information and Computer-Based Systems, by Eric Bauer
Copyright © 2010 Institute of Electrical and Electronics Engineers

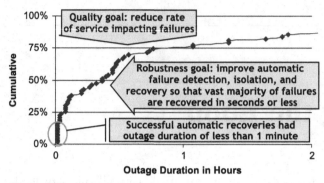

Figure 12.1   Example Cumulative Software Outage Duration Analysis

3. Take corrective quality actions to eliminate or minimize the root cause of the primary failure mode.

4. Take corrective robustness actions to automatically detect, isolate, and recover similar failures with little or no service disruption.

The tactical challenge is illustrated with an example: Figure 12.1 is an example of cumulative software outage durations for hundreds of instances of a highly reliable product operating over a calendar year in one enterprise. This system typically detected and isolated failures, and automatically switched over to standby modules in 2 to 6 seconds. Since this enterprise measures system usage in minutes rather than seconds, outage events are rounded up to the next minute. Thus, most of the events recorded with duration of 1 minute were probably only a few seconds, and thus are usually deemed successful automatic recovery events. However, more than 80% of the recorded events were longer than 1 minute, and thus exceeded the maximum acceptable service disruption latency. The purpose of field data analysis is to understand what corrective actions should be taken to both drive the quality goal of reducing the rate critical failures and drive the robustness goal of improving the system's automatic detection, isolation, and recovery so that the vast majority of inevitable failures that do occur will be automatically detected, isolated, and recovered in less than the maximum acceptable service disruption latency.

It is valuable to analyze field outages at two levels:

1. **As individual events.** Identifying specific corrective actions to improve automatic failure detection and/or shorten recovery latency from careful analysis of individual events gives insights into design changes/improvements and additional robustness test cases.

2. **As classes of events.** Statistical analysis of sets of outages over periods of months gives insight into architectural and design weaknesses, limi-

tations in robustness test plans, and weaknesses in test and quality activities.

This section discusses how enterprises measure service availability, how individual events can be analyzed, how classes of events can be statistically analyzed, and how anecdotal data can be solicited and considered. The insights from this analysis can be used as input to drive a product roadmap of reliability-improving features and testing, which is discussed in Section 12.2.

12.1.1 Measuring Service Availability

Enterprises often measure service availability impairments via one or more of the following techniques:

- **Manually created trouble or incident reports.** Problems that prompt end users to complain or otherwise trigger maintenance engineers to intervene are often considered formal incidents and documented in a trouble-tracking system. Records of service disruptions or outages will capture the time service was impacted, the time service was restored, and other details that enable enterprises to easily compute the service impact associated with each of these ticketed events.

- **Probes.** Service quality and availability can be probed via test clients. Enterprises offering networked services routinely test their services with automated tools and scripts. These probes may be colocated with the system being measured to eliminate service impact of networking and access facilities, or in end-user locations to measure performance likely to be observed by system users.

- **Alarms.** Systems should automatically raise critical alarms when service is impacted, and clear those alarms when service is restored. It is logically simple to compute the duration of each critical alarm event by calculating the latency between posting and clearance of critical alarms, and sum these latencies over a month or other reporting period to estimate service availability; some service assurance products do exactly this.

- **Performance data.** Many systems maintain detailed performance metrics for sessions, transactions, system throughput, and so on. For example, according to RFC 3261, SIP (Session Initiation Protocol) servers can return six categories of responses: 1xx provisional, 2xx success, 3xx redirection, 4xx request error, 5xx server error, and 6xx global failure; some of these return codes like "500 Server Internal Error" and "503 Service Unavailable," which clearly indicate the failure of a system. Careful analysis of request and response data can indicate how systems and solutions are actually performing.

Sophisticated enterprises will track the service availability, reliability, and quality of their critical systems on a quarterly, monthly, weekly, or even daily basis. Managers of the information systems, engineering, operations, or maintenance organization responsible for the system typically review this data regularly and compare it to performance targets. Tying the financial incentives or bonuses of these people to achieving key availability, reliability, and quality performance targets further motivates them to maximize the service availability, reliability, and quality characteristics that are used in financial incentive calculations. If performance drops below target, then the enterprise may take corrective actions that could include escalation to the system supplier and activation of business remedies, such as payment of liquidated damages by the system supplier.

A challenge for system suppliers is that they generally have no access to performance, alarm, or probe data for systems deployed and in commercial service at enterprises. Suppliers should have records of the outages that were escalated to the supplier's technical support organization, and those events should be carefully analyzed. Without special arrangement with the enterprise(s), suppliers are not likely to have visibility into the service disruption events that were addressed directly by the enterprise's maintenance engineers. Enterprise employees are generally smart and good at what they do; as they gain experience over time they are often able to address many—perhaps the vast majority—of failures and service impairments without escalating to the system supplier's technical support organization. Over time, suppliers may have less visibility into the typical problems enterprises experience with systems in production. This can result in enterprises complaining about poor software quality, reliability, or stability to system suppliers, yet the system suppliers don't fully appreciate either exactly what the customer is experiencing or know precisely what to do about it.

Best practice is for enterprises to share their outage data for critical systems with strategic suppliers so suppliers can analyze that data to drive service availability, reliability, and quality improvements. Sharing operational data for critical systems is often challenging for enterprises because it may expose end-user information and details of proprietary business operations and policies. Since different enterprises will inevitably have different data formats, analysis can be a huge task for system suppliers. As a result, sharing of outage-related data must be carefully considered, but it offers a valuable mechanism for system suppliers to improve the quality, reliability, and availability of systems deployed with strategic customers.

12.1.2 Analysis of Individual Outage Events

Since no single failure of a high-availability system should cause a service disruption to end users of longer than the maximum acceptable latency specified in the system's reliability requirements, a substantial service disruption or outage implies at least two failures. Two simultaneous failures are often called a *double-failure* situation; examples of double failures include:

- Primary hardware or software failure, followed by a failure to automatically detect the failure promptly.

- Primary hardware or software failure (which was promptly and automatically detected) followed by an unsuccessful (or unacceptably slow) automatic recovery action.

- An automatically detected hardware or software failure that is incorrectly isolated by the system so an inappropriate automatic recovery action is executed. Even if the inappropriate recovery action is completed successfully, by definition it cannot restore service..

- Human mistake while executing a procedure, such as entering a wrong IP address or configuration command, without appropriate automatic checking and/or a confirmation step to ask "Are you sure?" before performing a profound action.

- Hardware, software, or procedural error followed by a human mistake, such as human being accidentally removing the then-active FRU rather than the failed FRU, or incorrectly accepting an erroneous command at the systems' "Are you sure?" prompt.

- Failure when the system is operating in simplex mode, such as because of a previous but not yet repaired failure or during a maintenance action such as software upgrade.

- A design flaw that permitted a single failure to impact service.

In addition to traditional root-cause analysis of the primary defect(s) that escaped to the field and what should be done to prevent further defect escapes, one should also explicitly consider the failure(s) of the robustness mechanisms that enabled the primary failure to escalate into a service outage. Specifically, one should consider the following five items when analyzing field outages:

1. Was the failure detected fast enough? If not, then how could the failure have been detected faster?

2. Was the failure initially isolated to the correct recoverable module and was the right recovery action initiated? If not, then what caused the diagnostic failure, and what can be done to improve diagnostic accuracy?

3. Was the recovery action rapid and reliable? If not, then what should be done to improve it?

4. What robustness testing could have exposed the defect(s) that caused unacceptable automatic recovery?

5. What additional robustness test cases should be added to minimize risk of similar outages?

12.1.3 Statistical Analysis of Multiple Outage Events

As one can fail to see the forest for the trees, it is possible for teams to focus too closely on fixing individual problems to recognize architectural, design, process, or testing gaps in their design for reliability program. Examining the broader pool of outages complements detailed root-cause analysis of specific outages to enable better understanding of both general areas of weakness in the system and to set the impact of these weaknesses into context. For example, consider the hypothetical summary of outage analysis in results in Figure 12.2 of the sample system described in Chapter 9 compared to the downtime prediction and budget from Section 10.4.

The key insights from this summary analysis are:

- System availability prediction was close to observed performance in first 12 months of deployment following system release. Thus prediction model is "roughly right." Had the prediction been significantly off from actual performance, then one would have had to consider if the failures were typical or extraordinary. If the failures were extraordinary (e.g., due to an epidemic quality problem with a supplier, or a specific defect that caused many service outages), then the model may be acceptable for predicting typical downtime. If the failures were typical, then both the input parameters and model itself should be compared to actual performance to determine if and how input assumptions and/or the model itself should be changed. Note that availability models are not expected to be better than roughly right, but huge gaps should be analyzed and addressed to assure that predictions are sufficiently credible to be useful when making business decisions.

- Frontend blades experienced significantly more downtime than predicted. Actions should be taken to:
  - Determine if failure rate was higher than expected.
  - Determine if there were more silent (uncovered) failures than expected.

Component	Annualized, prorated unplanned hardware plus software downtime (in minutes)					
	Budget	Budget percentage	Predicted for release X.y	Predicted percentage	Actual, 12 months following release of X.y	Actual percentage
Frontend blades	2.25	43%	3.73	44%	6.41	62%
Backend blades	2.50	48%	4.21	50%	3.93	38%
Management blades	Failure of management blades does not impact user service					
Chassis, etc.	0.50	10%	0.48	6%	0	0%
Total	5.25		8.42		10.34	
Availability	99.9990%		99.9984%		99.9980%	

Figure 12.2 Hypothetical Outage Analysis of Sample System

- Determine if automatic recovery or switchover took longer than expected.
- Determine if automatic recovery or switchover actions were less likely to be successful than expected.
- Determine if manual recoveries took longer than expected (and if so, then why did they?).

Corrective actions should be taken to realign frontend blade behaviors that did not match expectations.

- Backend blades performed as expected.
- Chassis and related equipment caused no service outages in the 12-month period, which is expected given the very low predicted failure rates and mature fault tolerance mechanisms of these elements

If one has at least a handful of outage records from relatively similar system deployments, then one can perform simple analysis to understand what events are causing enterprises the most pain, and hence where effort might be productively applied to minimize future pain. Outage records generally include the following information, which can be insightful:

- **Date and time of event.** Are events uniformly distributed across day and night, or are they weighted to certain times of day (e.g., busy periods) or certain real-world events (e.g., popular events, electrical storms) or maintenance activities (e.g., shortly after system upgrades or reconfigurations, etc.) or something else?
- **System instance.** Are events uniformly distributed across system instances, or are a few systems generating more than their fair share of outage events? Note that repeated failures of a system instance could indicate diagnostic failure, meaning that the maintenance engineers did not properly diagnose and correct the true root cause of the failure from the first incident.
- **Capacity loss.** What aspect and portion of system capacity is lost? What failure signature does this pattern suggest?
- **Outage duration.** Does the outage duration suggest successful automatic recovery or successful repair by the maintenance engineer on duty? Long outage durations could indicate that problems were hard to detect, isolate, or recover, or perhaps the event was even escalated to other experts within the enterprise or to the system supplier's technical support organization.
- **Actual fix.** What recovery action was deemed by the maintenance engineer to actually resolve the problem? Actual fix options often include:
  - Recovered without intervention
  - Process or application restart
  - Soft reboot of blade or FRU
  - Hard reboot (i.e., reseating) FRU

- Soft or hard reboot of system
- Replace FRU
- Resynchronize, repair, or restore configuration or other data

- **Cause category.** Enterprises often assign cause categories to events, but the categories should be considered in context. For example, an enterprise might consider "documentation" to include both written materials provided by the system supplier as well as written procedures and records created by the enterprise, or "hardware" may include not only the system itself but also terminal servers, some IP gear, and other supporting equipment.

One should recognize that "outage pain" is generally characterized by the multiplicative product of capacity loss and outage duration. Long events that impact lots of users are obviously more of a business concern than short events that impact few users. Thus, it is often useful to look for similarities, trends, and patterns in the large and long duration events, and focus first on those events to maximize the benefit of analysis and corrective action efforts. Looking at the dataset from each of these perspectives should reveal whether outage events are essentially uniformly distributed across time, space, failure modes, and so on, or if there are patterns suggesting opportunities for further investigation and perhaps more focused corrective actions.

One should be aware that the reporting rate of outage events can vary between enterprises due to factors such as:

- **Definition of "primary functionality".** Systems often support several end-user, operations, administration, maintenance, and provisioning capabilities. While all enterprises will consider unavailability of critical end-user services to be an outage, some enterprises will also consider unavailability of management visibility, provisioning, or loss of redundancy to be outages as well.

- **How scheduled events are treated.** A small portion of scheduled maintenance activities like software upgrades will fail and some failures may impact service. If enterprises track scheduled work in a different system from troubles, then downtime for complications or failures of scheduled work may be recorded in the scheduled work management system rather than the trouble-tracking system. Analysis and calculations based on events in the trouble-tracking system will thus exclude any downtime from failures attributed to scheduled events that were captured in the scheduled work system.

- **Customer's policies and procedures.** Maintenance engineers, like everyone else, are busy and the paperwork associated with trouble tracking is not the highlight of their job. Thus, they may fail to report brief, small, or otherwise minor events if they are busy or lazy. In addition, enterprises may have policies to delay ("park") small outages that occur in peak hours into off-peak hours to minimize collateral impact to other users, or to delay resolution of outages on some lower-priority systems that occur in off-peak hours (e.g., nights, weekends) to normal business hours to minimize overtime expenses.

- **Compensation policies.** If compensation policies are tied to ticketed outage data, then there may be a bias to report or underreport to maximize the employees' bonus treatment. If service downtime or rate of emergency recovery actions negatively impacts their bonus payout, then they may underreport those events.

One should also recognize that outage durations can vary from enterprise to enterprise—and perhaps even across data centers in the same enterprise—based on differences in operational policies discussed in Section 5.11.4, "Robust Operational Policies."

12.1.4 Soliciting Anecdotal Remarks on System Performance

An enterprise's service availability expectations are often set into the broad and complex context of an enterprise's organization, historic performance and experiences, and many other factors, often collectively called "corporate culture." This culture often contributes to what is treated as exceptional (e.g., what triggers trouble tickets to be created) versus what is merely considered normal "background noise." Sophisticated enterprises often permit less background noise or variation in operation of their critical systems, while less mature enterprises may adopt a more casual operational policy and tolerate more noise or background variations. Discussion with appropriate maintenance and operations staff at enterprises can indicate how much operation noise is really occurring, and suggest what portion of service impairments may be known to the enterprise but not routinely reported to the system supplier.

The maintenance engineers who operate equipment on a daily basis often acquire great insight into the glitches and quirks in a system's behavior. While the first occurrence of the glitch or quirk might make it into a trouble ticket to the system supplier, these events may quickly be accepted as periodic reminders of the poor quality of the particular product, such as when the browser or some other application on your PC crashes and you remind yourself not to use that feature or application next time. For instance, if an enterprise learns that a system's stability degrades over time, it may mitigate this by scheduling a system restart once a week (sometimes called *software rejuvenation* by suppliers trying to put a positive spin on bad software). While the periodic reboot doesn't appear in the enterprise's outage database, it is a regular reminder to the enterprise of a system's poor quality.

When commercially feasible, it is often very insightful for architects, support, or quality engineers to discuss system availability, reliability, and quality with experienced maintenance engineers at sophisticated enterprises operating the system to calibrate and validate their assumptions about how the systems will actually operate in the field. The conversation can be framed around several broad topics:

- Discussion questions on **system measurement**:
  1. How do you measure the quality, reliability, and availability of this system?
  2. Do you report the quality, reliability, or availability of this system to enterprise leaders? If so, what metrics are reported and what targets are the metrics compared to?
  3. Does performance, quality, reliability, or availability of the system impact financial bonuses paid to enterprise management or staff? If so, what quantitative performance, quality, reliability, or availability metric value is required to achieve 100% of the applicable bonus target?
- Discussion questions on **outages and emergency recoveries**:
  1. What causes an enterprise trouble ticket to be created for an outage?
  2. What impairments are too small to be deemed an outage?
  3. How quickly would an enterprise outage trouble ticket be escalated to the system supplier's technical support team?
- Discussion questions on **planned maintenance actions**:
  1. What is the policy on installing security and stability patches? Are all of them installed? How quickly?
  2. What is the policy on installing software updates and upgrades? Are all of them installed? How quickly?
  3. How often is the system restarted?
  4. What approvals and preparation occur prior to execution of planned maintenance actions?
  5. Are service disruptions during planned maintenance actions recorded?
  6. What metrics are tracked for planned maintenance actions?
- Beyond these general operational policy questions, it may be possible to discuss specific questions about **system behavior, quality, and stability** such as:
  1. How stable is the system?
  2. How good is the system's automatic failure detection?
  3. How good is the system's automatic failure recovery?
  4. How good are the system's diagnostics?
  5. How good are the system's documented procedures?

Answers to these questions set the outage records into context within the enterprise(s) operating the system.

12.2 RELIABILITY ROADMAPPING

Customers often have long lists of must-have and nice-to-have features for new systems, yet practical business considerations often force both customers and suppliers to buy and deploy new systems before all of these features have been fully implemented. To encourage customers to deploy systems sooner, suppliers often share roadmaps of system features with customers to facilitate a dialog to enable the supplier to deliver early system releases with the minimum set of core functionality to meet the customers' initial deployment needs, and then deliver feature additions and improvements on a schedule that meets customers' needs. Ideally, customers get systems and software releases just in time and suppliers get sufficient timely revenue to meet the expectations of their business case.

Reliability is inherently a secondary product characteristic that customers consider for systems that offer acceptable functionality on an acceptable delivery schedule at an acceptable price. As with functionality and other product characteristics, customers will often accept initial (perhaps trial) versions of a system that are somewhat less reliable so long as the supplier offers a credible plan to deliver the service availability and reliability that the customer expects on an acceptable schedule. This flexibility enables system suppliers to deliver minimally acceptable systems for customer trials and evaluations, and drive service availability to meet and exceed the customers' expectations in system updates and future releases. Technically, this is achieved by assuring that the system's architecture makes it feasible that the customers' ultimate service availability and reliability expectations can be achieved, although some, many, or most of the design features required to achieve the expectation may not have been fully implemented in the initial release. A reliability roadmap explains to customers how all of the system features and testing required to achieve or exceed their expectations for service availability and reliability will be integrated into future system updates and upgrades. Assuming customers accept the feasibility and likelihood that the reliability roadmap will actually deliver acceptable service availability and reliability, and that the timing of these future updates and upgrades meets the business needs of both customers and system suppliers, then customers are generally willing to move forward with system purchase and deployment.

This section begins by reviewing what a reliability roadmap is, then reviews reliability-improving features and testing that are commonly included in a reliability roadmap.

12.2.1 What Is a Reliability Roadmap?

A credible reliability roadmap explicitly addresses the following:

- **Ultimate asymptotic availability target of the system.** Quantitatively specify what availability target the system is designed for. Nominally, the asymptotic availability represents the annualized service availability averaged over a large population of systems.

- **Quantitative best estimate or target for service availability of the current release.**

- **Best estimate or actual service availability performance for previous releases.**

- **Credible pre-release service availability targets for future releases** that achieve asymptotic availability target.

- **Planned or proposed features and testing to improve service availability and reliability** that credibly achieve by-release availability targets.

Reliability roadmaps are typically constructed to show how the system will achieve a quantitative service availability target by a specific release. Reliability roadmaps should be consistent with the system's service availability requirements in that if service availability is specified for unplanned hardware plus software downtime, then the reliability roadmap should show unplanned hardware plus software downtime. It is acceptable to separately roadmap different portions of downtime allocation; for example, one might separately roadmap unplanned hardware plus software downtime, and successful planned downtime.

Section 12.2.2 gives an example of unplanned hardware plus software reliability roadmap. A roadmap for successful and unsuccessful planned and procedural downtime could be constructed using a similar approach. A roadmap for unplanned hardware plus software plus successful and unsuccessful planned and procedural downtime could be created by combining downtime from two separate roadmaps.

12.2.2 Unplanned Reliability Roadmap Example

The section gives an example reliability roadmap for a hypothetical system that starts with a 99.99% unplanned hardware plus software service availability requirement in R1.0 and grows to a target asymptotic availability of 99.999%. Figure 12.3 shows the downtime improvement targets initially planned from R1.0 to R2.2. Note that roadmap charts are best illustrated with release number or calendar time on the X-axis and annualized downtime on the Y axis. Annualized downtime is a linear parameter that is generally easy for project team members and decision makers to understand; service availability (e.g., number of 9's) is a nonlinear parameter that few people intuitively grasp directly. As shown in Figure 12.3, one can easily overlay 99.95%, 99.99%, 99.995%, and so on availability lines onto a downtime chart.

Figure 12.4 shows the budgeted downtime targets behind the high-level visualization in Figure 12.3. Since this example covers unplanned hardware plus software, Figure 12.4 shows targets for those two categories by release. If

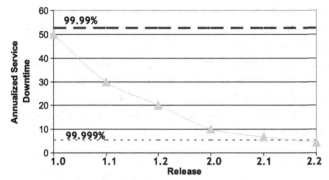

Figure 12.3 Sample Reliability Roadmap Visualization

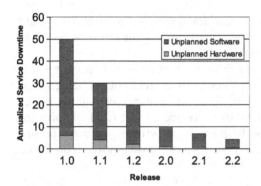

Figure 12.4 Sample Downtime Roadmap Visualization

the scope of the service availability requirement were broader, then additional budget categories (e.g., successful planned and procedural downtime, unsuccessful planned and procedural downtime) could be added. Likewise, budget categories could be exploded; for example, one could expand software-attributed downtime budgets to individual blades, subsystems, or modules.

Behind the downtime estimates of Figures 12.3 and 12.4 are release-specific plans that make it feasible and likely that each of these targets will be achieved. For example, the sample roadmaps for unplanned hardware and software downtime might be supported by the following feature plans:

- Release 1.0—initial release baseline—system supports full hardware redundancy with active-warm standby operations with 3-minute switchovers at the blade level.
- Release 1.1—data integrity and resource monitoring added and significant robustness testing campaign to improve hardware and software failure coverage.

- Release 1.2—design improved to shorten switchover times to approximately 30 seconds, and significant test campaign to improve reliability of switchover and recovery success.

- Release 2.0—redundancy architecture improves to active-active load sharing with 10-second switchovers, and significant test campaign to verify stability, reliability, robustness, and latency of active-active design.

- Release 2.1—throughput monitoring added to detect more silent failures, and additional robustness testing.

- Release 2.2—additional robustness testing, and quality and reliability improvements.

These specific feature plans will be complemented by both root-cause analysis and corrective actions from field outages and ongoing quality improvements, such as deploying static analysis and other tools to eliminate residual defects, and continuous improvements in code reviews and inspections, and so on. Note that roadmaps for planned and procedural downtime are useful for many systems, and they would include items like automation of procedures, rollback, shortened activation times, and so on.

Also note that maintenance or patch releases often significantly improve reliability and availability because they generally correct critical defects that escaped and were activated in the field. Since maintenance or patch releases seldom add functionality that is likely to introduce critical residual software defects, maintenance releases tend to have lower critical software failure rates and thus have higher reliability and service availability than major releases.

As field data becomes available it can be overlaid onto the roadmap alongside the original predictions. In analyzing field data, it is likely that reliability predictions will be adjusted based on observed failure rates, recovery times, mix of downtime contributions, and other factors. Thus, it is reasonable to revise roadmap predictions based both on changes in planned feature content and on refinements in prediction models and input parameters. Figure 12.5 shows an example of how to visualize integrating field data into a revised reliability roadmap. Behind this revision could be details explaining what input parameters were adjusted, if/how availability modeling was changed, and whether downtime budgets were changed.

12.2.3 Reliability Degrowth from Feature Development

Broadly speaking, software releases include a mix of new or improved features and fixes for defects that escaped into previous software deliveries. The focus of major feature releases is primarily on new features; the focus of maintenance releases is primarily on correcting defects of previous software deliveries. New or significantly modified features inevitably add residual defects that increase the critical software failure rate of the feature release. While

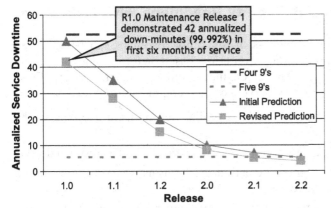

Figure 12.5   Revised Reliability Roadmap

many of these new defects will be found and fixed in subsequent maintenance releases, it is important to acknowledge the likely reliability degrowth associated with new features. This reliability degrowth in feature releases can be mitigated via:

- Improved quality processes that find and fix more defects before system release
- Improved failure coverage and robustness performance that increase the probability that critical failures will be automatically detected, isolated, and recovered with minimal service disruption
- Lowered availability expectations for a particular feature release

While a major feature release (e.g., "3.0") is likely to have more residual defects and hence lower availability than the most recent maintenance patch of the previous release (e.g., "2.2 maintenance release 2"), reasonable expectations are that:

- Major feature releases should have no more service downtime than previous major feature releases.
- Point releases should have less service downtime than the initial version of the major feature release they support.
- Maintenance releases should have less downtime than the feature, point, or maintenance release that they apply to.

Different markets and different customers will tolerate different balances of features, schedule, and service quality/reliability/availability. Product managers and decision makers must decide how to balance service availability and reliability against features and timing to meet both market and business expectations.

12.2.4   Validating Reliability Roadmaps with Field Data

Completeness and reasonableness of reliability roadmaps can be validated both by careful analyses of outage events and based on formal suggestions and anecdotal remarks of maintenance engineers and users of the system. These analyses and remarks often lead to concrete recommendations such as:

- Additional test cases to prevent similar defects from escaping to the field
- Additional code inspections or reviews to detect similar residual defects
- Improvements in failure detection mechanisms to assure faster, more accurate failure detection
- Improvements in failure recovery mechanisms to assure faster, more reliable failure recovery
- Additional robustness testing to assure effective and reliable failure detection, isolation, and recovery
- Improvements in diagnostics to enable faster, more accurate failure isolation
- Changes to documented procedures and release notes to minimize risk of failure
- Changes to system configuration to minimize risk of failure
- Rewriting failure-prone modules or interfaces
- Architectural or design changes to better contain failure

As acting on many of these recommendations will require development, test, documentation, or other resources to be allocated, it is essential to frame the priority of these recommendations into the broader business context.

As explained in Section 9.7, "Step 7: Prioritizing Gaps," most robustness-related improvements can be translated to estimates of the annualized minutes of pro-rated downtime saved. To simplify the estimation and decision process, it is generally most convenient to bundle related quality and robustness improvements into logical features that have both an R&D cost estimate and an estimated downtime—and hence availability—improvement. For example, if a system achieves an annualized downtime of about 40 minutes (~99.992%) and the system's target is 99.995% (26 down-minutes), then appropriate bundles of quality and robustness improvements that are estimated to accrue 14 annualized minutes of downtime savings can be mapped into upcoming releases to drive system availability to target.

12.3   PROBLEMS

The following problems consider a "target system" identified by the instructor:

1. What data might be available and useful to analyze to understand reliability and availability of field deployments of the target system?

2. Why might actual critical failure rates of the target system be different when system is deployed with different customers?

3. Why might observed (or recorded) critical failure rates of the target system be different with different deployments or customers even if the actual critical failure rates are the same?

4. Why might actual outage durations of the target system be different for different deployments?

5. What reliability-improving features and testing might reduce product-attributed hardware downtime for the target system?

6. What reliability-improving features and testing might reduce product-attributed software downtime for the target system?

7. What reliability-improving features and testing might reduce downtime for successful planned and procedural activities for the target system?

8. What reliability-improving features and testing might reduce downtime for unsuccessful planned and procedural activities for the target system?

Chapter 13

Design for Reliability
Case Study

This chapter presents a design for reliability case study of a hypothetical instant messaging system to illustrate the activities and linkages in system design for reliability and availability. While few businesses would consider instant messaging to be a mission-critical service that demands very high service reliability and availability, it is a simple service that all readers are familiar with and makes a suitable example. Design for reliability activities are similar for all system regardless of whether the system controls a website, manufacturing processes, enterprise logistics, financial information, or business processes, or delivers some other service. Enterprises will have different mission-critical services that would benefit from diligent system design for reliability, so readers can imagine how these concepts apply to their own organization's systems.

This example will consider a system developed by a supplier rather than a proprietary system integrated by an enterprise to clearly distinguish between the roles of the *supplier*, which develops and integrates the system, and the *enterprise*, which owns and operates the system. The supplier and the enterprise could be two organizations of the same enterprise (e.g., "supplier" can be the development department in an enterprise's information systems organization and "enterprise" can be the operations department in the same enterprise's information system organization), but for simplicity we'll assume that supplier and enterprise are different companies.

13.1 SYSTEM CONTEXT

Three aspects of system context are important to understand when planning reliability diligence:

Design for Reliability: Information and Computer-Based Systems, by Eric Bauer
Copyright © 2010 Institute of Electrical and Electronics Engineers

1. How critical is the system to the enterprise?
2. How does the target system fit into the enterprise's business processes or service solution?
3. What other systems does the target system interact with?

Each of these is discussed separately, followed by a summary.

13.1.1 Characterizing System Criticality

Staff and managers who use a system typically assume that the system is critical to the enterprise because it is central to their job. When asked, they will often say that they expect the system to be five 9's and operate 24/7/365 because they don't know how to frame the reliability and availability needs of one particular system into the broader context of criticality to the overall enterprise. Every enterprise operates within financial constraints; by understanding the criticality of the target system to the enterprise, decision makers can consciously decide how to balance the risk of system unavailability and service reliability against cost.

Some systems are so integral to business operations that unavailability of the service directly and immediately impacts the business. As a simple example, consider your local supermarket; since prices are no longer printed on most supermarket items, if the product information database that maps the UPC bar codes on items to price information is unavailable, then sales cannot be completed by cashiers. If sales cannot be completed by cashiers, then customers get upset and the business loses both revenue and customer goodwill. If the product information database is merely unavailable for a few seconds, then cashiers may notice the service disruption but few customers would be aware. If the cashier is unable to successfully scan items for perhaps 10 or 20 seconds, then the customers being checked out will notice. If none of the cashiers are able to successfully scan items for a minute or two, then all the customers on line to check out will probably become aware of the outage. At least some of the customers may get upset at the outage quickly as the checkout lines grow, their frozen foods begin to melt, and their personal schedules are wrecked because they can't finish their grocery shopping on time.

Some systems are so integral to real-time business operations that unavailability can cause a loss of business rather than simply a delay in revenue. For example, a two-minute outage of lottery system sales machines before a big drawing is likely to prevent many customers from being able to purchase tickets before the lottery sales deadline closes, and thus the lottery revenue is directly impacted. Likewise, unavailability of financial and commodity trading systems is likely to degrade or prevent the ability to trade, thus missing real-time market opportunities. Sophisticated customers often estimate the monetary impact on the enterprise for unavailability. For example, each minute of system downtime may be estimated to cost an enterprise a certain amount in wages for staff that are idle or in lost revenue or loss of customer goodwill or payments to customers with service-level agreements for service availability.

A simple operational metric for system criticality that can often be used is the average number of minutes between the time a system fails and the time an executive calls the IS/IT or other responsible leader demanding to know, "What happened, and when will it be fixed?" Readers can imagine if the phones in a call center suddenly stop ringing, or conveyors stop moving in a factory or logistics center, or critical information displays freeze, or other failures occur that critically impact the business, that an irate operations or production vice president will call IS/IT or maintenance manager on duty in minutes to demand a status report on the outage and an estimate of time to restore service. In contrast, some systems have ordinary availability expectations, such as copiers and printers that run out of paper or toner periodically and thus experience unplanned service outages; few readers can imagine a senior business leader calling the leader of the operations or IS/IT department minutes after a printer ran out of paper demanding to know when the printer will be restocked with paper.

The enterprise should align the system's availability expectations with the needs of the business, and the supplier may need to help put the service's criticality to the enterprise into quantitative service availability requirements.

13.1.2 Solutions and Systems

Systems operate in the context of an enterprise's overall solution of systems, business processes, and networking. Few systems deliver service directly to users without support of networking and other systems. For example, cash registers, mobile phones, conveyor belts, television set-top boxes, and so on all depend on networks to access complex services from enterprise solutions. The solutions tie together one or more systems with business processes and networking to offer valuable services to users, typically via some IP network.

End users will access our example instant messaging service across an end-to-end solution of the following components:

- **User device**, such as a laptop or smart phone, which renders the graphical user interface to the service.
- **Public wireless or wireline network.** If the user device is off the enterprise's premise, then user devices access the enterprise's IM service via a public wireless or wireline network.
- **Security device**, such as firewall or virtual private network element, will be used if client device was outside of the enterprise's intranet.
- **Local area network (LAN)** transports IP packets from the enterprise's premises, such as between local user devices and the IM server, as well as between other systems like security devices and authentication

servers. The LAN typically includes IP switches and routers, DNS and DHCP servers, Wi-Fi access points and cables.

- **IM server** (our example system).
- **Authentication system** that validates users' security credentials. The authentication server must be operational for users to successfully establish sessions with the IM server; unavailability of the authentication server does not impact existing user sessions.

Users access the instant messaging service via various facilities and devices, which must all be operational for an IM session to be possible, as shown in Figure 13.1. This architectural diagram is redrawn in Figure 13.2 as a pair of end-to-end *reliability block diagrams (RBDs)* to highlight exactly what elements must be available for a particular user-to-user IM conversation to be

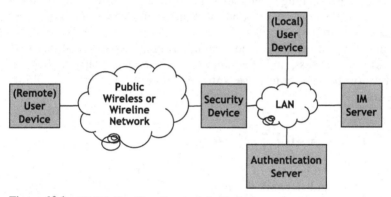

Figure 13.1   IM Solution User Connectivity Options

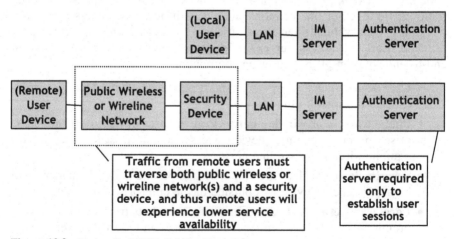

Figure 13.2   End-to-End IM Reliability Block Diagram

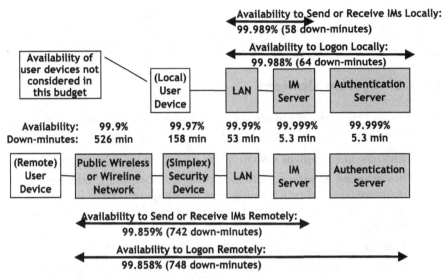

Figure 13.3   End-to-End IM Service Downtime Budget

available. Figure 13.2 makes it clear that the IM service availability experienced by an end user is impacted by far more than merely the unavailability of the IM server. Since service downtime is the sum of all elements and facilities in series in the reliability critical path, we can estimate end-to-end service availability by summing budgeted service downtime for each of the elements and facilities in the two scenarios.

Figure 13.3 gives a sample end-to-end downtime budget based on plausible estimates. Three primary insights from Figure 13.3 are:

1. **Service availability offered by a system is not the same as solution service availability experienced by an end user,** because end users often depend on devices, networking, and other support systems to access the service offered by the target system.

2. **Service availability experienced by end users in different network contexts can vary significantly.** Users at the same physical site as the target system are likely to experience much higher service availability than users accessing the service remotely. Users accessing the service from other continents or geographic regions are likely to experience even lower service availability because they are susceptible to greater wide-area networking unavailability.

3. **High availability of IM server, authentication server, and LAN improves service availability for all users, while availability improvements of security device benefits only remote users.** Replacing a simplex, non-redundant security device configuration with a redundant, highly available configuration will significantly increase service availability for remote users.

Considering end-to-end solution service availability helps customers calibrate their service availability expectations for elements across the solution and to manage the service availability experienced by system users.

13.1.3 System Context

In addition to the elements in the service delivery path that were enumerated above, the IM server also interacts with the following systems:

- **Element management system** monitors system operations and alarms.
- **Provisioning interface** enables enterprise operations, administration, maintenance, and provisioning staff to configure service for enterprise users such as creating new IM accounts and blocking accounts when necessary.
- **Backup server** backs up the contents of IM conversations.
- **Operations support server** monitors system usage and performance statistics. Enterprise operations and maintenance staff periodically review usage and performance statistics to assure that system configuration is adequate for current and projected load, and plan to grow or reconfigure system before system performance becomes degraded.

13.2 SYSTEM RELIABILITY REQUIREMENTS

Assume enterprise customers' high-level expectations for the IM server are "five 9's"and "24/7/365 operation" and that occasional planned service outages are acceptable for major software upgrades and major planned activities. For simplicity, assume that customers do not expect support for geographically redundant IM server configurations. Also, assume that the customer wants to include a service-level agreement for service availability in the contract that includes financial remedies. While the terms of the contractual commitment for service availability might not be negotiated until late in the sales cycle, the reliability requirements will include key details that can be used when proposing requirements for a formal service-level agreement.

The following sections detail how these very-high-level expectations might be translated into detailed requirements that can drive design and verification.

13.2.1 Defining Service Availability and Service Reliability

The primary function of the IM server is to "instantly" deliver messages between active human users. Since IM is inherently a conversational-style service, unavailability of service in one direction (e.g., inability to send messages) prevents conversational interaction, and thus is considered a service outage. Inability to log onto the IM server or initiate an IM session with an authorized active user is also considered a service outage. Service outages will be quantified by the percentage of active users impacted by an event; for example, if an outage event impacts 53 of the 100 users connected to the IM server, then the event will be characterized as 53% capacity loss. Events that impact less than 10% of users connected to the IM server (e.g., failures impacting a single user) are excluded from service availability measurements, but are considered in service reliability measurements. Assume enterprise customers will tolerate occasional service disruptions of up to 10 seconds for fault-tolerance mechanisms to automatically detect, isolate, and recover from failures or when executing planned procedures like installing security patches. Any messages lost in these brief service disruptions will be counted in service reliability measurements.

Service reliability of the IM server is the probability that an individual message, login attempt, conversation setup, or user provisioning action succeeds within the maximum specified time. Service reliability will be measured as defective message transmissions per million attempts; for instance, 10 DPM means that 10 out of every million IM messages sent fail to be received promptly by the other party. Service reliability measurements are valid only when the system is deemed available for service, meaning that service reliability is measured when the system is nominally up including during service disruptions that are deemed too short to be marked as service outages. Service (un)reliability is not technically counted for users impacted by chargeable service outages.

The supplier assumes that the following terms will be acceptable in any service-level agreement for product-attributable service availability:

- Outage time includes:
  - Service affecting unscheduled outage events that impact at least 10% of configured users for at least 10 seconds
  - Service affecting scheduled outages except during pre-agreed time period
  - Portion of the scheduled outage past the pre-agreed time period
- Outage time excludes:
  - Outage of standby elements (*simplex exposure*) that does not affect user service
  - Agreed scheduled outages that are confined to a pre-agreed time period

The scope of outage events attributable to the supplier will be determined by the extent of hardware, software, services, and support agreed between the enterprise and supplier. Specific measurement periods, arrangements for reconciliation of outage data, and remedies are important to define, but they are not relevant to system reliability and availability requirements.

13.2.2   High-Level Reliability Requirements

The discussion in previous sections leads to the following high-level availability and reliability requirements:

- **The system shall achieve product-attributable service availability of 99.999% (<5.3 annualized pro-rated down-minutes per year).**
- **The system shall automatically detect, isolate, and recover from all single hardware and software failures with less than 10 seconds of service disruption.**
- **The system shall have no single point of failure.**
- **No failure shall cause user configuration or instant message logs to be damaged or lost.**
- **Service reliability for logging onto IM server shall be at least 99.999% (<10 DPM) when system is available for service.**
- **Service reliability for sending and receiving messages shall be at least 99.999% (<10DPM) when system is available for service.**
- **Service reliability for establishing an IM session between two active and authorized users shall be at least 99.999% (<10 DPM) when system is available for service.**
- **Service unavailability due to software upgrade shall be less than 60 minutes per event.**
- **Service unavailability due to software patching shall be less than 30 minutes per event.**
- **Service unavailability due to system hardware growth shall be less than 15 minutes per event.**

Detailed requirements for failure coverage, switchover success probability, failure detection latency, and switchover latency will be set based on results of reliability and latency modeling and budgeting.

13.3   RELIABILITY ANALYSIS

13.3.1   System Design

Let us assume that our example IM system is built from the following elements:

- **Load balancers** (active-standby pair). Assume load balancers share a virtual IP address and they distribute traffic from client devices across a load-shared pool of frontend computers. If the active load balancer fails, then the standby load balancer will rapidly and automatically promote itself to active and continue service.

- **Frontend computers** (load-shared pool) terminate traffic from client devices, and handle authentication, authorization, access control, and user interface support for active users. Frontend computers interact with the enterprise's authentication server to validate logon credentials and enforce usage policies, such as blocking communications as necessary. Frontend computers interact with backend computers to monitor user status and to implement instant messages in conversations. Frontend computer failure is detected by the active load balancer, and causes the load balancer to send user traffic to another frontend computer. The other frontend computer will retrieve information on the status of the user's active conversations to reestablish their IM session status with little or no user-perceptible service disruption. Assume that the IM server supports two different interface mechanisms to client devices: HTTP and Message Session Relay Protocol (MSRP [RFC4975, RFC4976]). HTTP traffic is handled by the HTTP server process, and MSRP related traffic is handled by MSRP server process. Each of these servers is completely independent; failure and recovery of one server process will not impact the other process.

- **Backend computers** (active-active pair) maintain status information on all users *presence* and active IM conversations, notify frontend servers when status of a monitored user changes, serialize messages from frontend servers and publish messages to frontend servers, and maintain persistent records of IM dialogs. User status is replicated across both backend computers and each IM conversation is randomly assigned to one of the two backend computers. Frontend computers will detect backend computer failure by expiration of a request timeout, and that will cause frontend computers to redirect failed operations to the other backend server. Backend computers will be architected so that if backend capacity becomes a bottleneck, then active-active redundancy can be enhanced to N + 1 load sharing.

For simplicity, assume that the system is built from commercially available rack-mounted computer hardware and a pair of rack-mounted load balancers, and networked with a pair of rack-mounted active-active Ethernet switches. Assume frontend and backend computers use popular open-source operating system, database, middleware, and protocol stacks. The supplier integrates these commercially and open-sourced software modules with appropriate business logic software to implement the IM system.

13.3.2 Reliability Diligence for Sourced Hardware

Ideally the supplier will select hardware designed and manufactured by hardware suppliers with high-quality design and manufacturing processes and a history of delivering highly reliable hardware backed by excellent technical support and an attractive warranty policy. Using a hardware supplier that the system supplier has had good experience with is recommended; using a hardware supplier that the enterprise customers have had good experience with is even better because that should slightly reduce the rate of procedural failures because enterprise maintenance staff are likely to be at least somewhat familiar with the hardware supplier's equipment. If the system supplier has no experience with the hardware supplier, then it is appropriate to complete a basic audit of the supplier's design, manufacturing, and quality processes. Suppliers who are registered to quality standards like ISO 9000 are required to have written process documents and quality records, so high-quality suppliers should be able to demonstrate that mature processes were repeatably executed in the design, test, and manufacture of the hardware.

Ideally, the system will use a hardware product model that has demonstrated highly reliable operation in the field. Given the pace of innovation and product line evolution, the supplier may opt for a new hardware product model that has little or no previous field deployment. In cases when no field data is available, the system supplier should ask the supplier to demonstrate that the same high-quality design and manufacturing processes used for previous models in the product family were used for the new model, and thus that this product model is likely to perform at least as reliably as previous product models. Section 15.10 enumerates a set of hardware design for reliability assessment questions that are helpful when initiating a reliability discussion with a hardware supplier.

13.3.3 Reliability Diligence for Sourced Software

Leveraging mature operating system, middleware, tools, and other software can increase software reliability as well as shortening development intervals. Other things being equal, software with millions of hours of operational time is likely to be more reliable than new software or software with limited operational deployment because most or all of the defects have been exposed—and hopefully fixed—in the more mature software. Fewer residual software defects in a mature software component generally means there are fewer software defects that will be exposed in integration and deployment of the system. When technical possible and commercially feasible, it is generally best to reuse open-source or commercially available software, or reuse the supplier's own software assets.

Software suppliers are often unaware of exactly how reliable their software applications or components actually are in field operation because:

- They are likely to be unaware of how often software crashes in the field or how often it is rebooted.
- They are unlikely to know exactly what caused every software crash, and hence don't know if the root cause is attributable to their

software, to the enterprise/user operating the software, to a co-resident software application, to some integration issue, or to a combination of factors.

Thus, you should check the reputation of the supplier with its customers and verify that high-quality development processes are in place to assure that consistent, repeatable, high-quality software is delivered by the supplier. A subset of the questions is Chapter 15, "Appendix: Assessing Design for Reliability Diligence," may be useful in facilitating a conversation with the supplier on its software reliability. A key is to determine how the supplier's staff knows they have completed enough testing to discover (and fix) sufficient defects that the software will be acceptably reliable in field operation. There are lots of painful and wrong answers to the question "How do you know when your software is ready to send to customers" that are more or less "best effort in time available" or "ready-or-not, here it comes." Some immature organizations even employ strategies like the "mattress model,"[1] in which the testers are rolled off the project (or sent on vacation) the week before the release decision so the rate of defect discovery drops off so the metrics look nice, or otherwise manipulating defect data to make the software look better than it is. Thus, the real question is whether the software supplier's release criteria are sufficient to assure that released software is sufficiently reliable to meet the system's needs for quality, reliability, and availability.

Software Acquisition Capability Maturity Model (SA-CMM) [SACMM] from the Software Engineering Institute at Carnegie-Mellon University is a good framework for sourcing software with quality; suppliers and enterprises may find it useful to assess their internal processes against SA-CMM and address notable gaps.

13.3.4 Enumerate Recoverable Modules

Each of the four IM server hardware elements from Section 13.3.1 is independently recoverable onto redundant elements:

- **Load balancer.** Hardware failure of active load balancer is recovered onto standby load balancer.
- **Frontend computer.** Hardware failure of a frontend computer is recovered by load balancer rerouting traffic to operational frontend computers.

---

[1]The mattress model envisions that the software is like an old mattress infested with insects. When you hit the mattress, the bugs come scurrying out so they can be found and addressed. When you stop hitting the mattress, the bugs stop coming out of it. If your completion metric is "no high severity bugs seen in X days," then if you stop hitting the mattress (i.e., testing it) more than X days before making a software release decision, you are likely to pass your release criteria.

- **Backend computer.** Hardware failure of backend computer is recovered by frontend computers directing all service requests to the other active backend computer.

- **Ethernet switch.** Assume Ethernet switches are running active-active. Each computer and load balancer is configured with redundant network interfaces with one of each element's interfaces connected to one active switch and the second interface connected to the other switch. Link aggregation is used by the computers and load balancers to mitigate failure of a network interface, cable, or Ethernet switch.

Recoverable software modules map onto IM server hardware elements from Section 13.3.1 as follows:

- **Load balancer software modules.** The commercial load balancer runs proprietary software that is embedded in the element. Although there is high availability software, management software, middleware, and other software alongside the load-balancing software, the reliability and complexity of this software is managed by the supplier of the load-balancer. Thus, the IM server reliability analysis will not consider details of load balancer software.

- **Frontend computer modules.** In addition to normal operating system software and middleware, each frontend computer hosts the following IM server modules:

  - **HTTP server process** accepts HTTP traffic from client devices and interworks with backend processes to deliver IM service to users. A single multithreaded HTTP server process instance runs on each frontend computer, and that process can be restarted following failure.

  - **MSRP server process** accepts MSRP and related traffic from client devices and interworks with backend processes to deliver IM service via MSRP clients. A single multithreaded MSRP server process instance runs on each frontend computer, which can be restarted on failure.

  - **Control daemon** starts the HTTP and MSRP server processes, monitors their health, and provides management visibility and controllability, including process restart and frontend computer reboot. If the control daemon fails, then the frontend computer is restarted. The control daemon runs at a higher priority than the other server processes and manages overload control.

- **Backend computer modules.** In addition to normal operating system software, middleware, and database management software, each backend computer hosts the following IM server modules:

  - **Presence server** tracks the status of each user (e.g., available online, not online). There is one presence server process running on each backend computer; one presence server is designated "primary" and other presence server process instances are designated "secondary." All frontend server processes direct presence updates to the primary presence server and presence queries are distributed across all operational presence server instances. Secondary presence server instances monitor availability of primary presence server; if primary presence server becomes unavailable, then secondary presence servers elect a new primary.

- **Conversation server** mediates IM conversations between users on HTTP and/or MSRP server processes. Conversation servers control IM conversations, including serializing, distributing, and logging each message. Conversation servers are independent, so one or more process instances can run on each backend computer. Frontend server processes pick a conversation server instance round robin for each new conversation. If round robin selection does not work satisfactorily, then future releases of IM server can use a more sophisticated load-balancing algorithm.

- **OAM server** provides management visibility, controllability, and access to the IM server for operations, administration, maintenance and provisioning by enterprise maintenance staff. One OAM server process instance is configured as the primary (active) unit and another backend server hosts a second OAM server process instance that is configured as the secondary (standby) instance. To balance system load, the primary presence server and primary OAM server should be configured on different backend server instances. The OAM server runs at higher priority than either presence or conversation server process instances, but lower priority than the control daemon.

- **Control daemon** starts the OAM server, presence server, and conversation server processes, monitors their health, and implements management visibility and controllability, including process restart and backend computer reboot. If the control daemon fails, then the backend computer is restarted. The control daemon runs at a higher priority than the other server processes and manages overload control.

- **Ethernet switch software modules.** The commercial Ethernet switch runs proprietary firmware that is embedded in the switch. The Ethernet switch is considered a black box for purposes of this analysis.

13.3.5 Construct RBDs

Figure 13.4 gives a reliability block diagram (RBD) for the IM server supporting HTTP user devices. Both the load balancers and Ethernet switches are simplified as black boxes that lump hardware and software failures together. The frontend computers are arranged with N + 1 load-shared redundancy.

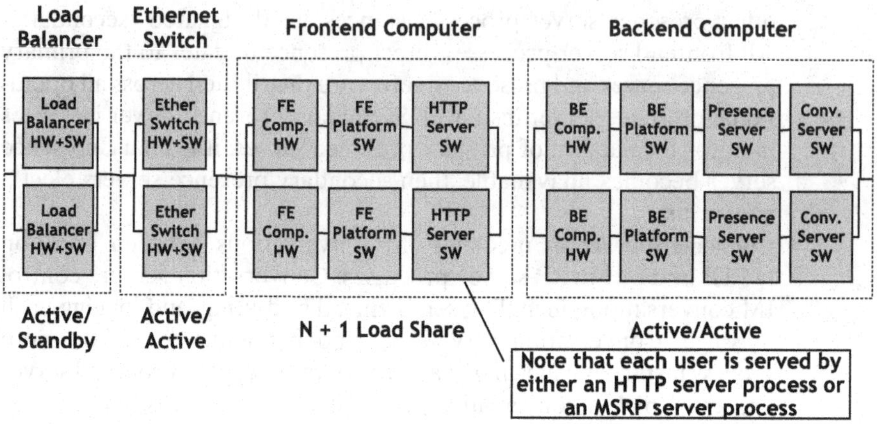

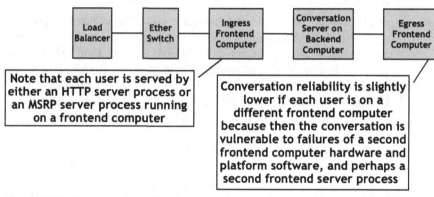

Figure 13.4 IM Server Reliability Block Diagram for HTTP Access

Figure 13.5 IM Conversation Reliability Block Diagram

Each frontend computer is modeled as computer hardware running platform software hosting an HTTP server process. The MSRP server is not shown in this RBD because individual users access the IM server via a client device via HTTP rather than MSRP. The backend computers are arranged in active-active redundancy. Note that control daemons and OAM process are excluded from the RBD because failure of those processes does not directly impact user service. The RBD for MSRP service is identical to Figure 13.4, except the "HTTP Server SW" block is replaced with "MSRP Server SW."

Individual RBDs can be constructed for different service scenarios or to access different system functionality, and each of these RBDs can be analyzed to understand the system's reliability and availability characteristics. For example, instant messaging is different from many servers because conversations inherently involve more than one user device simultaneously. While Figure 13.4 illustrates the RBD for service to an individual user, the simplified reliability block diagram for an active conversation in Figure 13.5 adds one frontend computer for each party in the conversation to support communications with each party's client device. For instance, if an IM conversation was between two HTTP user devices, then potentially two different frontend computers could be involved (one for each party). If HTTP server and MSRP server have different reliability characteristics, then IM conversation reliability might vary depending on the protocols used by users (i.e., HTTP-to-HTTP conversation reliability may be somewhat different from MSRP-to-MSRP or HTTP-to-MSRP).

13.3.6   Failure Mode Analysis

The IM server delivers various services to users; the primary reliability metrics of these user services are deemed to be the following:

- **Session accessibility:** ability of a user to connect to the IM server
- **Session retainability:** ability of a user session to remain operational until the user requests session termination (logoff)
- **Conversation accessibility:** ability to successfully initiate or accept an IM conversation
- **Conversation retainability:** ability to retain a viable and operational conversation until one party terminates the conversation
- **Message delivery:** ability to accurately deliver each message to all parties in proper order

Failure mode analysis for the IM server should consider the impact of component failure on each of these primary metrics. Table 13.1 gives the failure mode analysis for a backend computer; similar tables should be constructed for frontend computers, load balancers, and Ethernet switches. More detailed analysis can be completed on finer-grained modules, for example, on middleware and database management system components.

13.3.7   Characterize Impact of Procedures

The service impact of all planned procedures should be explicitly considered for the same service quality vectors used in Section 13.3.6, "Failure Mode Analysis." For example, consider the planned procedure of growing the IM server configuration to add another frontend computer to increase system capacity. Assume that in the first release of the IM server the strategy to grow the number of frontend computers is as follows:

1. Install new rack-mounted frontend computer hardware and connect to Ethernet switches.
2. Install frontend IM software on computer.

Table 13.1 Failure Mode Analysis for Backend Computer

Component	Session accessibility	Session retainability	Conversation accessibility	Conversation retainability	Message delivery
Backend computer hardware	No impact	No impact	No impact because frontend computers will retry to operational presence and conversation servers	Impact; conversations hosted by backend computer are lost [1]	Impact; messages in conversations hosted by backend computer may be lost on failure [1]
Backend platform software	No impact	No impact	No impact because frontend computers will retry to operational presence and conversation servers	Impact; conversations hosted by backend computer are lost [1]	Impact; messages in conversations hosted by backend computer may be lost on failure [1]
Presence server	No impact because frontend computers will retry to an operational presence server	No impact	No impact because frontend computers will retry to an operational presence server	No impact	No impact
Conversation server	No impact	No impact	No impact because frontend computers will retry to an operational conversation server	Impact; conversations hosted by backend computer are lost [1]	Impact; messages in conversations hosted by backend computer may be lost on failure [1]
OAM Server	No impact	No impact	No impact	No impact	No impact
Control Daemon	No impact [2]	No impact [2]	No impact [2]	No impact [2]	No impact [2]

Notes:

1. While it is possible to design mechanisms in which frontend HTTP and MSRP servers will recover conversations onto another operational conversation server that were lost when a conversation server failed, we assume that schedule pressure prevented the IM server team from implementing those mechanisms. If conversations are not recovered, then there is no point in retransmitting an unconfirmed (presumably lost) message to the conversation server that recovers the conversation. Detecting failed conversation servers, recovering conversations onto other conversation server instances, and resending lost messages should be a candidate feature on the IM server's reliability roadmap.

2. Although failure of control daemon does not impact service, the initial release of IM server requires presence server, conversation server, and OAM server to be shut down to restart the control daemon. Enhancing system design to permit failed control daemon to be restarted without impacting running processes should be a candidate feature in the IM server's reliability roadmap.

Table 13.2 Service Impact Analysis of Frontend Computer Growth

Procedure	Session accessibility	Session retainability	Conversation accessibility	Conversation retainability	Message delivery
Growing IM server configuration by adding an additional frontend computer	Unavailable while IM server is gracefully shut down and restarted	Unavailable while IM server is gracefully shut down and restarted	Unavailable while IM server is gracefully shut down and restarted	Unavailable while IM server is gracefully shut down and restarted	Unavailable while IM server is gracefully shut down and restarted

3. Use OAM server to add new frontend computer to IM server configuration.

4. Gracefully shut down all frontend and backend computers in IM server configuration (including new computer), thereby making service unavailable to users.

5. Start up backend and frontend computers in recommended order, thus restoring service availability.

6. Verify operation of new frontend computer.

7. Reconfigure load balancers to distribute traffic to new frontend computer.

Based on this strategy, one can complete the procedural impact analysis in Table 13.2. Dynamic configuration mechanisms could be added to IM server to support hardware growth without requiring the entire system to be shut down and restarted; such a mechanism could be considered for the IM server's reliability roadmap.

Similar analyses can be completed for all planned procedures. Procedures that produce unacceptably long service disruptions can be redesigned, automated or system architecture changed to make service disruption acceptably short; note that redesigned procedures or software changes to lessen impact of procedures is often included in reliability roadmaps.

13.3.8 Verify Adequacy of Failure Detection

One should review the product error categories in Chapter 3, "What Can Go Wrong," to identify:

- What error scenarios are applicable at IM server system level?
- What error scenarios are applicable for each major module?

One then considers whether those failures will be rapidly and reliably detected. For example, this section will consider only the conversation server on the backend computer.

13.3.8.1   Field-Replaceable Unit Errors

The primary responsibility for detecting errors of FRU hardware lies with the hardware supplier for the frontend and backend computers, the load balancers, and the Ethernet switches. Reliability diligence for sourced hardware should verify that hardware suppliers have included mechanisms that rapidly and reliably detect inevitable hardware failures and that those mechanisms have been verified via hardware fault insertion testing and demonstrated good performance in field operation.

13.3.8.2   Programming Errors

The conversation server process is inherently vulnerable to typical programming errors like referencing uninitialized or incorrect pointers, infinite loops, logic errors, and process or thread hang or abort. The control daemon on the backend computer will regularly exchange messages with the conversation server process to assure that conversation server is operational. The control daemon will be configured to be notified if the conversation server process dies and will also monitor process size and CPU usage of the conversation server to assure that they are within normal operating parameters.

13.3.8.3   Data Errors

Both frontend and backend computers are vulnerable to file system corruption following a power failure when the operating system is unable to synchronize and gracefully close all files before the system stopped. Thus, both computers must be configured to automatically check and repair file systems on startup, rather than waiting for manual input before executing the check and repair.

Since the conversation server logs all conversations, it is inherently vulnerable to full file systems that prevent the logging operation from completing successfully. The control daemon on each backend computer will monitor free disk space on each file system and raise minor, major, and critical alarms as appropriate. The conversation server will carefully monitor all file system I/O, and create new log files if previous files were changed or deleted (perhaps as part of log file backup operations).

The conversation server will have a low-priority thread that periodically audits the conversation data by verifying with applicable frontend server processes that each conversation that the server is managing is actually still valid, and will gracefully terminate any conversations that have ended. Since the initial release of IM server does not support automatic recovery of conversations following conversation server failure, there is no data shared between conversation servers that could get corrupted or out of sync.

13.3.8.4 Redundancy Errors

Since the initial release of the IM server doesn't support automatic recovery of conversations onto a redundant conversation server, this category is not applicable to the conversation server itself. Redundancy errors are generally applicable both at the system level and to the mechanisms that control failure recovery. For the initial release of IM server, one should assure that a failed conversation server can be successfully restarted and returned to service by the control daemon without having to restart the backend computer.

13.3.8.5 System Power Errors

System power errors are applicable to both the entire system (e.g., power failure to the rack hosting all computers, load balancers, and Ethernet switches) as well as power failure of individual elements. As mentioned in Section 13.3.8.3, "Data Errors," frontend and backend computers may be vulnerable to file system corruption on power failure. Beyond assuring that a single computer can automatically recover from file system corruption on power failure, system-level testing should also assure that the entire system will start up properly if one or more elements have slower startup because they must check and repair the file system before starting IM server software.

13.3.8.6 Network Errors

The dual network interfaces on the frontend and backend computers and the load balancers should be configured with one connection to each of the Ethernet switches and link aggregation to maintain network communications in the event of failure of one network interface, a single cable, or one Ethernet switch. Failure of Ethernet switches and cables connecting backend computer to one Ethernet switch should be tested to verify proper operation of link aggregation.

Since the conversation server uses a network to communicate only with frontend HTTP and MSRP server processes hosted on computers in the same rack via short physical cables and a single Ethernet switch between each of the network interfaces, dropped or corrupted network packets are unlikely, as are brief network connectivity outages. Failure of a frontend computer or a frontend HTTP or MSRP server process that the conversation server interworks with is a credible failure risk, but that is addressed in the context of the failure mode analysis covered in Section 13.3.6, "Failure Mode Analysis."

13.3.8.7 Application Protocol Errors

Since the conversation server communicates over a network only to HTTP and MSRP server processes rather than directly with third-party components, the scope of application protocol errors is likely to be limited. Nevertheless, it is possible that developers of one or both server processes will have slightly different interpretations of the communications protocol specification, and thus a request or response might be received that is inconsistent with the expectations of the developers of the conversation server process. Thus, the conversation server should carefully validate all messages received before acting on them to prevent different interpretations of a protocol specification (e.g., a frontend server process setting a length field to integer −1 to indicate field not used, but the conversation server interpreting the value as an unsigned integer of 255 if length field is one octet or 65535 if length field is two octets).

13.3.8.8 Procedural Errors

Procedures typically occur at the system level, and there are no procedures specifically applicable to the conversation server. Each of the planned procedures should be individually reviewed to assure that the principles in Section 5.11, "Procedural Considerations," have been fully considered.

13.3.9 Failures of Robustness Mechanisms

There are three general robustness mechanism failures to consider: detection failure, isolation or diagnostic failure, and recovery failure. Detection failure is the primary risk to address because every minute of undetected failure can be a minute of service outage. In addition, proper failure detection will expose diagnostic failures and recovery failures because the primary failure will not automatically clear in the expected timeframe.

For the conversation server, consider a failure scenario like a deadlock on resource or data structure used by the conversation worker threads; in this case the thread that responds to queries from the control daemon will respond successfully, leading the control daemon to presume that the conversation server is fully operational when some conversation worker threads are actually stuck waiting on a deadlock. Since the worker threads are blocked, no IM messages will be passed and thus users will experience message delivery failures and apparent conversation retainability failures. Assume that the communications protocol used between frontend servers and conversation servers requires acknowledgment and relatively short timeouts are used. This enables frontend servers to promptly detect unavailability of a conversation server, raise an appropriate alarm, and use other conversation servers for new conversations until this conversation server is recovered. Thus, frontend server processes provide another layer of detection of conversation server unavailability.

A third layer of failure detection can be provided by implementing a self-test server that establishes one HTTP client session to each HTTP server process and one MSRP client session to each MSRP client process and then performs a handful of operations to verify that conversations can be established and terminated properly. Note that this test server would typically bypass the load balancer by using the specific IP address of each frontend server, but it could be configured to send traffic to the load balancer to verify correct operation of the load balancer. This self-test server could be enhanced to directly test the presence server (e.g., by querying presence data from all operational presence servers and verifying that responses are all consistent) and the conversation server (e.g., by emulating a frontend server that directly communicates with conversation server). This self-test server could be run automatically by the master control daemon or on demand to assist maintenance engineers in diagnosing system troubles.

13.4 DOWNTIME BUDGETING

Since the target customers tolerate occasional service downtime when executing planned activities, the reliability modeling and budgeting will focus on downtime caused by unplanned hardware and software failures. We begin with a first-draft downtime allocation across the major elements in the system reliability block diagram as shown in Figure 13.6.

The initial downtime budget was driven by the following logic:

- Load balancers and Ethernet switches are of similar complexity, and thus should have similar initial downtime allocations; 15 seconds of

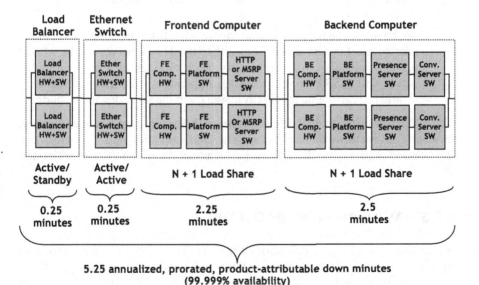

Figure 13.6   Initial Unplanned Hardware plus Software Downtime Budget for 99.999%

annualized downtime is likely to be quite conservative for mature and highly reliable elements operating in redundant configuration, but it is a reasonable starting point for conversations with the suppliers of those elements.

- Since 99.999% availability works out to 5.25 annualized prorated down-minutes (actually 5.26, but we round to quarter-minutes for convenience) and 0.25 minutes are allocated for pair of load balancers and 0.25 minutes are allocated for pair of Ethernet switches, we are left with 4.75 down-minutes for the frontend and backend computers. Frontend and Backend computers are likely to have similar hardware configurations, but the backend computer hosts two service-critical software processes (presence server and conversation server) while the frontend computer hosts only one frontend server process for any individual user. Note that MSRP devices will access IM server through the MSRP server and HTTP browsers will access IM server through the HTTP server and those servers may have different software failure rates, different software failure coverage, different recovery latencies, and different recovery success probabilities, and thus HTTP clients and MSRP clients may experience slightly different service availability. However, since there is no compelling reason to establish different downtime budgets for the two different frontend clients, the same budget will be used for both. Since there are two service-critical processes on the backend computer compared to one service-critical process on the frontend computer, we will give the backend computer a quarter-minute more downtime allocation than the frontend computer. Thus, the frontend computer is allocated 2.25 down-minutes and the backend computer is allocated 2.5 down-minutes.
- We have chosen to model the service availability experienced by a single user of the IM server, and thus either the HTTP server or the MSRP server is included in the reliability block diagram at a time. Since IM server and MSRP server processes implement similar functionality, it should be reasonable to initially assign them the same downtime budgets.

The initial downtime budget often changes as the system design moves forward, modeling is performed, feasible system characteristics and behaviors are determined, and eventually system performance is measured and estimated from lab testing.

13.5 AVAILABILITY MODELING

There are several different options for modeling unplanned hardware and software downtime of the IM server. For simplicity, assume that the downtime of each set of major redundant elements will be modeled separately, and then the downtime will be summed.

- **Load balancers.** Developers will contact load balancer supplier to determine the optimal way to configure the pair of load balancers and estimate the service downtime predicted for that optimal configuration.

- **Ethernet switches.** Developers will contact Ethernet switch supplier to determine the optimal way to configure the pair of Ethernet switches and estimate the service downtime predicted for that optimal configuration.

- **N + 1 load-shared frontend computers.** Individual frontend and backend computers will be modeled separately, and then service downtime modeled across an N + 1 load-sharing pool of each type of computer.

- **Individual frontend computers** can each be modeled as simplex elements in which critical hardware failures and critical software failures are likely to have somewhat different recovery times.

- **Backend computers** are modeled as an active-active pair of identical simplex elements in which hardware and software failures have different failure rates and recovery characteristics.

Somewhat different modeling approaches can be taken based on engineering judgment, the modeling tools available, and other factors.

A key insight that the modeling should reveal is that the failure coverage, switchover latency, and switchover success of the N + 1 pool of frontend computers and active-active pair of backend computers are highly influential, as well as the failure rates and availability of individual frontend or backend computers. Essentially, if the system detects and recovers from failures of frontend and backend computers with negligible service disruption, the failure rate of individual frontend or backend computers is less important.

After constructing the model, one should work with appropriate subject matter experts to estimate the feasible and likely values for all input parameters. Some input parameters, like hardware MTBF or failure rate and switchover times, will be relatively easy to find or measure; other input parameters, like failure coverage and software failure rate, are often much harder to reliably estimate. One should plot sensitivity analyses (e.g., Figure 7.9—Failure Rate Sensitivity Analysis) of parameters with significant estimation uncertainty to characterize how influential those parameters are on the system availability prediction.

When feasible and likely input parameters are used in the model for initial system release, the result is often a prediction for more system downtime than stipulated in the system requirements. If the gap is acceptable for the current release, then:

- Detailed reliability requirements can be written to capture the values of highly influential parameters that were deemed feasible and likely. These detailed requirements should drive formal testing to assure that the system achieves performance consistent with the predicted system availability.

- Formal reliability roadmapping, as described in Section 13.6, "Reliability Roadmap," can be executed for the next release.

If the predicted availability is not deemed acceptable for this release, then reliability roadmapping should be completed so decision makers can consider whether to increase investment in reliability-improving features and testing in the initial release, or lower customers' availability expectations for initial release, or simply accept higher risk of failing to meet service reliability and service availability requirements in the initial release. Detailed reliability requirements for initial release will be driven by this decision.

13.5.1 Latency Budgeting

One of the high-level reliability requirements of the IM server given in Section 13.2.2 is that failures shall be detected, isolated, and recovered with less than 10 seconds of service disruption. One should construct latency budgets for recoveries controlled by the IM server application itself. As a minimum, any single failure should be detected, isolated, and recovered in less than 10 seconds so that if the user retries an operation 10 seconds after a failure, the retry will succeed. Ideally the system will be capable to detect, isolate, and mitigate a critical failure fast enough that the user's request can succeed, albeit taking a bit longer than normal. For example, the timeout for conversation setup messages between frontend servers and conversation servers should be much shorter than the conversation setup timeout between clients and MSRP or HTTP server so that the frontend server has sufficient time to detect a failed conversation server and retry the request to another conversation server rather than having the user receive a failed conversation setup response.

13.6 RELIABILITY ROADMAP

A roadmap of reliability-improving features and testing should be constructed if a system is predicted or known not to be meeting its reliability or availability requirements. For the example IM server, the reliability feature roadmap would be constructed as follows:

1. Construct candidate features to mitigate each unacceptable service disruption scenario identified in the failure mode analysis (e.g., enabling active conversations to be automatically recovered after failure of a conversation server process).

2. Propose candidate features to improve failure detection based on scenarios identified from failure detection and duplex failure analyses (e.g., creating a self-test process that verifies proper functioning of all key services of each critical process).

3. Solicit other reliability- or availability-improving features that are suggested by developers, support engineers, or others.

4. Estimate the availability benefit of each of the candidate features. If reliability modeling is inadequate or inappropriate to quantitatively estimate the availability benefit of each feature, then one can qualitatively bucket the features based on what system characteristic they will improve (e.g., improved failure detection, improved fault tolerance, faster recovery, reduced critical failure rate) and expected availability benefit (e.g., high, medium, low, very low).

5. Estimate the development and test effort for the highest-benefit features in each bucket.

6. Identify the most appropriate suite of features to include that is affordable and satisfies other business constraints, and estimate the likely system availability assuming those features are implemented.

7. If the set of features proposed for one release is insufficient to reach the system's availability requirement, then repeat for future releases.

In addition to feature changes, one should also assess the adequacy of robustness testing and plan for sufficient robustness testing of future releases. Continued—perhaps even increased—investment in robustness testing should assure the effectiveness of automatic failure detection, isolation, and recovery, thus reducing unplanned service downtime.

Quality improvement activities, such as increasing the use of static analysis tools or code inspections, may also be useful to consider when constructing a reliability roadmap. One should also consult with support engineers and subject matter experts, and perhaps even customers, to determine if product documentation, procedures, training, and support are sufficient or if they need to be improved. It may be appropriate to enhance stability testing, and perhaps system release criteria, to assure that the overall system is sufficiently tested.

The bottom line is that the reliability roadmap should include sufficient investment in features, testing, and other activities to make it both feasible and likely that the system's reliability and availability requirements will be achieved.

13.7 ROBUSTNESS TESTING

Robustness testing for IM server will be done at three phases of development:

1. **Unit testing.** Developers will verify that failures within each unit of design and across interfaces to the unit of design will be automatically detected and contained to prevent the failure from cascading to other parts of the system. Unit testing will also verify that alarms are raised to the fault management system when appropriate.

2. **Integration testing.** Integration testing will verify that failures are properly contained to prevent failure cascades and that automatic failure detection and recovery mechanisms function properly. Proper operation of each redundancy arrangement should be verified, such as by triggering a failure in each active unit of supported active-standby pairs or one active instance in each load-sharing or active-active redundancy arrangement.

3. **System-level robustness testing** verifies that the actual service impact of failures is no worse than specified and completes enough robustness test cases and switchovers to verify the adequacy of failure detection and reliability of failover.

System architects, integration testers, system testers, and product support engineers plan robustness testing by meeting to decide which error scenarios in each of the eight error categories from Chapter 3, "What Can Go Wrong," are applicable to both the IM server and components of the IM server. Each of these applicable error scenarios is classified by likelihood of occurrence in the field and ease of test execution. The team considers a test to be easy to execute if:

- No additional test tools, equipment, or fixtures need be purchased to perform the test.
- Someone on the team knows how to perform the test; ideally, someone on the team has successfully performed the test before.
- The test is relatively quick and easy to set up and execute.

The team also earmarks each scenario with whether it is best tested at the unit, integration, or system level. The test cases are then sorted by error category with highly applicable and easy-to-execute scenarios at the top and low-applicability, hard-to-test scenarios at the bottom.

Each of the sorted lists of error scenarios is reviewed to decide which tests to include in the first system release, and perhaps which to propose for subsequent releases. While some categories (e.g., programming errors) are more applicable error scenarios than other categories (e.g., system power), at least one robustness test case should be included from each error category. To help decide how much robustness testing is appropriate, some development teams allocate a fixed portion of overall test effort to robustness testing (e.g., 20% for early releases of highly available systems and somewhat less for mature systems with proven failure detection, containment, and recovery mechanisms). The result will be a list of error scenarios for unit testing, integration testing, and system-level testing for each of the error categories for the target release. Note that not all categories will be covered by all phases of testing; for instance, system power and procedures are likely to be tested only at system-level robustness testing.

The list of applicable error scenarios can be revisited for each system release to add additional scenarios based on new features and root-cause analyses of field failures, and to change ease of testing based on experience and acquisition of new test tools and equipment. Test scenarios that have consistently passed in previous releases can be automated and moved to regression test plans or retired, and other test scenarios can be introduced. By expanding the breadth of error scenarios covered by robustness testing, failure coverage should grow.

13.8   STABILITY TESTING

Stability testing will verify that the system achieves the transactional reliability requirements under a heavy and mixed traffic load. Each stability test run will last for at least 72 hours with three simulated days of 6 hours of maintenance followed by 18 hours of heavy usage. The first 6-hour maintenance period includes creating and provisioning thousands of test users; subsequent maintenance periods include data backups and minor re-provisioning or reconfiguration of many users to simulate heavy maintenance activity. All test users will be active (simulated logon) during the heavy-usage period and establishing IM session and exchanging IM messages at the full advertised capacity of the system configuration. At least once in each heavy-usage period, all simulated users will reconfigure several aspects of their user static profile information (e.g., business title or e-mail address) and once an hour in the heavy-usage period all simulated users will reconfigure some aspect of their dynamic profile information (e.g., textual status note available to other system users). Test tools shall be constructed to assure that requests of simulated users will occur randomly throughout the heavy-usage period to minimize the risk of all simulated users simultaneously attempting an operation and thus pushing the system into overload. Seventy-five percent of the simulated users will become inactive during maintenance periods while the remaining 25% will continue operating at same work load as during the heavy-usage period. Thousands of simulated users sending messages at full advertised throughput of the system for 54 hours (three 18-hour heavy usage periods) plus additional traffic in 18-hour maintenance periods should include many thousands of IM sessions and perhaps millions of individual messages. At the end of the test run, testers will review logs for simulated clients to assure correct system behavior was observed by all clients and will review system logs to assure that the system experienced no exceptional situations or alarms. Performance statistics will be measured throughout this period and key performance indicators, including transactional reliability for user and provisioning operations, will be computed and compared to requirements. Results of each stability test run are reported to the project team.

Stability test runs will be performed every two weeks in the second half of the system test interval. While stability test runs can be attempted at the start of the system test interval, by design they are inherently challenging for the system and thus are often less likely to pass in the beginning of the test interval before sufficient software defects have been discovered and corrected. Repeating the stability run every two weeks both assures that the system remains stable and gives the project team clear and quantitative data on performance of key quality indicators like service reliability and latency of message delivery. Sophisticated development teams will use biweekly stability runs to incrementally improve performance of key quality indicators, and thus some positive changes in performance may be observed from one run to the next. The results of the stability run on the release candidate software are presented to decision makers as evidence that the release both meets its key quality and performance requirements, and is completely stable under sustained heavy load.

13.9 RELIABILITY REVIEW

A best practice is to complete a reliability review of a system early in the development cycle before development and test plans are committed. The reliability review is an opportunity for decision makers, stakeholders, and members of development and test teams to together decide if it is likely that the reliability requirements will be met with the development and test plans of record. Ideally, a reliability review should cover the following topics:

- **Customers' expectations for service reliability and service availability,** including clear and quantified definitions of total and partial outages.
- **Historic reliability and availability performance of previous systems and releases.** This should cover root-cause analysis of recent outage events, including corrective actions taken.
- **Overview of system reliability and redundancy,** including:
  - **Reliability block diagrams.**
  - **Failure mode analysis results** demonstrating that likely failures and procedures will not produce unacceptable service disruptions.
  - **Architecture-based availability model results** demonstrating the feasibility of achieving customers' expectations.
- **Proposed new reliability, availability, and robustness improving features** and roadmap for improvements in future releases.
- **Robustness testing.** Given system complexity and historic performance, is adequate robustness testing planned?
- **Stability testing.** Given system complexity and historic performance, is adequate stability testing planned?

- **Release criteria.** Given system complexity and historic performance, have appropriate quality, reliability, and stability release criteria been established?
- **Conclusion.** Concluding remarks should cover:
  - **Best estimate of service available at system release.** Considering historic performance of the system itself and development processes, as well as the plans of record, what is the best estimate of service availability for this system release?
  - **Reliability risks.** What exceptional reliability, availability, or stability risks exist for this system release, and what mitigation actions are appropriate?
  - **Recommendations.** If the best estimate of service availability is below customers' availability expectations for this release, then recommendations to decision makers can include one or more of the following three basic options:
    1. Increase investment in reliability-, availability-, and robustness-improving features and/or testing.
    2. Lower customers' availability expectations for this release.
    3. Accept increased risk of failing to meet customers' availability expectations.

13.10   RELIABILITY REPORT

Sophisticated customers for some high-availability systems will insist on evidence of reliability diligence that assures that it is feasible and likely that the system will achieve the customer's reliability and availability expectations. A written reliability report is a convenient way to demonstrate this diligence. Fundamentally, a written reliability report organizes the high-level design for reliability artifacts that are created during the design and development process and that are typically covered in a reliability review meeting (see Section 13.9). An outline of a typical reliability report is shown below; a sample reliability report is included in [Bauer09].

Executive Summary
- **Product Overview** reviews product's primary functionality, features, and configurations highlighting availability- and reliability-related aspects.
- **Architecture Overview** reviews the product's hardware and software architecture highlighting availability- and reliability-related aspects.
- **System Availability Estimates** reviews system availability estimates of key system configurations.

Reliability Requirements reviews the system's high-level reliability requirements.

Reliability Analysis reviews qualitative reliability diligence.

- **Reliability Block Diagrams** gives RBDs, noting the presence or absence of any single points of failure.
- **Failure Mode Analysis** gives redundancy strategies, estimated recovery latencies, and service impact of component failures.
- **Duplex Failure Analysis (optional)** reviews service impact of a primary failure followed by a failure of the high-availability software either to detect the failure or to successfully recover the failure.
- **Impact of Planned Activities** reviews the service impact of successfully executed planned activities like software upgrade and hardware growth.

Reliability Prediction reviews quantitative availability prediction of unplanned product-attributable service downtime.

- **Modeling Methodology** describes the modeling technique (e.g., continuous-time architecture based Markov modeling) and strategy (e.g., granularity of modeled components).
- **Model Assumptions** reviews the key assumptions, including how input parameters were estimated.
- **Unplanned Downtime Model Results** shows quantitative modeling results.

Appendix. Markov model state transition diagrams should be included if Markov modeling was used.

As the reliability report is intended to be shared with potential and actual customers, highly proprietary information should not be included. Suppliers often elect to protect reliability information, like sensitive architectural and design details, with nondisclosure agreements. Actual field performance information must be carefully generalized to avoid disclosing highly proprietary data on how the system is performing in other customers' (often their competitors) enterprises. Enterprises with integrity will respect a supplier's desire not to disclose sensitive details on the system configuration, operational policies, and overall performance of the enterprise's competitors; after all, the supplier probably doesn't want its details shared with its competitors, either.

If one plans ahead, writing a reliability report is often a matter of copying and pasting existing artifacts into a document, adding a bit of prose to connect the artifacts, reviewing, revising, and posting the document. For example, after completing a reliability review, it is often only a modest incremental effort to repackage the less sensitive information into a written reliability report.

13.11 RELEASE CRITERIA

Assuming the IM server development organization is an experienced team with mature processes, a standard suite of release criteria must be met to qualify for release to the field. Most release criteria are straightforward, such as:

- 100% of test cases executed.
- At least 95% of test cases pass.
- No open critical defects and no major defects that cannot be worked around.
- Stability testing demonstrates complete stability and acceptable system performance.

One release criterion question that decision makers should be asking relates to test adequacy:

Has the team completed sufficient testing to expose and correct enough residual software defects that the system software will be acceptably reliable in field operation?

The quality manager for IM server development should have a methodology to estimate the number of undiscovered critical software defects and thus be able to directly address this question based on data.

At the review meeting in which IM server decision makers decide whether to release the system to customers, concrete statements of reliability- and availability-related information should be presented for consideration, such as

- **System demonstrated complete stability during 74-hour testing of mixed user and administrative traffic, mostly at engineered capacity.**
  - **Session connection demonstrated 30.7 DPM for 65K attempts against a target of <= 10 DPM.**
  - **Conversation initiation demonstrated 12.0 DPM for 920K attempts against a target of <= 10 DPM.**
  - **Message delivery demonstrated 2.4 DPM for 22M attempts against a target of <= 10 DPM.**
- **8 to 11 residual (unknown) critical software defects are estimated; based on historic data, this should produce an acceptably low software failure rate.**
- **Best estimate of product-attributable, prorated, unplanned hardware plus software downtime based on lab and field data is 11.4 minutes (99.9978%) against a target of 5.3 down minutes (99.999%).**

This information, along with other product and quality information, enables business leaders to make appropriate decisions about releasing a system to customers.

13.12 FIELD DATA ANALYSIS

The product's support manager reviews all high-severity trouble tickets and customer incidents every week to assure that root causes of incidents are understood as well as possible and that appropriate corrective actions are

planned. Corrective actions are often either bug fixes in an upcoming maintenance release or a change to customer documentation detailing a workaround
or recommended configuration or policy change. Every month a team reviews
all reported outages to validate duration, capacity loss, and attributability and
the product's quality manager computes and reports quality statistics, including service availability. Every quarter the product's quality statistics are compared and validated with quality statistics maintained by strategic customers
that track and report scorecards on the system's performance in their
enterprise.

Semiannually, or quarterly if the system has sufficiently large deployment,
outage incidents are statistically analyzed to determine the actual causes of
system downtime to validate downtime budgeting, parameter estimates, and
performance of predictive models. One analyzes observed downtime and
event rate by category (e.g., hardware, software, product-attributable procedural) to assess performance against budget; this can highlight areas for
product improvement and/or guide revisions to system's downtime budget.
One analyzes events to estimate actual outage rates, durations, and impacts by
category, and can often compute observed values of key modeling parameters
like critical software failure rate or typical outage duration for software-
attributed failures. These actual parameter estimates can be used as input to
the predictive model to create a "hind-cast" prediction to assess how close
the model is to actual results when actual input is used. The hind-cast prediction is likely to be rather different from actual performance because many
relatively rare events (e.g., failures of specific FRUs or software modules) are
likely not to have occurred, and the events that did occur may have been fairly
unusual because each outage is somewhat unique. A second factor is that critical failures are often not uniformly distributed across software and hardware
modules, because a particular residual software defect or hardware design or
manufacturing flaw was activated repeatedly and thus outage data can be
skewed compared to what a model would predict. While the quantitative prediction from the model is likely to be significantly different from the observed
value for a 3- or 6-month window, the model should conceptually reflect actual
system behavior. If long-term actual system behavior is profoundly different
from what the model predicts and those differences are not explained by
unusual quality problems or special customer circumstances, then one should
consider if the model should be reworked to more accurately capture how the
system actually behaves.

Chapter 14

Conclusion

This chapter reviews system design for reliability activities and how they fit into the overall system development process. Concluding remarks are also given.

14.1 OVERVIEW OF DESIGN FOR RELIABILITY

Service reliability and service availability can be designed into a system just as ordinary features and functions are designed into a system. Figure 14.1 illustrates how the design for reliability activities flows together across the system development lifecycle; the sections below review each activity individually.

14.1.1 Reliability Requirements

For most commercial, industrial, enterprise, and government systems that are not human life critical (i.e., excludes medical electronics, aerospace, nuclear power control, etc.), brief and occasional service outages and transactional errors are an accepted cost for competitive system functionality at reasonable system cost. One begins any design activity by characterizing the key requirements of the system being designed. For reliability, one must characterize:

- **Maximum tolerable service disruption** (often several seconds), in which automatic failure detection, isolation, and recovery are expected to operate.
- **Service availability expectation** or maximum unplanned service downtime per system per year. Overall service downtime requirements are often captured as service availability, which is the percentage of time

---

Design for Reliability: Information and Computer-Based Systems, by Eric Bauer
Copyright © 2010 Institute of Electrical and Electronics Engineers

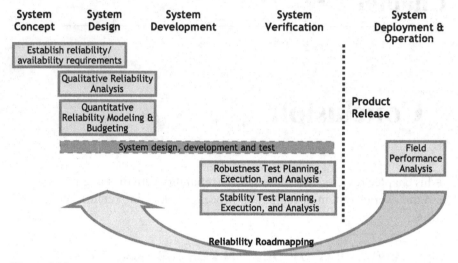

Figure 14.1   Design for Reliability Process

that the primary functionality of a system is available for users. Highly available systems are often expected to achieve four 9's (99.99%, 53 annualized, pro-rated product-attributable down-minutes), four-and-a-half 9's (99.995% or 26 annualized, pro-rated product-attributable down-minutes), or five 9's (99.999% or 5.3 annualized, pro-rated product-attributable down-minutes).

- **Service reliability expectation**, which is the maximum tolerable rate of service or transactional errors while the system is operational (i.e., available or not down). Service reliability is sometimes expressed as either the percentage of valid service requests that are correctly delivered to the requesting user with acceptable service quality (e.g., service latency is within specification), or as the number of defective operations per million attempts (DPM).

These reliability and availability expectations can be driven by:

- The service or application offered by the system
- The expectations of system users
- Service-level agreements offered by enterprises to users, or contractual performance commitments made by supplier to enterprise
- Performance of historic and competitive systems
- Industry standards
- Legal or regulatory considerations

Defining high-level and detailed service availability and reliability requirements is detailed in Chapter 8.

14.1.2 Qualitative Reliability Analysis

Given the maximum acceptable service disruption latency requirement, system architects partition the system into suitable recoverable modules with appropriate failure detection mechanisms to assure that it is feasible for the maximum service disruption latency requirement to be met. Redundant hardware is often required to avoid accruing significant downtime on hardware failure. Having designed the system with hardware redundancy, the hardware redundancy can be leveraged to reduce downtime following software failure as well. System architects will also assure that failures are contained to the smallest practical unit of design, which will often be smaller than hardware field-replaceable units. Architects must also assure that suitable overload control mechanisms are designed, as well as secondary failure detectors to assure that faults that are not detected the instant they are activated will be promptly detected before the error cascades into a critical failure. These principles are covered in Chapters 4, 5, and 6.

A thorough analysis of the "paper" architecture and design can assure that the system design makes it feasible and likely that the reliability requirements will be met. This analysis can expose weaknesses in system architecture and design early enough in the development process that they can be fixed inexpensively and with minimal disruption to the development program. In addition, a thoughtful reliability analysis can guide the system's campaign of robustness testing. The qualitative analysis verifies that the system is capable of promptly detecting, isolating, and recovering from errors with acceptable service disruptions, and that it is feasible to meet the system's reliability requirements. The principles of reliability analysis are covered in Chapter 7 and practical aspects are covered in Chapter 9.

14.1.3 Quantitative Reliability Modeling and Budgeting

Establishing a budget and managing to it is a time-honored technique for managing money, and it also works well for managing service downtime. By allocating specified service downtime across elements of the system, developers have more concrete targets for how reliable and robust individual modules must be so they can create appropriate quality targets to manage failure rates and create appropriate designs for failure detection, isolation, and recovery so it is feasible and likely that the downtime budget—and hence availability requirements—can be met.

Service availability requirements are generally impractical to directly verify via lab testing because critical failures will be very rare in the released system. The best practice is to construct mathematical models based on the system's architecture and behavior to estimate the feasible and likely service availability of the system. Mathematical modeling allows system architects to vary key parameters to determine their sensitivity and thus determine the optimal budget of parameter values to make it feasible and likely that service availability requirements will be met. A suite of key parameter values like downtime allocations, recovery time latencies, and switchover success probabilities that modeling shows should achieve the system's availability requirements are captured as targets. These optimal values and behaviors are often directly verifiable via lab testing, and thus should be captured as detailed design requirements that will drive development and testing. Reliability modeling and budgeting are covered in Chapters 7 and 10.

14.1.4 Robustness Testing

Robustness testing confronts the system with likely error scenarios to verify that the failure containment, detection, isolation, and recovery mechanisms work properly. Testers and developers can use the qualitative reliability analysis to identify the most likely error scenarios in each error category, and are careful to verify proper operation of each recovery mechanism. Analysis of robustness test results can drive improved estimates of key parameters in architecture-based availability models. Robustness testing is covered in Chapter 11.

14.1.5 Stability Testing

Testing the system under a prolonged heavy load of mixed end-user and OAM&P traffic running mostly at the system's full engineered capacity is a best practice for assuring system stability and characterizing service reliability. While stability testing is not designed to verify failure detection, isolation, or recovery mechanisms, it does assure that the architecture and design of the system itself is robust enough to endure a heavy sustained load. Stability testing is covered in Chapter 11.

14.1.6 Analysis of Field Performance

Over time, deployed systems will inevitably experience critical failures. Some of these failures will escalate into service outages because one or more secondary failures prevented the system from automatically detecting, isolating, and recovering the primary failure within the maximum acceptable time. Section 12.1 reviews how field outage data can be analyzed to drive improvements in future releases.

14.1.7   Reliability Roadmapping

If reliability performance does not meet expectations, then a release-by-release roadmap of availability- and reliability-improving features and testing should be constructed and executed. System architects, developers, testers, support engineers, and others often have ideas to improve failure detection, isolation, and recovery; testers can always do more robustness testing; and inevitable service outages from field deployments will highlight areas for further availability and reliability improvement. By organizing reliability features and testing into bundles, one can estimate changes in reliability-related parameters and estimate service availability of future releases. By taking the ratio of estimated down-minutes saved from availability modeling to the estimated development and test costs of the associated feature bundle, one can estimate the annualized cost-per-down-minute-saved. While this is likely to be a very soft metric, this can be used to roughly compare different bundles of robustness-related features to better prioritize reliability-related activities by system releases. Section 12.2 reviews how to construct a reliability roadmap to facilitate methodical planning of system improvements on a release-by-release basis.

14.2   CONCLUDING REMARKS

As networked systems and applications become more integrated into personal behaviors, commercial activities, and government operations, expectations for always-on, always-available application services increase. Since failures and disruptions of hardware, software, and other infrastructure ingredients required to support networked application services are inevitable, highly available systems must be designed to be both reliable and robust. Reliable systems have a very low rate of failure, and hence a low rate of service disruption. Robust systems contain the impact of inevitable failures, rapidly detect the failures, automatically activate the proper recovery actions, and rapidly restore service with minimal service disruption. The guiding principle of highly available systems is that no single failure shall cause an unacceptable service disruption; the implication is that any unacceptable service disruption (outage) is the result of a primary failure and at least one failure of an automatic failure containment, detection, isolation, or recovery mechanism. As this book has shown, high service availability and service reliability can be methodically designed into a system like any other feature via diligent system design for reliability. By qualitatively and quantitatively managing service reliability and service availability throughout the development lifecycle, a development team can efficiently manage achieving, and eventually exceeding, customers' expectations for reliability and availability.

14.3 PROBLEMS

1. Explain the activities throughout the system development lifecycle that assure that a clear service availability requirement is properly implemented prior to system release.

2. If system reliability or availability of field deployment did not meet customers' expectations, then what activities could a development team undertake to meet the customers' expectations in the next release?

Chapter 15

Appendix: Assessing Design for Reliability Diligence

Since system *design for reliability (DfR)* fits naturally into typical development processes, it is generally easy to assess how complete a project's design for reliability diligence is by asking a few straightforward questions to the individuals executing the applicable processes. Although questions like "Do we have appropriate reliability requirements?" or "Have we done appropriate reliability analysis?" are too vague to generally produce useful answers, more concrete questions can be asked for each DfR activity. The notion of a DfR assessment is to ask engineers involved in each activity several concrete questions and carefully listen to their answers. Often the individual engineers and managers recognize the risk the project is taking due to incomplete reliability diligence and will suggest specific actions to address significant gaps.

System reliability diligence is assessed across the eight major DfR activities presented in this book:

1. Reliability requirements
2. Reliability analysis
3. Reliability modeling and budgeting
4. Robustness testing
5. Stability testing
6. System release criteria
7. Field availability
8. Reliability roadmap

Although hardware reliability was only lightly covered in Section 1.7, a set of basic hardware reliability assessment questions are included in Section

Design for Reliability: Information and Computer-Based Systems, by Eric Bauer
Copyright © 2010 Institute of Electrical and Electronics Engineers

1.8, "Hardware Reliability." These questions can be asked of the original equipment manufacturer or internal hardware design team to verify that appropriate hardware reliability diligence was completed. Properly evaluating the responses to these hardware reliability questions will require a deeper knowledge of hardware reliability and quality than has been presented in this book. Nevertheless, hardware reliability diligence is an important topic to be considered when hardware is included in the system delivery, even if the hardware is designed and developed by others.

15.1 ASSESSMENT METHODOLOGY

A DfR assessment is typically completed in five steps:

1. **Identify appropriate subject matter experts.** Rarely will a single engineer or manager be fully aware of the status of all aspects of a system's design for reliability diligence, and thus it is best to evaluate each topic with an appropriate expert. Table 15.1 gives the typical roles of subject matter experts to address each DfR assessment category.

Table 15.1   Recommended Experts for DfR Assessment Vectors

DfR assessment vector	Role of typical expert
Reliability requirements	System engineer who writes system requirements
Reliability analysis	System architect who creates high-level system design
Reliability modeling and budgeting	System architect or reliability engineer who is responsible for assuring that system's reliability requirements are met
Robustness testing	System tester who performs software or hardware fault insertion testing, adversarial testing, negative testing, break-and-destroy testing, etc.
Stability testing	System tester who performs long-duration stability or endurance testing
System release criteria	Quality or project manager who monitors and manages development and test metrics
Field availability	Quality manager who monitors problem reports from the field or product support engineer who works issues reported by customers
Reliability roadmap	Product manager or system engineer who works feature roadmap for future system releases

2. **Initial interviews with subject matter experts.** Meet with each of the subject matter experts and ask whether and how each of the assessment questions is addressed by the project. As they describe what diligence has been completed, ask if the expert believes that the diligence has been sufficient. Experts often have deep insights into the risks in their area of expertise, but often have not had an opportunity to fully articulate those risks. Use the assessment questions to facilitate this discussion and capture all appropriate feedback from the discussion.

3. **Draft assessment report** identifying gap items, risks, proposed mitigations, and recommended priorities.

4. **Review draft assessment report with subject matter experts** to assure that current status and plans are accurately captured in the report and that proposed recommendation and priorities are appropriate.

5. **Present final assessment report** to project leaders and decision makers. Ideally, decision makers will accept high-priority recommendations and commit resources to complete those recommended mitigation steps.

Each assessment question can be evaluated with one of the following four options:

1. **Covered.** Project's current or planned reliability diligence adequately covers this item.

2. **Partial gap.** Project's current or planned reliability diligence partially covers this item, but one or more specific gaps present a risk of failing to meet customers' reliability/availability expectations.

3. **Gap.** Project's current or planned reliability diligence does not adequately cover this item.

4. **Not applicable.** This activity is not applicable to the system under consideration.

As different systems will have different reliability/availability expectations, individual assessment questions will have different degrees of importance for different systems. Thus, many of the assessment questions will be highly applicable to any particular system, some will have modest or little applicability, and a few will be "not applicable." Projects will naturally focus their gap closure efforts on the highly applicable items that were assessed as "gap" or "partial gap." Gaps in lower-applicability items can be addressed as business priorities permit.

Partial and complete gaps identified via a DfR assessment are best presented qualitatively with the following key data:

- **Item.** Exactly what is the gap in diligence, for instance:

  Switchover success probability not quantitatively specified in system requirements.

- **Risk.** Characterize the technical or business risk of current or planned reliability diligence, for instance:

  Switchover reliability not formally verified by system testing, causing elevated risk that automatic failovers will not succeed. Unsuccessful failovers of deployed systems will require manual recovery, thus prolonging service downtime and increasing customers' operating expense.

- **Proposed mitigation.** Propose a specific mitigation action to address the risk, such as:

  Baseline quantitative switchover success probability requirements to drive formal verification by system test.

- **Priority or business risk.** Characterize how severe the business or technical risk of this gap is, relative to other DfR and/or project risks, such as high, medium, or low.

Depending on the extent of gaps exposed in the first DfR assessment, it may be appropriate to repeat the DfR assessment a year or two later to confirm results of mitigation actions, and to identify further areas for improvement.

15.2   RELIABILITY REQUIREMENTS

Rigorous product development processes rely on system requirements being fully documented and agreed early in the development cycle so that architects can construct appropriate system architecture; developers can design, code, and unit test appropriate software; and testers can appropriately test the system. If system requirements for reliability are captured as verifiable functional requirements, then the same development processes that assure that ordinary functional requirements are planned, managed, implemented, and completed with quality will assure that reliability features are also completed with quality. If market or technical expectations are not captured in system requirements documents, then the project risks having the system's architecture and high-level design overlook implicit market expectations and requirements, or coding and unit testing omit them, or system test failing to verify them.

Thirteen general reliability requirements questions are listed here. Formal, testable requirements in an appropriate controlling document can be assessed as "covered." Requirements that are not documented but informally understood to apply (and hence may not be rigorously implemented or tested) may be assessed as "partial gap." Other items can be assessed as "gap" or "not applicable," as appropriate.

1. **Is "total service outage" sufficiently defined and documented so that system architects, developers, testers, and support and quality engineers will agree on whether a particular failure event should be classified as a total outage?** Service outage definition should explicitly enumerate which system services are covered and crisply define exactly

the minimum chargeable outage duration that should imply the maximum acceptable (i.e., non-outage) service disruption duration.

2. **Is "partial outage" sufficiently defined and documented so that system architects, developers, testers, and support and quality engineers will agree on whether a particular failure event should be classified as a partial outage, and how to prorate the partial outage event?** Partial outage definition should characterize both how less-than-total system outages will be quantified and what the minimum chargeable capacity loss is. Partial capacity loss outages are generally normalized as the percentage of provisioned or configured users who were impacted and partial functionality loss outages are generally normalized as the percentage of system interfaces or categories of functionality that were impacted. There may be a minimum percentage loss threshold to assure that "outage" classification applies only to events impacting more than one user.

3. **What is the system's product-attributable service availability requirement?** Typically a quantitative service availability rating will be given for a major system configuration such as "standalone configuration 99.98%; clustered configuration 99.995%."

4. **Is the maximum acceptable service disruption for automatic failure detection, isolation, and recovery specified?** This will often be no more than a few seconds.

5. **Are maximum switchover/failover latencies specified for each set of redundant modules?** Switchover times should be specified for each active-standby, active-active, and other redundancy arrangement.

6. **Is minimum switchover/failover success probability specified?**

7. **Is the minimum percentage of software failures that are automatically detected, isolated, and recovered in maximum acceptable service disruption latency (i.e., "software coverage") specified?**

8. **Is the minimum percentage of hardware failures that are automatically detected, isolated, and recovered in maximum acceptable service disruption latency (i.e., "hardware coverage") specified?**

9. **Are the maximum cold (system) restart and warm (application) restart times specified?**

10. **Is the maximum acceptable service disruption duration for planned maintenance activities specified (e.g., software upgrade, update, patch, and system growth or degrowth)?** Critical, online systems are often required to support procedures for hitless or non-service-impacting maintenance activities that result in minimal service disruption. Requirements should clearly specify the maximum acceptable impact and disruption to primary functions of a system due to execution of planned maintenance activities; will existing sessions be impacted? Will new service requests be impacted? Will some transactions be impacted?

11. **Is a software rollback or revert mechanism supported to efficiently recover from a failed or toxic software upgrade?**

12. **Is geographic redundancy support specified?**

13. **Are service reliability key performance indicators (KPIs) like maximum rate of properly formed key functions/transactions that can fail (e.g., maximum rate of defects per million operations) specified?**

15.3 RELIABILITY ANALYSIS

Reliability analysis covers nine basic qualitative reliability diligence questions.

1. **Do reliability block diagrams of hardware and software for primary system configuration(s) exist?**

2. **Are there any single points of failure?** A single point of failure (see Section 5.1, "Robust Design Principles") is a hardware or software module that is required for service delivery but is not protected via automatic failure detection, isolation, and recovery mechanism to assure that module failure will not cause an unacceptable service disruption. High-availability systems should have no single points of failure.

3. **Are there any single points of repair?** A single point of repair (see Section 5.1, "Robust Design Principles") is an FRU that will cause service to become unavailable when the FRU is repaired or replaced. For example, the backplane is often a single point of repair because repairing or replacing a backplane generally requires the chassis to be depowered, thus shutting down a single chassis system.

4. **Is the nature and duration of service impact for failures of major modules understood?** Note that this is often referred to as "failure mode analysis" or "failure mode and effects analysis."

5. **Is the nature and duration of service impact for planned activities understood?**

6. **Are commands available for maintenance engineers to trigger and test switchover/failover mechanisms?**

7. **Are confirmation messages (e.g., "Are you sure?") presented to maintenance engineers prior to executing service-impacting actions?**

8. **Are safe stop points supported during upgrade procedures/scripts?** *Safe stop points* are documented points in the written procedure where maintenance engineers can safely suspend a procedure if a failure occurs, or if it is necessary or appropriate to pause (e.g., because the procedure will not complete within the allocated maintenance period).

9. **Will feature activation, configuration, or deactivation affect any other end user's service?** For example, will changing an individual user's configuration on a particular service cause other users of that service to experience a service disruption due to software reconfiguration or restart?

15.4 RELIABILITY MODELING AND BUDGETING

Reliability modeling predicts system downtime based on estimates of failure rates, success probabilities, latencies, and other parameters. Modeling should be used to verify the feasibility and likelihood of achieving a system's service availability requirements. Ask these nine modeling questions:

1. **What type of mathematical model is used to predict unplanned hardware and software downtime?** Architecture-based Markov modeling is common, but other modeling techniques are also used.

2. **What type of modeling is used to predict downtime for successful and unsuccessful planned and procedural activities?** Algebraic models are common, but other modeling techniques can also be used.

3. **Is imperfect (< 100%) failure coverage used in the model to address the portion of critical hardware and software failures that will not be promptly detected and properly isolated by the system automatically?**

4. **Have model's input values for automatic recovery latency (e.g., switchover/failover) been validated by lab measurement?**

5. **Have model's input values for success probabilities (e.g., switchover success, failure coverage) been validated by analysis of robustness test results?**

6. **Have software failure rates been calibrated against field performance of previous releases, and tailored based on added features and test results for this release?**

7. **Does the best estimate of unplanned downtime meet the reliability budget and system requirements for this release?**

8. **Has duration of service impact for successfully executed planned and procedural activities been validated by lab measurement?**

9. **Has success probability of planned and procedural activities been calibrated against field performance of previous releases and tailored based on added features and test results for this release?**

Reliability budgeting divides the high-level downtime requirement into individual allocations that can be managed separately. The following questions assess typical downtime budget categories. Alternate downtime factorizations can be used, and thus these questions can be altered to track with the downtime factorization used for the system under consideration.

1. **What portion of service downtime is allocated to software-attributed causes?**
2. **What portion of service downtime is allocated to hardware-attributed causes?**
3. **What portion of the downtime is budgeted for the system's successful planned/procedural activities?**
4. **What portion of the service downtime is allocated for failed planned/procedural activities that are attributed to system and/or the system supplier?**

15.5 ROBUSTNESS TESTING

Robustness testing verifies that the system automatically detects, isolates, and recovers from plausible and likely failures with minimal service impact. This assessment category should evaluate the adequacy of the robustness test coverage in each of the eight robustness error categories described earlier in Chapter 3, "What Can Go Wrong."

1. **Are the system's automatic detection, isolation, and recovery from Programming Errors adequately verified?** Common programming errors to consider include:
   - Memory leak or exhaustion (including excessive fragmentation)
   - Shared resource conflict
   - Tight or infinite loop
   - Remote execution failures and hangs, including remote procedure call failures
   - Thread stack or address space corrupted
   - Reference uninitialized or incorrect pointer
   - Logic errors
   - Non-memory resource leaks
   - Process abort, crash, or hang
   - Thread hang or abort
2. **Is the system's automatic detection, isolation, and recovery from Data Errors adequately verified?** Common data errors to consider include:
   - File system corruption, including from disorderly disk write on power-down
   - Disk partition or file system full
   - Database corruption
   - Database mismatch between active and standby versions
   - Shared memory corruption
   - Linked list breakage
   - File not found
   - File corrupted

- Record not found
- Record corrupted
- Corrupted executable
- Checksum error
- Cannot access file or write protected

3. **Are the system's automatic detection, isolation, and recovery from Redundancy Errors adequately verified?** Common redundancy failures to consider include:

   - Switchover reliability—execute sufficient switchovers to assure mechanism is acceptably reliable.
   - Failover to failed (redundant) hardware.
   - Failed failover.
   - Site failure to verify georedundancy.
   - Failure of high availability process(es).

4. **Are the system's automatic detection, isolation, and recovery from Networking Errors adequately verified?** Common IP networking failures to consider include:

   - Failure of adjacent or supporting network elements
   - Corrupted IP packets
   - Dropped IP packets
   - IP packets out of sequence
   - Disruption of (external) IP infrastructure
   - Disruption of intershelf IP infrastructure on multishelf network elements
   - Disruption of intrashelf IP infrastructure on blade-based systems
   - Recovery from regional network or power failure (triggers re-registration or reconnection storm)
   - IP port unavailable
   - Inconsistent real-time clocks

5. **Are the system's automatic detection, isolation, and recovery from Application Protocol Errors adequately verified?** Common application protocol errors to consider include:

   - Invalid protocol syntax
   - Invalid protocol semantics
   - Unexpected or illegal message sequences
   - Out-of-range parameters, including illegal command codes
   - Malicious messages
   - Overload, including denial-of-service attack

6. **Are the system's automatic detection, isolation, and recovery from System Power Errors adequately verified?** Common programming errors to consider include:

   - Network element power failure and restoration
   - Fuse failure and replacement

- Shelf power failure and restoration, for multishelf systems.
- Single power feed failure on systems with redundant power feeds
- Test backup power generators in systems designed for them
- Overvoltage
- Undervoltage/brownout

7. **Are the system's automatic detection, isolation, and recovery from FRU Hardware Errors adequately verified?** Common hardware failures to consider include:

- Processor failure
- Disk failure
- Power converter module failure
- Clock failure
- Clock jitter
- Ethernet switching failure
- Memory device failure
- Bus error or failure
- Transient failure or signal integrity issue
- Application-specific component failure

8. **Are the system's automatic detection, isolation, and recovery from Procedural Errors adequately verified?** Common procedural errors to consider include:

- Wrong (including out-of-range) inputs to OAM&P commands.
- Verify presence and appropriateness of warnings on all service-impacting commands prior to deliberately impacting service to prevent a single keystroke error from disrupting service.

15.6 STABILITY TESTING

Stability testing demonstrates that the system is acceptably reliable under an extended heavy load of mixed user and operational activities. This category assesses nine questions of adequacy of stability testing.

1. **What is the duration of each stability test run?** Seventy-two hours is typically the minimum acceptable duration, but longer runs are used for some systems.

2. **How is the traffic load varied throughout the stability test run?** Best practice is to maintain full engineered load of user traffic on the system for majority of stability test run, and to simulate heavy maintenance activities during one or more simulated maintenance periods of light user traffic.

3. **How broad is the mix of end-user services during the stability run?** Best practice is to simulate a typical service mix.

4. **Is user provisioning performed during the stability run?** Best practice is to simulate adding new users and modifying existing users during the stability run. Some user provisioning should be performed during peak traffic periods. After all, users are often added during normal business hours when system is fully utilized, rather than waiting until maintenance periods.

5. **What maintenance operations are performed during stability test?** Backups, performance monitoring operations, routine diagnostics, and other normal maintenance operations should be performed during simulated maintenance periods in stability runs.

6. **What traffic measurements are made during stability testing?** Are these measurements sufficient to determine acceptable throughput was achieved during the stability test run?

7. **What key performance or service quality measurements are made during stability testing?** Best practice is to verify the system's key performance and service quality requirements during stability testing. Thus, defects per million operations (DPM), quality-of-service, and other performance metrics should be collected and evaluated against system's requirements.

8. **What system failure measurements are made during stability testing?** Best practice is to check for component failure, continuing memory/resource growth, switchovers, processor overload, buffer/queue overflow, etc.

9. **How are results of stability testing evaluated?** What are the minimum pass criteria for a stability test run?

15.7 RELEASE CRITERIA

Product development teams must use some release criteria to determine when sufficient system testing has been performed and results are adequate for software to be officially released to customers. Primitive product development teams may use casual best-effort-in-time-available criteria that are driven primarily by calendar dates (e.g., schedule or contract says to deliver software on a particular date, so the software will be shipped on that date, ready or not). Mature product development teams will consider five factors to assure that:

1. Specified functionality has been formally verified.

2. Product documentation and supporting artifacts and processes are complete and verified.

3. Results of formal testing (including robustness and stability testing) are acceptable.

4. All known critical defects have been corrected, or workarounds documented.

5. There are likely to be few enough unknown critical defects left in the software that critical software failure rate will be low enough to assure reliable operation.

Typical product quality activities primarily focus on formally assuring that the first four factors are addressed, but estimating the number of unknown residual defects is often not formally considered. Since unknown, high-severity residual defects are the primary driver of critical software failures in field operation, it is important for highly available systems to carefully consider whether sufficient testing has been completed to drive the number of unknown residual defects to a small enough number that acceptably reliable operation is likely. The following four questions help assess the adequacy of a product's residual defect prediction and assessment methodology:

1. **How is number of unknown residual, high-severity defects predicted prior to product release?**

2. **What is the maximum acceptable number of predicted residual, high-severity defects at product release?**

3. **How (and how often) is the defect prediction method validated and calibrated against historic releases?**

4. **How is the maximum acceptable number of predicted residual defects set and how often does it change?**

15.8 FIELD AVAILABILITY

Analyzing critical failures and outages that occur during commercial or production operation of a system is essential to discover whether the system is meeting its reliability and availability requirements, to identify areas for improvement, and to validate and calibrate prediction models and methodologies. The following five questions enable one to assess the adequacy of a system's field availability data analysis.

1. **Is actual product-attributable service availability (or downtime) known?** Is it known for individual releases, or is it known only at the aggregate level across multiple releases?

2. **Root-cause analyses (RCAs) have been completed for what portion of critical field failures that occurred in past 12 months?**

3. **Do outage RCAs routinely include improvements in robustness test plans?**

4. **When was the last time that the product's downtime budget was compared with actual field performance?**

5. **When was the last time that the product's availability model input parameters and predictions were compared and validated with actual field data?**

15.9 RELIABILITY ROADMAP

If field availability is not meeting the system's service availability requirements or the market's availability expectations, then a reliability roadmap should be used to manage reliability improvement activities to close the gap. Early releases of a product can also benefit from a reliability roadmap to assure that high availability is promptly achieved. Adequacy of a product's reliability roadmap can be assessed via the following six questions:

1. **Are quantitative reliability/availability targets captured in a reliability roadmap for future releases?**
2. **Are reliability/availability/stability-improving features or testing associated with future releases to support quantitative reliability/availability targets?**
3. **Are reliability/availability/stability-improving capabilities and testing planned, managed, and tracked as features for future releases?**
4. **Are the benefits of planned reliability/availability/stability-improving features and testing quantified (e.g., to improvements in unplanned or planned downtime)?**
5. **Does modeling suggest that it is feasible and likely that quantitative reliability/availability targets will be met with the proposed reliability/availability/stability-improving features?** For example, is availability degrowth (i.e., increase in downtime) anticipated and managed when substantial new or modified code is introduced (e.g., additional robustness testing or availability-improving features added to compensate for additional residual defects likely to be introduced)?
6. **Does engineering judgment and experience suggest that the reliability roadmap will achieve its targets?** Can one credibly assure a (possibly dissatisfied) customer that the reliability roadmap is credible?

15.10 HARDWARE RELIABILITY

This section enumerates several reliability-related items to review with the system's hardware supplier(s) to assure that adequate hardware reliability diligence was executed. Thoroughly assessing the adequacy of a hardware supplier's response requires knowledge of hardware design, reliability, and quality that is beyond the scope of this book. An appropriate expert should verify that that acceptable hardware reliability diligence was completed by suppliers to assure that hardware is likely to have an acceptably low failure rate throughout the system's designed service life. Here are six questions for cursory hardware reliability assessment:

1. **What is the designed service life of the FRU(s)?** After how many years of continuous operation is the hardware return rate likely to climb above the predicted hardware return rate? 3 years? 5 years? 10 years? 20 years?

2. **What is the maximun hardware return rate requirement of the FRU(s)?** What percentage of installed FRUs should customers expect to return per year?

3. **Are hardware return rates tracked for individual (FRUs)?**

4. **What is the observed hardware return rate for each FRU?**

5. **What is the no-trouble-found or no-fault-found rate for each FRU?**

6. **Is a formal hardware failure root-cause analysis program in place to drive corrective actions?**

Abbreviations

8i = Eight-ingredient framework

COTS = Commercial off-the-shelf

CPLD = Complex programmable logic device

CPU = Central processing unit

DDoS = Distributed denial-of-service attack

DfR = Design for reliability

DNS = Domain name service

DoS = denial-of-service attack

DPM = Defects per million

DRAM = Dynamic random access memory

DSP = Digital signal processor

ECC = Error checking and correcting, as in error checking and correcting random access memory

FCAPS = Fault, configuration, accounting, performance, and security management

FIT = Failure in time, refers to number of hardware failures in 1 billion hours

FMEA = Failure mode and effect analysis

FRU = Field-replaceable unit, such as a hot-swappable hard disk drive or a processor blade

FPGA = Field programmable gate array

HA = High availability

HALT = Highly accelerated life testing

HFI = Hardware fault insertion/injection

HTTP = Hypertext Transfer Protocol

IC = Integrated circuit

IEEE = Institute of Electrical and Electronics Engineers

IETF = Internet Engineering Task Force, which develops and promotes standards for the Internet.

I/O = Input/output

ITU = International Telecommunications Union, an international standards body

IP = Internet Protocol

JTAG = Joint Test Action Group, or the interface to IEEE 1149 Boundary Scan functionality

MOP = Method of procedure

MPEG-4 = Fourth video encoding standard from the Motion Pictures Expert Group

MPLS = Multiprotocol label switching

MSRP= Message Session Relay Protocol, Standardized by Internet Engineering Task Force in RFCs 4975 and 4976

MTBF = Mean time between failures

MTBO = Mean time between outages

MTTR = Mean time to repair

MTTRS = Mean time to restore service

NFF = No fault found

NTF = No trouble found

N + K = Load-sharing across N elements required to deliver advertised service load and K redundant elements

NEBS = Telcordia's GR-63-CORE National Electrical Building Standard (NEBS) [GR-63-CORE]

OAM = Operations, administration, and maintenance

OAM&P = Operations, administration, maintenance, and provisioning

OEM = Original equipment manufacturer

POST = Power-on self-test

RBD = Reliability block diagram

RCA = Root-cause analysis

SFI = Software fault insertion or injection

SIP = Session Initiation Protocol, standardized by the Internet Engineering Task Force in RFC 3261

SNMP = Simple Network Management Protocol, defined by the Internet Engineering Task Force

SONET = Synchronous optical networking

VoIP = Voice-over-Internet Protocol

X.805 = ITU-T standard on "Security architecture for systems providing end-to-end communications"

References

[Bauer09] "Practical System Reliability," Eric Bauer, Xuemei Zhang, Doug Kimber, IEEE Press, 2009.

[CERT] Carnegie-Mellon Computer Emergency Response Team, www.cert.org.

[Coverity09] "Coverity Prevent™ 4.4 Checker Reference," Coverity, Inc., 2009.

[CWE] "2009 CWE/SANS Top 25 Most Dangerous Programming Errors," http://cwe.mitre.org/top25/.

[Demarco86] "Controlling Software Projects: Management, Measurement and Estimation," Tom Demarco, Prentice-Hall, 1986, ISBN: 978-0131717114.

[DoDD8500.1] Department of Defense DIRECTIVE NUMBER 8500.1, October 24, 2002, "Information Assurance (IA)".

[GR-63-CORE] NEBS Requirements: Physical Protection, Issue 2, April 2002, Telcordia.

[Hanmer07] "Patterns for Fault Tolerant Software," Robert Hanmer, John Wiley & Sons, Ltd., ISBN 978-0-470-31979-6, 2007.

[Humphrey89] "Managing the Software Process," Watts S. Humphrey, Addison-Wesley Professional, 1989, ISBN: 978-0201180954.

[IEEE610] "IEEE Standard Glossary of Software Engineering Terminology," IEEE Std 610.12-1990(R2002).

[IEEE1149] IEEE Std 1149.1 "IEEE Standard Test Access Port and Boundary-Scan Architecture," Reaffirmed 27 March 2008.

[Lyu95] "Software Fault Tolerance," Michael R. Lyu, John Wiley and Sons, Inc., 1995.

[Lyu96] "Handbook of Software Reliability Engineering," Michael Lyu, McGraw-Hill, 1996, ISBN 978-007039400, www.cse.cuhk.edu.hk/~lyu/book/reliability.

[McDermott08] "The Basics of FMEA", Robin E. McDermott, Raymond J. Mikula, and Michael R. Beauregard, Productivity Press, 2008, ISBN 978-1563273773.

[MIL217F] MIL-HDBK-217F "Military Handbook Reliability Prediction of Electronic Equipment," U.S. Department of Defense, December 1991.

[Musa89] "Software Reliability Engineering," John Musa, McGraw-Hill, 1989, ISBN: 978-0079132710.

[NIST] "Guide for Applying the Risk Management Framework to Federal Information Systems: A Security Life Cycle Approach," NIST Special Publication 800-37, Revision 1, National Institute of Standards and Technology, U.S. Department of Commerce.

[NRIC] Network Reliability and Interoperability Center website, www.nric.org.

[NRICBP] NRIC Best Practice website, www.fcc.gov/nors/outage/bestpractice/BestPractice.cfm, available from www.nric.org.

[O'Connor04] "Practical Reliability Engineering," Patrick D. T. O'Connor, Wiley, 2002, ISBN: 978-0470844632.

[Pukite98] "Modeling for Reliability Analysis," J. Pukite and P. Pukite, IEEE Press, 1998.

[Rauscher06] "Eight Ingredients of Communications Infrastructure: A Systematic and Comprehensive Framework for Enhancing Network Reliability and Security," Karl F. Rauscher, Richard E. Krock, and James P. Runyon, Bell Labs Technical Journal, 10.1002, John Wiley & Sons, Ltd., 2006.

Design for Reliability: Information and Computer-Based Systems, by Eric Bauer
Copyright © 2010 Institute of Electrical and Electronics Engineers

318   References

[RFC4975] RFC 4975, "The Message Session Relay Protocol (MSRP)," B. Campbell, R. Mahy, C. Jennings (Eds.), The Internet Society, September 2007.
[RFC4976] RFC 4976, "Relay Extensions for the Message Session Relay Protocol (MSRP)," C. Jennings, R. Mahy, A. B. Roach (Eds.), The Internet Society, September 2007.
[SACMM] "Software Acquisition Capability Maturity Model?(SA-CMM?)Version 1.03," Jack Cooper, Matthew Fisher (Eds.), March 2002, TECHNICAL REPORT CMU/SEI-2002-TR-010 ESC-TR-2002-010, www.sei.cmu.edu/reports/02tr010.pdf.
[SAF] Service Availability Forum website, www.saforum.org .
[SR332] "Reliability Prediction Procedure for Electronic Equipment, Issue 2," January 2006, Telcordia Technologies.
[SR2785] "Software Fault Insertion Testing (SFIT) Methodology," Telcordia SR-2785.
[Stamatis03] "Failure Mode and Effect Analysis: FMEA from Theory to Execution," D. H. Stamatis, ASQ Quality Press, 2003, ISBN 978-0873895989.
[TL9000] "TL 9000 Quality Management System Measurements Handbook Release 4.0," Quality Excellence for Suppliers of Telecommunications Forum (QuEST Forum), www.tl9000.org, December 31, 2006.
[Trivedi02] "Probability and Statistics with Reliability, Queueing, and Computer Science Applications," 2nd Edition, New York, John Wiley & Sons, 2002.
[USCERT] United States Computer Emergency Response Team, www.us-cert.gov/.
[X.805] "Security Architecture for Systems Providing End to End Communications," ITU T Recommendation X.805, International Telecommunications Union, October 2003.

Photo Credits

Design for Reliability: Information and Computer-Based Systems, by Eric Bauer
Copyright © 2010 Institute of Electrical and Electronics Engineers

About the Author

ERIC BAUER is reliability engineering manager in the Wireline Division of Alcatel-Lucent. He originally joined Bell Labs to design digital telephones and went on to develop multitasking operating systems on personal computers. Mr. Bauer then worked on network operating systems for sharing resources across heterogeneous operating systems, and developed an enhanced, high-performance UNIX file system to facilitate file sharing across Microsoft, Apple, and UNIX platforms. That work led him to work on an advanced Internet service platform at AT&T Labs. Mr. Bauer then joined Lucent Technologies to develop a new Java-based private branch exchange (PBX) telephone system that was a forerunner of today's IP Multimedia Subsystem (IMS) solutions, and later worked on a long-haul/ultra-long-haul optical transmission system. When Lucent centralized reliability engineering, Mr. Bauer joined the Lucent reliability team to lead a reliability group, and has since worked on reliability engineering on a variety of wireless and wireline products and solutions. He currently focuses on reliability of Alcatel-Lucent's IMS solution and the network elements that comprise the IMS solution. He has been awarded 11 U.S. patents, coauthored "Practical System Reliability" (ISBN 978-0470408605), and has published several papers in the *Bell Labs Technical Journal*. Mr. Bauer holds a BS in Electrical Engineering from Cornell University, Ithaca, New York, and an MS in Electrical Engineering from Purdue University, West Lafayette, Indiana. He lives in Freehold, New Jersey.

Index

Design for Reliability: Information and Computer-Based Systems, by Eric Bauer
Copyright © 2010 Institute of Electrical and Electronics Engineers

Printed in the United States
By Bookmasters